Issued by the Ministry of Information in co-operation with the War Office
and the Ministry of Home Security

Beating the INVADER

A MESSAGE FROM THE PRIME MINISTER

IF invasion comes, everyone—young or old, men and women—will be eager to play their part worthily. By far the greater part of the country will not be immediately involved. Even along our coasts, the greater part will remain unaffected. But where the enemy lands, or tries to land, there will be most violent fighting. Not only will there be the battles when the enemy tries to come ashore, but afterwards there will fall upon his lodgments very heavy British counter-attacks, and all the time the lodgments will be under the heaviest attack by British bombers. The fewer civilians or non-combatants in these areas, the better—apart from essential workers who must remain. So if you are advised by the authorities to leave the place where you live, it is your duty to go elsewhere when you are told to leave. When the attack begins, it will be too late to go ; and, unless you receive definite instructions to move, your duty then will be to stay where you are. You will have to get into the safest place you can find, and stay there until the battle is over. For all of you then the order and the duty will be : " STAND FIRM ".

This also applies to people inland if any considerable number of parachutists or air-borne troops are landed in their neighbourhood. Above all, they must not cumber the roads. Like their fellow-countrymen on the coasts, they must " STAND FIRM ". The Home Guard, supported by strong mobile columns wherever the enemy's numbers require it, will immediately come to grips with the invaders, and there is little doubt will soon destroy them.

Throughout the rest of the country where there is no fighting going on and no close cannon fire or rifle fire can be heard, everyone will govern his conduct by the second great order and duty, namely, " CARRY ON ". It may easily be some weeks before the invader has been totally destroyed, that is to say, killed or captured to the last man who has landed on our shores. Meanwhile, all work must be continued to the utmost, and no time lost.

The following notes have been prepared to tell everyone in rather more detail what to do, and they should be carefully studied. Each man and woman should think out a clear plan of personal action in accordance with the general scheme.

Winston S. Churchill

From Winston Churchill, May 1941

(see page 42)

.... We shall never surrender!

BEATING THE INVADER:
BEESTON & CHILWELL
IN WORLD WAR TWO AND THE FLOODS

Compiled by Judith Church

Profits from the sale of this book will be donated to *The Vascular Fund, St Mary's Hospital, Praed Street, London, W2 1NY,* in grateful thanks to Mr John Wolfe, Consultant Vascular Surgeon, and his team.

This book is printed in Arial 12 point type for the benefit of the partially-sighted.

ISBN 0 9553849 0 7
        978 0 9553849 0 5

Published by Chilwell Publishers, © 2006
25 Haddon Crescent, Chilwell, Beeston, Nottingham, NG9 5JU

Produced by Robin Hood Publishing, Attenborough, Nottingham, NG9 6AP

CONTENTS

FOREWORD

By John Brunton

The roll-call of battles: Dunkirk, El Alamein, Normandy, and so many more. Speak of the fighting spirit of British troops in the face of German aggression and the very real threat posed by Adolf Hitler during the years of World War II, 1939-45. With the stories of those battles, and so many more on land, sea and in the air, their detail has long been sifted and analysed by historians over the six decades since the end of hostilities. Yet if our understanding of British military endeavour, of victories and of such reversals of fortune inevitable in any long campaign, has fuelled so many books over the period, it is equally true to say that the domestic picture, what war meant on the home front has not. Which makes this book so especially apposite now.

From a range of sources, Judith has set out with twin, clear goals, of talking to those who were there and could remember, and asking them to set down their memories of World War II as they could recall them in Beeston, where Judith grew up.

Yet the end result, by the nature of her research, exceeds that brief to provide a varied social and personal picture of those tumultuous times and their immediate aftermath.

As a result, this book now stands as a tangible record to the times. It recalls such events as the bombing of Beeston, and notably the direct hit on a house in Mona Street, which, while it occasioned loss of life also contained the story of a miraculous escape.

There's an account of Beeston's own *Dad's Army*, the Home Guard who, had the Nazis invaded, would have been the country's final military reserve.

There is also an account of the war effort as it related to the Central Ordnance Depot, Chilwell, and the affecting story of William Mackrell's ordeal as a prisoner of war. Judith's account does not, however, end in 1945 with peace in Europe and later, the Pacific.

Inextricably linked is the winter of 1947. As if Britain hadn't been battered enough by the hardships of war and rationing, then came the harshest winter of the 20th Century, still recalled by those who lived through it and remember the extent of flooding; another misery with which Beeston people so stoically coped.

As well as the social document which you now have in front of you, there's another, more personal reason why Judith has undertaken and completed this task. Two years ago she needed major surgery. Such was its complexity that surgery could not be carried out in Nottingham, but meant that she had to go to St Mary's Hospital, Paddington. Her treatment there necessitated a 20-hour operation where surgeons worked in shifts, and she in turn received, in the course of its duration, 40 pints of blood. Proceeds from this book, she has determined, will go to funds at the renowned hospital, by means of her own, heartfelt, thanks. That her treatment has been a success says so much for the wonders of modern medicine.

This book, however, is about the indomitable spirit of another age. It's about fortitude, adapting to change, however unwelcome, and dovetailing the consequences in whatever ways possible, to allow life to carry on. It is about war, without the military battles - but war nonetheless.

This is a compelling chronicle of how Beeston, like Judith's, my home town too, embraced that challenge.

John Brunton is a features writer with the Nottingham Evening Post

5

ACKNOWLEDGEMENTS

Thank you to everyone for contributing their memories of daily life in the Second World War and the turmoil of the 1947 floods. Some of these recollections were first published in *Beeston Heritage* and *Beeston Echoes,* the magazines of the Beeston & District Local History Society. The relevant magazines are no longer available.

Thank you to the following for their particular help and contributions;

Mrs Sheila Martin for permission to publish her late husband's recollections of the bombing of Mona Street,

Mrs Helen Jenkins for researching and writing the history of the Central Ordnance Depot and *Radar,*

Mr Alan Oxley for three articles, the *Salute the Soldier Week* programme on page 81, the photograph on page 95, and invaluable help as usual,

My husband Doug Church for help with photography and computer work,

Mrs Paula Hammond for the newspaper article on page 154,

Mr Alan Clayton and Mr Bill Spowage for proof-reading,

The Beeston & District Local History Society for allowing the use of illustrative material from their archives. Not all dates and sources are known but have been added where possible. Information other than that in contributor's articles is from contemporary press accounts, various encyclopaedias and the BBC Radio 4 programme *Making History,*

Thank you also to everyone who has helped in any way but is not mentioned above.

Cover pictures, The Beeston War Memorial plinth on page 6 and Arromanches on page 122 photographed by Doug Church.

Photographs on pages 27 and 152 property of Mr Geoffrey Drinkwater.

Photographs of the D-Day landings were purchased in Arromanche.

Pictures of the Central Ordnance Depot on pages 21,125,126 and 157 from *Chilwell 1939-1945.*

Barton Ferry and Thrumpton Ferry pictures property of Judith Church.

Sketches on pages 34, 35, 74 and 105 by Anna Church and Julia Church.

Written, researched and designed by Judith Church.

Inscription on the plinth of Beeston War Memorial

INTRODUCTION

The horrors of World War One led to it becoming known as 'The War To End All Wars'. But only 21 years later, in 1939, this country was at war with Germany yet again when Adolf Hitler refused to withdraw his troops from Poland in his mission to conquer Europe and beyond. The conflict escalated until most other countries were drawn in and what became World War Two finally ended in August, 1945, after two atomic bombs were dropped on Japan resulting in their unconditional surrender. The war in Europe had ended in May, 1945 when Hitler took his own life prior to the liberation of Berlin by Russian troops under Marshall Zhukov.

It is now over sixty years since the end of the Second World War. With the passing of the years and the people involved, memories are fading of this time of great fear, hardship and deprivation and it has largely been consigned to the history books. So in order to try to fully appreciate the sacrifices that were made this collection of memories of some of the local people who lived through it is published as a tribute to the 146 people from the Beeston area who lost their lives and those who fought and struggled so that we are able to live peaceably today. And hopefully to ensure that it doesn't happen again. "We must never forget."

Luckily, Beeston and district escaped the worst of the bomb damage that was inflicted on the manufacturing areas of the country. However, daily life became very difficult but despite the air raids, shortages and food rationing etc., everyone worked together to overcome the hardships and make the best of the situation. A real community spirit pervaded.

Ration books were prepared in 1938 when war seemed inevitable, but they were not needed until 1940 after many ships carrying food to us were torpedoed and restrictions really began to bite in 1942 when supplies of food to the shops became sporadic. Ration book coupons were only valid at the shop where the individual was registered for meat and groceries and long queues formed when word got round that provisions had become available. A good hot meal could be bought cheaply from subsidised British Restaurants. Surprisingly, the nation was healthy on its slim rations.

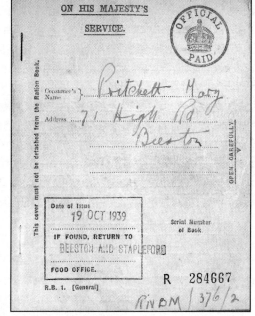

In 1939 the government expected air attacks to take place on London and the provincial cities so evacuation

of infants and school children was recommended. Happily, the youngsters of the Beeston area didn't have to leave home. Families in other parts of Nottinghamshire looked after children evacuated from Birmingham, London, Leeds and Sheffield. After some time, when the air attacks hadn't materialized, the children returned home but were evacuated again in 1940 when London suffered under the Blitz and also later when Germany fired V1 flying bombs and V2 rocket bombs at us.

In the absence of the men who were away fighting for their country women had to take on extra jobs and responsibilities in addition to their work and family commitments. All sectors of industry had to be maintained. Agriculture, commerce, the service and manufacturing industries and the munitions factories all had to employ a large female workforce. Many young women joined the armed services. Others became members of the Women's Voluntary Service or worked on the farms as members of the Women's Land Army; some became bus drivers and conductresses and factory workers etc. They worked alongside the firemen or drove ambulances, assisted with Civil Defence work which included Air Raid Precautions, and generally cared for the young and old. Most of the older men joined the Local Defence Volunteers, later called the Home Guard, along with the ones too young to be in the armed services. The Home Guard was operational until the threat of invasion disappeared in 1944. Both men and women spent free time fire watching or working as Air Raid Wardens. There were no exceptions; everyone had to play their part in the War Effort.

Air raid shelters were dug in back gardens and nothing was thrown away or destroyed. Food scraps and vegetable peelings were saved for animal food and old clothes were altered to fit younger family members or taken apart and remade to wear again. Even bath water was limited to a depth of five inches. The government launched a 'Dig for Victory' campaign and many dug up their ornamental gardens to grow fruit and vegetables for their own consumption and any surplus would be traded for other items in short supply when available. More vegetables were eaten to eke out the small meat ration. Many people kept hens in their back gardens to ensure a supply of fresh eggs. The alternative was dried, powdered egg. And by 1945 whale meat was appearing in the shops.

There were, though, benefits for children in wartime because school meals were subsidised so more families were able to afford them and orange juice and cod liver oil were introduced along with a mass immunisation programme for diphtheria.

There were joyful celebrations when the war finally ended in August 1945. Street parties were held all over the Beeston area with jelly, custard and blancmange and other treats that had been saved for the celebrations. People expected life's luxuries to soon be available. They wanted to buy new clothes, meat, eggs and bacon, chocolate and sweets again. Unfortunately, the reality was just the opposite. Britain had been ravaged by six years of war and was bankrupt. Shortage of basic necessities meant rationing had to be increased. Bread rationing was introduced in 1946 due to a world scarcity of grain. The immediate post war years were a time of constantly making do, of producing meals from supplies even more meagre than wartime, of continually darning and patching clothes and generally going without.

Worse was to come, however. Heavy rain in February 1946 caused flooding in Beeston Rylands and the winter of 1946/7 was very hard. Thick snow lay on the ground until Easter, hundreds of sheep died in the fields, winter crops were ruined and there was an acute shortage of fuel. Clothing coupons were cut once more and food rations reduced yet again. Thousands of people all over the country were still homeless after the bombings and had to be accommodated in military camps. When the snow and ice thawed Attenborough was isolated, Beeston Rylands, the southern area of Beeston and parts of Chilwell were badly affected by floods. But as the year wore on and the weather improved a gradual all-round recovery took place. Things remained tight for some while, though, and clothes rationing didn't end until 1949. Identity Cards, introduced in 1939, were abolished on 21 February 1952. Eggs, flour, soap and milk came off ration in 1950, tea in 1952 and confectionery in 1953. At long last, on 3 July 1954 all rationing officially ended. The war had lasted six long years but the effects were felt for many years after that.

COUNTY OF NOTTS.
NATIONAL SERVICE COMMITTEE

BEESTON

RECRUITING

WEEK

NATIONAL SERVICE
MEANS   YOU

A PARADE OF UNITS OF THE FIGHTING AND CIVIL DEFENCE SERVICES WILL BE HELD ON SATURDAY, MAY 13, 1939

Parade will assemble at 2 p.m. at the Dovecote Lane Recreation Ground, and will return to the Dovecote Lane Recreation Ground at 3.30 p.m. for a

MASS MEETING AND DEMONSTRATIONS BY THE FIGHTING SERVICES

Speaker: ALD. W. BAYLISS, J.P.

The Parade will take the following Route:

Dovecote Lane, Queens Road, Humber Road, High Road, Wollaton Road, Broughton Street, Park Street, Cromwell Road, Imperial Road, Chilwell Road, Station Road, Queens Road, Dovecote Lane.

COME AND SEE

THE MODERN MECHANISED ARMY UNITS, R.A.F. BOMBERS AND CIVIL DEFENCE SERVICES, INCLUDING THE AUXILIARY FIRE BRIGADE, AIR RAID WARDENS, FIRST AID AND DECONTAMINATION UNITS.

RECRUITS FOR ALL SERVICES URGENTLY REQUIRED

Beeston Gazette & Echo, 5 May 1939

AIR RAID WARNINGS

In time of war, the following Code of Signals will be adopted.

PRELIMINARY CAUTION MESSAGE.—Confidential caution—not made public—to selected public officials, to enable them to take necessary preliminary action on threatened raid. Telephone Code: "Yellow."

CANCEL CAUTION MESSAGE.—On removal of threat of raid. Telephone Code: "White."

PUBLIC WARNINGS

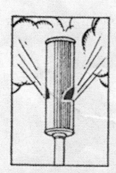

ACTION WARNING.—Signal of two minutes' duration, consisting of either (1) a fluctuating or "warbling" signal of varying pitch, or (2) a succession of intermittent blasts of about five seconds' duration, separated by a silent period of three seconds. Telephone Code: "Red."

RAIDERS PASSED MESSAGE.—A continuous signal of two minutes' duration at a steady pitch. Telephone Code: "Green."

STREET SIGNALS.—Police Constables and Air Raid Wardens will repeat the public signals :—

Repeating Action Warning.—**Whistles** blown in sharp blasts.

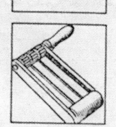

Local Gas Warning.—**Hand Rattles.**

Cancelling Gas Warning, or repeating the "Raiders Passed" signal if no Gas present.—**Hand Bells.**

Hand Bells will thus become, in effect, our **"All Clear"** signal.

From *ABC of ARP, 1939*

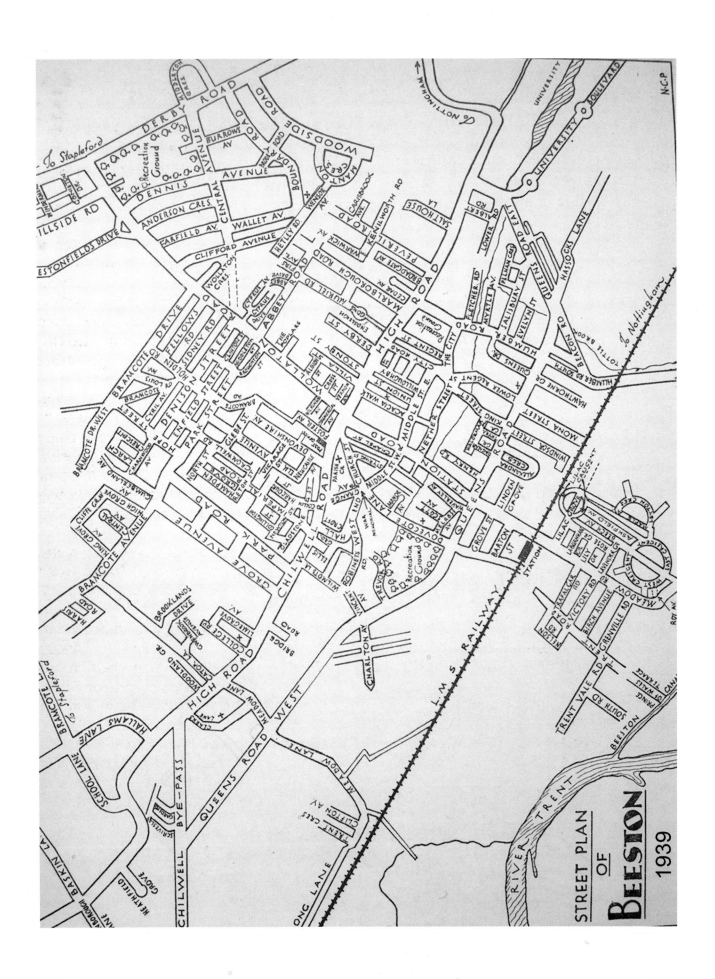

STREET PLAN
OF
BEESTON
1939

MY WAR TIME EXPERIENCES AS AN AIR RAID WARDEN 1938-1945
By Margaret Cooper

These started unofficially in September 1938 when I volunteered to help my father who had already been appointed as Head Warden for the B area of Beeston. This comprised the area from the left hand side of Wollaton Road, Station Road etc. to the Chilwell boundary and from Derby Road to the river.

In the days prior to the outbreak of war we were engaged in the assembling and distribution of gas masks to the public and instructions in the art of fitting the various types from the large containers for the babies, to the Mickey Mouse ones for the toddlers and the small, medium and large for older children and grown-ups. The whole area was divided into sectors, each of which comprised a compact group of streets and houses and was in the care of a Senior Warden and five or six other Wardens.

I was allocated to sector B14 with Mr Walter Price (Mr Stanley Price's father) as Senior Warden with Mr Burnett, Mr Jack Sibley, Mr Eugene Perry, Mr Norman Barnes and later Mr James Pittam, as my companions. Our area was Montague Street, Middleton Street, Clinton Street and the southern section of Denison Street. Each of us was responsible for checking gas masks and blackout precautions in a particular street. Mine was Clinton Street and I was expected to visit the residents regularly generally during daylight hours to see if they were OK, if gas masks were in order or needed changing and discuss any problems concerning blackout

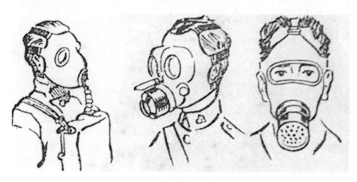

Gas Masks

General Service   Civilian Duty   Civilian

arrangements in the house. Later on when some properties had air raid shelters erected in their gardens it was necessary to discover if the residents were using these or whether they preferred to shelter indoors. It was also important to discover the number of occupants in each house and if any were regularly absent on shift work etc.

At the outbreak of the war my sister and I had already enrolled as Air Raid Wardens and been supplied with tin hats, whistles, special respirators and white armbands with black Ws upon them. Later we were to receive uniforms of a black jacket and trousers, greatcoat and shoes. My father, as Head Warden received (via our home phone) details of enemy planes coming across, by various warning colours: <u>yellow</u> - coming over North Sea, <u>purple</u> - coming over the coast in our direction and <u>red</u> - enemy planes imminent, this latter was when sirens were sounded. This information was quickly passed to Senior Wardens who then notified their team. In the beginning we were expected to be out patrolling our area on a yellow warning but later on this was changed and generally we were called out on a purple warning. From September 1939 to August 1940 all was quiet here and this gave time for us to receive training for our task and first aid revision courses together with instruction on gas attacks. The latter was done at weekends in a specially constructed hut on the Round Hill field. Into it was let off various gases e.g. phosgene etc. and we had to crawl on all fours with our respirators on and identify the gases.

Most weeks we would be called to a sector meeting to be told vital instructions in case of raids and casualties and how to fill in our incident forms.

Meantime, public shelters were erected and one was placed in Middleton Street for our area.

A Warden's post was erected in our garden providing a small meeting room and an area with sleeping accommodation. It was realised that it would be necessary to have Wardens available during the day to man the post and the telephone and so permanent Wardens were employed for these duties and voluntary Wardens were used for night times at the post. Incidentally after the war, the post became our garage!

The first incident in the Beeston/Chilwell area occurred on the night of August 25th 1940 - (this was the same night as the first raid on London). Our sector was on patrol as usual and hearing a plane overhead had taken refuge in the public shelter on Middleton Street. Suddenly, we heard a swishing noise and then Mr Burnett - a World War I veteran said, "Get down - it's bombs!" We learnt afterwards that the bombs had been dropped on the Long Eaton Fabric Company premises on the Chilwell bypass. No one was in the building - which was severely damaged, but I do not think there were any casualties. We believe the enemy was aiming for Chilwell Depot.

Empire News, 25 May 1941

During the next months there were more 'alerts' especially when the nights were clear. The night of November 14/15th 1940 was one such and the sirens sounded early and soon the enemy planes were overhead and we feared the worst. The sky seemed full of these heavily throbbing planes but they continued on to the west without releasing their load here. We knew some people were receiving a terrific bombing. It was Coventry!! Our hearts sank as we heard the news - so many ex-Beeston folk were living there and above all, our Sector Warden (Walter Price's son) was working there. It was a long night on duty as there was a likelihood of the enemy planes dropping unused bombs on the way back to their base. Later we learnt that Stan Price was safe but hundreds had died and there was terrific damage to buildings including the cathedral. (Official figures for that night were 568 dead and 863 seriously hurt. Out of 75,000 buildings 60,000 were destroyed or badly damaged). The next day's radio news bulletin opened with the playing of the *Coventry Carol* - a most poignant moment!

An incident much nearer to home occurred in late February/March 1941. For some reason, I was alone at the junction of Montague Street and Denison Street when I heard a great swishing of a bomb very close. I immediately lay down in the gutter and feared the worst. After a few moments all was quiet so I got up and began to explore around the houses in Denison Street and at the back of No.30 I found a huge crater. By this time some of my sector had arrived and I was able to report the find. Then began the job of evacuating the whole of the lower part of that street. Fortunately most people had not gone to bed as the raid occurred before midnight. However there were some amusing incidents - someone couldn't leave without her pet bird – someone else must finish some cooking! etc., etc.

Eventually, all were taken to emergency accommodation. The area was cordoned off and for a time the buses on Wollaton Road were re-routed to avoid unnecessary vibration. The bomb squad from Chilwell arrived the next morning and the huge bomb was defused by a very brave officer.

Later that year a solitary bomber dropped the last of its load (?) at the top of Elm Avenue on the house of Mr and Mrs Cressy. It was believed that a light was seen there which enabled the enemy to score a direct hit on the house and the occupants. Immediately afterwards there was a great cloud of thick smoke and as we came nearer to investigate it seemed to envelope my house on Park Street but fortunately it was not damaged.

It was unusual for raids to take place in the day time but during 1941 when I was teaching at Nether Street School, we had an 'alert' one afternoon and everyone had to process in an orderly manner to the air raid shelters in the playground. These had long stone seats on either side which would accommodate about 70 children each. No lighting was provided so we spent the time singing songs until the 'all clear' went. It seems that the plane was aiming for Ericsson's (now Siemen's, Beeston Rylands).

1941 brought the most terrific raid in this area on the night of May 8/9 when Nottingham was bombed. This started with the dropping of the most ghastly pink flares which appeared to circle the city. Then followed the heavy bombers and the thuds as bomb after bomb was dropped causing terrible casualties as the Co-op bakery and the Dakeyne Street shelter received direct hits. A month earlier bombs were dropped on Mona Street, Windsor Street and Cator Lane.

Later on we were to hear of the Germans' 'secret weapon' the guided missile - the V2. These rockets attacked in the daylight but we saw few of them in this area.

During these war years normal activities carried on though evening meetings tended to finish earlier to enable people to reach their homes before the raids began. I was able to attend Ranger meetings in Nottingham each week as buses with dimmed lighting continued to run. Theatre and concert halls continued.

Most firms, schools and businesses had to take precautions for fires from incendiary bombs, so workers were organised in groups of firewatchers.

When I transferred to a school in Bulwell in December 1941 I was expected to take my turn at fire-watching in a very old four storey building where the two fire-watchers were placed in the Head's room - at the very top of the building. We slept either on the floor or on the top of a large table! Fortunately, there were no raids when we were on duty. On other nights, the lady wardens were expected to take their turn to sleep at the warden post. This was very easy for my sister and me and generally we managed to have a quiet night and to be awakened by the arrival of the permanent Wardens about 7am.

As the war continued more of the local inhabitants were involved in street fire-watching and trained in the use of stirrup pumps etc. Some teenagers with cycles were employed as messengers and stationed at the Town Hall. Both of my younger sisters did these duties before they joined the Women's Auxiliary Air Force.

In spite of the possible dangers which we faced whenever there was an 'alert', there was a great feeling of working together and comradeship from both young and older folk.

Over sixty years on it is good to realise that our efforts were worthwhile and helped in some small measure to save England in its darkest hour.

* * * * *

NOTICE
FIRE   GUARD   TRAINING
TO ALL FIRE GUARDS:-

I.-Street Party Leaders are now forming classes for training, in accordance with Government
Syllabus, for men and women fire guards in Street Parties.

II.-Fire Guards at Business Premises are required to take training as directed by their Employers.

III.-Fire Guards performing duties under the direction of this Council will be trained by the
Council's Instructors.

Issued by THE FIRE GUARD STAFF OFFICER,
Beeston and Stapleford Urban District Council,

Fire Prevention Office,
123, High Road, Beeston.   September 1st, 1942

DUNKIRK AND THE HOME GUARD

Late May and early June 1940 saw approximately 335,000 officers and men of the British Expeditionary Force as well as French soldiers safely evacuated from Dunkirk, northern France, and the surrounding beaches. British warships and small vessels, a great number privately owned, crossed the Channel and picked up troops whilst under constant attack. Many little ships such as fishing vessels, lifeboats and motor yachts responded to the call to rescue our men. The strength of the German forces had been seriously underestimated and the British and French were cut off in north-east France by the German advance to the Channel and it looked probable we would be invaded. The small boats were able to enter shallow water to take the men off the beaches and back to England safely. Some boats made up to seven trips before Dunkirk fell to the Germans. Winston Churchill called it a "miracle of deliverance". Sadly not all the troops could be rescued and many of those left behind were taken prisoner for the duration of the war, (see pages 106-120 for a first-hand account from a prisoner of war). Immediately after the evacuations Hitler proclaimed a war of total annihilation against his enemies.

In May 1940 when invasion seemed imminent a home defence militia was formed called the Local Defence Volunteers. Thousands of men volunteered, about five times the number expected. Members were either too old or too young for the armed forces or in occupations vital to the war effort and therefore wouldn't be conscripted. In July at the instigation of the Prime Minister, Winston Churchill, the name was changed to the Home Guard. It was some time before uniforms were issued and the only guns were shotguns and air rifles that had been handed in by members of the public in response to an appeal. Pickaxes, crowbars, bayonets, knives etc. would also be used if the need arose. Eventually the Home Guard were issued with World War One rifles and gradually more up to date weapons were made available. In 1942 compulsory enrolment applied in areas where the units were below strength.

They guarded munitions factories and aerodromes and organised roadblocks etc. If the Germans invaded, the Home Guard would be expected to delay the enemy until our fighting forces could be deployed. By the time it was disbanded in December 1945 the Home Guard had become an efficient army of about two million men.

* * * * *

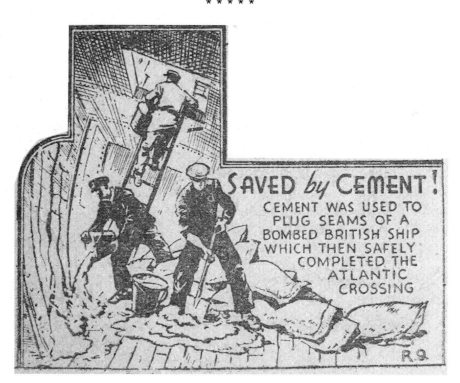

Tank Express, September 1941

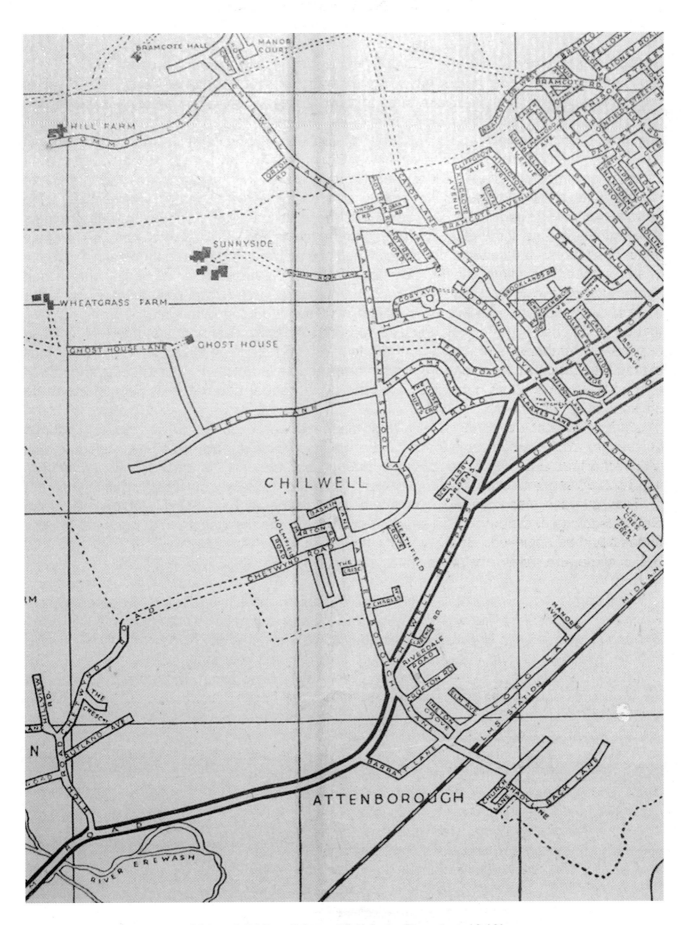

Map of Chilwell from 'Guide to Beeston 1946'
(Before the Inham Nook Estate was built)

BEESTON AND CHILWELL 1939-45
By W H Ashton

On the 3rd September 1939, we were in Christ Church, Chilwell in the largest congregation I can remember. The vicar had a terrible statement to make - "*We are at war!*" Father was at home building blackouts: substantial ones of plywood on a wooden frame (meant to stop flying glass as well as prevent light showing to help the enemy bombers).

On 4th September our A.T.S. (Auxiliary Territorial Service) girls arrived to be billeted until the accommodation (huts) for them in Chilwell Depot could be prepared. We had our first alert - which this small boy slept through - and were then told not to return to school after the holidays until the air raid shelters were ready. Who said war was all bad? It was quite amazing how quickly the shelters were built, especially those at Ericsson's. They were queer things, built as towers above ground level because of the low water-table level near the river. Many of the household shelters were permanently full of water, making more play areas.

I remember our history master at school explaining 'patriotism' by reminding us we had beaten attempts in 1588 (Spain), 1805-15 (France) and 1918 (Germany) to impose a single state of Europe upon us. It was now our duty to prevent another attempt.

Life for us, the children, went on quietly and ordinarily, we even managed normal holidays in June 1940 on the Isle of Wight, but from then on the raid alerts became more regular until the night the bombs began to drop. It was the only time in my life I was genuinely frightened although the effort not to show it was helped by the anger generated at the inability to do anything about it!

Later on any boy who had a bike could be - and was expected to be - a Civil Defence Messenger. This way we could feel we were fighting back in our own small way. We had only two instructions: first - *get the message through* and second - *if another messenger was knocked out to get his message through too*. This duty led to my only 'war wound' when the bomb that hit the Meadow Dairy, now site of the Beekeeper Inn, in Chilwell blew me off my bike and grazed my knees (it also knocked my mother - on fire-watch - to the ground, happily unhurt.)

Air raids were always very noisy affairs in Chilwell due to the number of anti-aircraft guns around the Depot. During these raids Mona Street in Beeston was badly damaged and Chilwell had several incidents - luckily deaths and injuries were slight. Ericsson's (now Siemen's) was machine gunned in daylight but without any serious damage. We saw stray German planes - though since every schoolboy could recognise any plane instantly we always had plenty of time to duck. We even saw a V1 flying bomb later in the war.

One of the greatest joys was acting as eyes of the Home Guard in their war games with the occupants of Chilwell Depot; for in those days small boys knew every ditch and hedgerow intimately and so we were virtually invisible - after all war was really a game for us. We had of course all volunteered for the old Look, Dodge and Vanish (LDV later the Home Guard, sometimes called Look, Duck and Vanish) but were turned down on what we considered the flimsiest of reasons (too young).

Mother was called up for 'war work' as soon as I was 12 years old and became Deputy Local Fuel Overseer. She was also closely engaged with the adoption by Beeston of the Destroyer H.M.S. *Active* early in 1942. Beeston raised over £250,000 for *Warships Week* in the process. Much knitting and collecting for the officers and crew brought many messages of thanks.

Probably my greatest personal sorrow came when our young Alsatian bitch was offered as a war dog. We had

Beeston Gazette & Echo

BEESTON WARSHIPS WEEK
FEBRUARY 7 TO 14, 1942
Our aim is to raise at least
£210,000
In order to pay for
H.M.S. ACTIVE
THE NAVY IS SACRIFICING ALL THEY HAVE

18

difficulty feeding her and dad was worried about her reaction to bombing so we had to say "good-bye". Mother had at least two citations for her work 'on active service'. Unfortunately these have been lost in the intervening years.

Our mothers had a wonderful ability to utilise our rations in such a way that even growing children never really went hungry. I now believe that, in part, this meant the mothers going short but we did not realise this at the time. We had, of course, the British Restaurants, in Chilwell aptly held in the Memorial Hall, built to commemorate our saviours of Britain in World War One. These helped out with what was really a very healthy diet, i.e. without junk food.

As I remember the charges in the BRs were: main course 5d, soup 2d, bread 1d, sweet 2d and tea 2d. (All pre-decimal prices)

As the war dragged on much talk was of the Second Front. We knew in advance roughly when this was to be for our original ATS girl had been moved into the Depot and replaced by Pam, a young lady from Aston University, where she studied music, who was an MT Driver in the ATS, usually driving 5 ton trucks. She was on the regular run from Chilwell to Southampton. She was therefore away for several days at a time and almost invariably arrived back in the middle of the night, badly in need of a bath (not always limited to the standard five inches of water). This meant many disturbed nights but the many problems or inconveniences we had we saw as our part in the war effort and accepted them as such, as we did with all the rules and regulations, identity cards and restrictions which were a normal part of our lives.

I suppose that we thought of ourselves as being in the front line although Beeston as a place, escaped most of the horrors of the war. However as people, the citizens of Beeston and district did their bit and made their sacrifices like all the rest of the country and when it was all over we could hold our heads high and say "we did our best!"

ATS girls training at Bramcote Hills Park, with Bramcote Hills House in the background. This was formerly the home of John Sherwin Gregory, during the war ATS girls were lodged here. The house was demolished in 1966.

CENTRAL ORDNANCE DEPOT, CHILWELL: THE BEGINNING AND 1939–45
By Helen Jenkins

The 8th Viscount Chetwynd, Godfrey John Boyle (also a Texas Sheriff!), was a qualified civil engineer, (having been a Director of Vickers Ltd, ship builders and machine-gun makers). He was asked by the Director General of Munitions' Supply to overlook the building and running of a large Factory for preparing explosive charges.

In 1915 he chose Chilwell as the place for the Factory because it had all the necessary requirements. It was away from any largely populated areas for safety reasons. It was near to a main railway line and, as jobs in the lace industry were declining, many people wanted work.

The Factory was built very quickly and in March 1916 shells were being filled. This made Chilwell a target for air raids. One million shells had been filled by 2nd September and nearly every large shell fired by the British during the Battle of the Somme was filled here.

By October 1916 there were about 6,000 employees, a third of them female. The first women to be taken on were employed as crane drivers in the Filled Shell Store.

Up to early 1918 there had been several explosions which had been very minor compared with the one on the evening of 1st July 1918, when 134 people died and hundreds were injured.

King George V on a visit to Chilwell in December 1916, with Lord Chetwynd

Chilwell Shell Filling Factory workers at Attenborough Station after a shift change in August 1918. In order to accommodate the large numbers of workers using the station the platforms had to be lengthened in 1916.

Early in 1935 the then derelict old Shell Filling Factory was being turned into a depot to provide accommodation for the Army's vehicle fleet.

The RAOC (Royal Army Ordnance Corps) Workshop was set up in 1936 to look after the Army's transport requirements. During 1939 - 1945 vehicles and spares came out of the old Shell Filling Factory endlessly. Chilwell had been selected as the ideal place to centralize the Army's mechanical transport because of its closeness to the car industry factories and it was the connecting link between the factories and the Army, for whom the

Churchill Tank, one of many issued from Chilwell

first few months of the Second World War were known as 'The Phoney War', with not much happening on the Western Front. Vehicles and spares were brought to Chilwell ready for issue later.

Initially, the RAOC was a non-fighting force, with no infantry training. Their main job was to supply MT stores and other supplies to their colleagues in action. This lasted for 18 months into the War, after which soldiers were trained, and then went as infantrymen into action; where many died. Those who remained at Chilwell were joined by many RAOC conscripts.

After Dunkirk, thousands of battle-weary survivors who had to be fed and accommodated came to Chilwell from France. Supplies had to be maintained for the Army at home and abroad and these survivors had to be quickly re-equipped to take their places defending their country.

Chilwell was an important target for the Germans and there are many accounts of bombers and enemy aircraft overhead, but none found their target.

In 1942 REME (Royal Electrical and Mechanical Engineers) was formed from the men who had trained in electrical and mechanical engineering at RAOC and 'Chilwell Ordnance Workshop' became a War Office controlled No. 8 Central Workshop.

Chilwell continually expanded and by the end of World War Two the Army had nearly one million vehicles and spare parts, the majority of which were supplied by Chilwell or its storehouses in other parts of the country.

THE WOMEN'S LAND ARMY

The Women's Land Army was established in 1917 because of the shortage of labour on the farms as many men were away fighting, or had been killed, in the First World War. The organisation was reformed in June 1939 when war loomed again and there was a need to increase food production as we wouldn't be able to import in quantity.

At its peak 80,000 women worked with the Land Army enabling thousands of acres of unused land to be brought into cultivation. The uniform consisted of brown breeches, green jerseys and brown felt hats. They performed all the necessary farm tasks including ploughing, haymaking, growing cereals and vegetable crops and harvesting. They looked after the animals and were responsible for milking, lambing, poultry keeping etc. Many were employed as rat catchers. Their work continued for some years after the war ended until the farm workers were able to take over again. The Women's Land Army was disbanded in November 1950.

REGISTRATION FOR FIREWATCHING

ALL women born between the 21st September, 1897, and the 20th September, 1922, who should have but have not registered must do so not later than the 10th October, 1942. Anyone failing to comply with this Order becomes liable under the Defence Regulations, 1939, to heavy penalties. This Order also applies to all men who have attained the age of 18 and those who have moved into the district since the previous registration in 1941. Registrations can be made at the following Fire Prevention Offices, viz :-

BEESTON AND STAPLEFORD

123, High-road, Beeston
35, Nottingham-road, Stapleford

At the times specified in paragraphs 8 and 9 of the Registration Notice.

LONG EATON

70, High-street, Long Eaton.

Monday, Tuesday and Thursday : 9 a.m. - 5.00 p.m.
Wednesday and Friday : 9 a.m. - 7.30 p.m.
Saturday : 9 a.m. - 12.30 p.m.

(signed)

C. H. WRAGG,
Clerk to the Beeston & Stapleford
Urban District Council.

Wm. E. STANLEY,
Clerk to the Long Eaton Urban
District Council.

3rd October 1942

A SCHOOLBOY REMEMBERS WORLD WAR TWO
By Geoffrey Drinkwater

It is Sunday morning in the late summer of 1939 and I'm just 11 years old. My lanky figure is emphasized by my short, grey, flannel trousers held up by what is every schoolboy's pride: a snake belt. Out of these trousers protrude a pair of long, thin legs, the lower parts of which are covered with grey, woollen socks. They've been hand-knitted by my mother along with my grey, woollen pullover and both are edged with a black, gold and green stripe, indicating that early in September I am to become a pupil of the Henry Mellish County Secondary School.

Daily Express
2nd September 1939

Over my shoulder, attached by a thick piece of sisal string, hangs a lunch-box sized cardboard container. If I peep inside, I can smell the new rubber that makes up my gas mask. I never take it out, except when at gas mask practice, because I have been brought up to do as I am told. It will be close by me for most of the war, shortly to come, the threat of which I have been aware of for the last year or so.

I am reminded of this as I pass through the entrance porch into the Sunday School Hall of Chilwell Road Methodist Church, Beeston. I can see a bucket of sand, a bucket of water and a stirrup pump, so named because it has, at the top of a vertical brass cylinder, a piston attached to a two-handed grip that looks like an inverted horse rider's stirrup. I have seen one of these pumps demonstrated by people called Air Raid Wardens. They deliver either an impressively forceful jet of water for extinguishing a blaze or a spray specifically for damping down the area around an incendiary (fire) bomb. These bombs are quite small, weighing about 10 lb and are made mainly of magnesium, which burns with an intense heat. If a jet of water is directed at one, it explodes into fragments. As there aren't any air raid shelters here at the church, Sunday School will soon have to be held at Church Street Boys' School.

If I think back a few months, I can recall a further reminder of what the future might hold. I am standing with my family in a crowd of several hundred people at the Nottingham end of University Park between the Pavilion and the Highfields Lido (later to be replaced by the D H Lawrence building and the Djanogly Centre). The local ARP (Air Raid Precautions) organization has arranged a demonstration of an aerial gas attack. Although I have just once previously seen low-flying biplanes, when my dad took me, sitting on a cushion on the crossbar of his bike, to Castle Donington airfield, the dramatic impact of witnessing the approach from the south of two low-wing monoplanes is not reduced. Flying very low at rooftop height are two Miles Magisters, painted in the bright yellow livery of RAF Training Command. As they pass over, above the deafening engine noise we hear two loud explosions, accompanied from the ground by clouds of white smoke, simulating poison gas. The demonstration has served its purpose: we take home with us a fearful apprehension of impending war.

We have heard the siren during pre-war air raid practices at day school, when we have to get under our desks. This now familiar sound summons my mum & dad and brothers Ken (14) and John (8) and myself on the first night of the war, 3rd September 1939, and we take cover, complete with gas masks issued to us in 1938, in the large pantry under the stairs at our home at 56 Park Street, Beeston. I am trembling with fear for several hours until the continuous note of the 'all clear' takes us, our way lit by a candle in a pale green enamelled holder, back to our beds.

It isn't long before my dad decides that we must have a better form of air raid shelter. Every year, we are quite used to helping dig a two-foot deep trench to fill with leaf compost for dad's sweet peas, so it seems a quite familiar task and something of an adventure when we're asked to help dad dig a six-foot trench. The problem, then, is to find some suitable covering for the top so that we can pile the loose earth over it.

On my frequent visits to my Grandma Drinkwater at 3 Factory Lane, Chilwell, over the back garden wall, I have noticed abandoned

From 'ABC of ARP' 1939

pigsties and the various sheets of steel used for the roofs. I know that they can be accessed from the nearby Wilmot Lane so it is there that I go to scout around. There I find old metal advertising plaques. One of them has a dark blue background with a white representation of a West Highland Terrier and a caption advertising Spratt's Bonio, a fortified dog food. This and others I load on to my trolley that I've made out of old pram wheels and drag them home.

They are just the right size for placing across the top of the trench but we need something to support them. This is no problem as we never throw anything away and we soon fish out of a corner half a dozen discarded pieces of angle iron from the sides of old beds. We shovel the soil over the top, leaving an old stepladder at one end for access. Job done.

In this early part of the war, I realise that my dad is eligible for 'call-up'. Born in 1900, he was conscripted into the army in 1918. Now, at the age of 39, he accepts employment with the Myford Engineering Company and, as he is involved in work vital to the war effort, he is classified as being in a Reserved Occupation (exempt from military service). He has to work an alternating pattern of three weeks on days followed by three weeks on nights. As he regularly has to adjust his sleep pattern from days to nights and vice versa, this is a punishing regime for him and us. When dad is sleeping during the day, it imposes on my two brothers and myself a strict embargo on playing in the backyard whilst, indoors, mother makes us walk on tiptoe and speak in hushed tones.

There are no further air raid warnings for several weeks as we're entering a phase of the war when nothing much happens and the radio broadcasts repeatedly report, '*All quiet on the Western Front*'. It is dubbed, '*The Phoney War*'. It's not the only thing that's phoney. Inspecting our carefully constructed trench we notice that we have inadvertently created one emergency provision in place of another — a water supply two feet deep.

During the next year we are provided at the bottom of the garden with an Anderson Shelter, half of which is below ground. Predictably, this also fills up with water. Some time later, workmen arrive to pump it out and provide an effective waterproof concrete lining, four inches thick. Access to the shelter is at the end, through a

---

YOU HAVE BEEN WARNED!

If you get a choking feeling and a smell of musty hay,
You can bet your bottom dollar that there's PHOSGENE on the way.

But the smell of bleaching powder will inevitably mean,
That the enemy you are meeting is the gas we call CHLORINE.

When your eyes begin a twitching and for tears you cannot see,
It isn't mother peeling onions, but a dose of C. A. P.

If the smell resembles pear-drops then you'd better not delay,
It's not father sucking toffee, it's that ruddy K. S. K.

If you catch a pungent odour as you're going home for tea,
You can safely put your shirt on it, they're using B. B. C.

With garlic, horse-radish or onions, mildly on the air,
They're broadcasting MUSTARD, damned 'hot stuff', beware!

And remember, while geraniums look pleasant in a bed,
Beware their smell in war-time, if its LEWISITE you're dead.

Lastly, when a powder of a greyish-white is seen,
Don your respirator, or its agony from ARSINE.

Wartime Poem

---

gap in the corrugated iron, about 2ft 6in high and two-feet wide, so to keep out the draught we need a cover that we can lift off when getting in and replace when we're safely inside. And what do we make this out of? That's right — the metal advertising plaque for Spratt's Bonio.

After hearing on the wireless in 1940 about the invasion of Holland by German parachute troops, I learn that there is an imminent danger of invasion here and that a glider-borne attack is possible. I have seen anti-glider obstacles on my school field, in the form of short lengths of telegraph pole set into the ground. Like so many kids, I am a local itinerant — here, there and everywhere. So it's not surprising that on one of my forays to Dovecote Lane Recreation Ground to play cricket with my brothers and

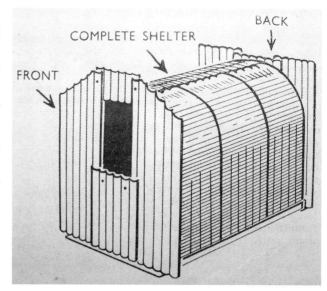

Anderson Shelter, from 'ABC of ARP' 1939

pals, I notice that several old cars have appeared — scattered around on the Boys' Brigade sports ground, on the opposite side of Queens Road. One of these cars is of little known make — a *Bean* — a large, sedate saloon, painted blue and black. It will stand there until after the war, when Phil Williams, the son of the Boys' Brigade Captain, will put in some petrol, charge up the battery, crank the engine and it will start!

Towards the end of 1940 and well into 1941 we frequently experience intense enemy aerial activity, sometimes for several consecutive nights. It seems that we are below the track of German aircraft en route for targets not in the immediate locality. Consequently, we regularly shelter in the 'Anderson', sometimes occupying the stools we have placed in it from 10pm until dawn and taking with us blankets, an eiderdown, torches, thermos flasks and a chamber pot.

It is during one of these raids, probably targeting the Chilwell Ordnance Depot, that I can hear a low-flying bomber and the staccato rattle of machine guns. Situated at the bottom of Sutton's field (now a recreation ground) on Cator Lane, is a searchlight together with an emplacement containing World War 1 type twin-mounted Lewis machine guns, specifically for firing at an aircraft that has been spotted by the searchlight. I conclude that exactly this has happened to the bomber and that it is returning fire in an attempt to extinguish the searchlight.

I learn later that a bomb has scored a direct hit on an air raid shelter at a house in Bramcote Lane, Chilwell, situated just north of the junction with Lynton Road, killing the occupants including an *ATS* (*Auxiliary Territorial Service*) girl, who is most likely attached to a unit at the Chilwell Ordnance Depot. A number of these girls are compulsorily billeted at private addresses.

As I have a school friend, Geoffrey Garton, who lives down the Rylands, the Trent at Beeston is part of my patch. Whilst cycling by the river along the towpath towards Attenborough, we come across a fresh bomb crater only a matter of 20 yards from the bank, near Mitchell's brown boat-house. There are a couple of craters nearby but they're quite small, indicating that the bombs have failed to detonate.

There are many searchlights in this area but apart from the one mentioned earlier I am not aware of their location — only their existence, as witnessed by the beams of light probing the sky during enemy aerial activity. People soon learn to identify the distinctive sound of a high-flying German aircraft that can only be described as a one per second pulsing, 'hm — hm — hm'. On hearing this they say with certainty, 'Oh, that's a Jerry'. There are considerable numbers of anti-aircraft guns if one is to judge from the sight and, more often, the sound of firing and shell-bursts, but I am only aware of the location of two of them. There is a battery of 4.5-inch naval guns in the copse on Beeston Fields Golf Course and some Bofors (quick-firing single or double-barrelled anti-aircraft guns) and 3.7-inch guns on the Ordnance Depot site. I soon become able to identify the calibre of guns that are firing, namely, the heavy crump of the 3.7s and the very concussive and loud noise issuing from the 4.5s, as distinct from the characteristic ringing reports as the Bofors guns fire their clips of five 40mm shells that can only be mimicked as 'don-don-di- din-do…..n.'

After a night raid when anti-aircraft gunfire has taken place, a favourite pastime of boys is to comb the streets in search of shrapnel (jagged pieces of shell casing) in order to see who can find the largest piece. My own prize specimen is a large shiny piece of shrapnel some four inches long displaying the narrowly spaced lines indicating that metal turning has taken place during manufacture.

After one of these raids, my curiosity to inspect any damage is helped by the information provided by a young policeman we have lodging with us. I get on my bike, made up from bits of several old bikes, and scour the area for damage. Riding up Wollaton Road I notice, across the ends of Denison Street, Sydney Road, Fellows Road and Bramcote Drive, barriers displaying the notice "NO ENTRY DELAYED ACTION BOMBS". I learn many years later that it is one of these bombs that fell only ten yards or so from Margaret Cooper, when patrolling as an Air Raid Warden in Denison Street (see page 14). After another raid around this time, I see similar notices near the top of Station Road in respect of bombs that have failed to detonate in the National Provincial Bank on the south side of Beeston Square (now the site of Bird's Bakery shop), and in Shaw & Marvin's Dye Works on the east side of Station Road. On another occasion I go down to what is known as Depot Corner near the junction of Attenborough Lane with High Road, Chilwell and there view a remarkably deep crater across the whole width of the road and pavements, caused by a high-explosive bomb probably weighing at least 500lb.

Bomb damage to the Queens Hotel near Mona Street

On the 8th April 1941 my post-raid biking around after the previous night's air raid brings me to the corner of Queens Road and Mona Street where the corner of the Queens Hotel has been hit and a nearby house on Mona Street almost destroyed. I learn many years later that this house is the home of George Martin one of my contemporaries attending Church Street Junior Boys' School. It turns out that when the bomb struck, George and his brother were asleep downstairs and were led to safety through the rubble by their father from upstairs who, with their mother, had narrowly escaped injury by taking shelter under the iron bedstead. (see page 36). A high explosive bomb has fallen on Acacia Walk, Beeston, causing slight damage but no casualties. I discover that incendiary bombs have been scattered across Beeston from Park Street and Glebe Street to Middle Street, Dagmar Grove and Windsor Street. The first strikes a house at the north-east corner of the junction of Park Street and Cromwell Road and is dealt with by the Park Street (North) fire watching squad under the leadership of George Chamberlain. The team operates on the basis of a nightly rota, which is pinned to a homemade display board in the Chamberlain family's front garden opposite our house on Park Street.

Frequently, mum asks me to "run across the road and see if your dad's on fire-watch tonight", which means that between dusk and dawn he has to be at home and available for duty. Each squad is equipped with a ladder, stirrup pump and water buckets, sand buckets and sandbags, and each member has had some training in the method of tackling an incendiary bomb. It is a two-man technique: the stirrup pump operator works at a safe distance; the 'fireman' lies on the floor with the hosepipe held aloft in one hand whilst directing a spray of water around the bomb. Each member wears a steel helmet and, when on duty, patrols the area during an air raid. In one such raid my father and elder brother, Ken, are patrolling together when they hear the loud low-pitched howl of a dud anti-aircraft shell and dad, having been a soldier in the First World War, quickly falls flat on the ground, pulling my brother down with him.

When an air raid is imminent, known officially as a 'red alert', warning is given by the siren located in Wollaton Road on the top of Parkes' lace factory (formerly the Anglo Scotian Mills and in 2005 converted to private apartments). My own family, however, has the means of a much earlier warning (officially, a 'purple alert'). We know that Jack Baugh (pronounced *boar*), a resident in the Larch Crescent area and member of the Auxiliary Fire Service will receive such a warning by telephone and will immediately ride his James autocycle to the Fire Station. His route will take him down Park Street past our house and, upon hearing the characteristic phut-phut-phut of his engine, my parents will say, "There goes Jack Baugh, the sirens will be going soon". And, sure enough, they do.

The events of the night of 8/9 May 1941, the heaviest air raid of the war on Nottingham, are vividly etched in my mind. Perhaps we're getting blasé, as we're not in the Anderson shelter but sitting around the dining room table. We hear the easily recognizable noise of an aircraft making a diving attack,

Stirrup Pump used by Mr Underwood, a resident of Abbey Road, Beeston during World War Two

passing directly over our house, and then, as the bombs fall, the loud screeching whistle of their descent, like an express train with its brakes on. Such is the noise and shock of the bombs exploding that we think one has landed very close. There is then total silence followed by the unmistakable noise of our front windows breaking as they are sucked outwards into the street by the vacuum created by the bomb blast — despite the fact that at the beginning of the war, we have glued on to them a special lace fabric to prevent lethal glass splinters.

When we first hear the bombs falling, all of the family dives under the table and, at the instant of the explosion; my mother spills a cup of hot tea all over me. I am clad only in my winceyette pyjamas and my immediate mental reactions, in slow motion, are that the scalding sensation is all part of being killed by the bomb.

I go outside next morning to see that Park Street is covered with a layer of brick rubble and dust. A little over 100 yards from home I discover that the top of Elm Avenue and a section of Glebe Street have been hit by a stick of five bombs, the first badly damaging the end house (later to become part of "The Elms" Nursing Home) and killing the lady occupant who had left the Anderson shelter and gone back into the house. One or two bombs have fallen at the rear of the Pollard's house at number 2 Bramcote Road, on the tennis lawn fronting onto Glebe Street (later to become the site for two modem bungalows). I can see that these bombs have made only small craters so they must have failed to explode. As I return home, I notice small wafers of pale, grey ash falling through the air that I later discover are the burnt remains of paper from the Boots Printing Works on Station Street, Nottingham, destroyed by fire in the raid. I meet my friend Derek Thornhill, who lives at 26 Cromwell Road, much closer to the exploding bomb. He tells me that his mother, brother Brian and himself had been sheltering since the beginning of the raid, in the cellar. His father, Tom, was out on patrol with his across-the-road fellow Special Constable, Jim Wright. Sometime after 2am, since all had gone quiet as if the raid had come to an end, they came back into the sitting room. At about 3am he goes on to describe the falling bombs, in the same way as myself, as sounding like an express train. Surprisingly, hearing no sound of the exploding bomb, they were first aware of breaking glass as the windows fell outwards and the contents of the fireplace came inwards. This reported timing gives credence to the conjecture that the lady killed in the Elm Avenue house, thinking that the raid was over, had returned indoors and may well have shown a light. The German bomber in question may have been a solitary raider that had become detached from the main force that had already made for home.

During this raid the value of steel helmets is illustrated in two incidents. At the time of impact of the bombs, Mr Albert Gibson, wearing his dark blue Special Constable's steel helmet is attending to the needs of nature in the outside toilet of his home at 24 Cromwell Road, being about fifty yards from the point of impact. The explosion brings tumbling down on his head some large tins of paint that have been sitting on the shelf above. He is without injury.

In the other more potentially serious incident, Mr Walter Simpkins is patrolling several hundred yards from the point of impact on Imperial Road outside the orphanage (later to become Silverwood Nursing Home). A large piece of masonry strikes his Air Raid Warden's helmet, which he later shows me. It has in it a significant dent. If he had not been wearing this he would undoubtedly have been seriously injured or killed.

Water storage tanks for use in situations where no water can be extracted from the mains, are erected and situated in a street or accessible off-street location. Extraction is by means of lightweight two-wheeled trailer pumps powered by a Coventry Climax engine that has a cast aluminium cylinder block (of a type later to be used in the Hillman Imp car). The tanks are five feet deep, ten feet wide and thirty feet long and are built of black-painted prefabricated sheet steel to contain several thousand gallons of water. One such a tank has been assembled at the side of the Chilwell Road Methodist Church. By now, at the back of the church are brick-built air raid shelters. Others may also be seen in many side streets, built on the street itself. That they are a hazard in the blackout is illustrated by the fact that a fellow member of the 6th Beeston Boy Scouts, who is serving as an ARP (Air Raid Precautions) volunteer cycle messenger boy, has recently collided with one of these shelters in the blackout and has knocked himself unconscious.

Our Scoutmaster, Henry (Skip) Middleton is an employee at the Chilwell Central Ordnance Depot and I think later that perhaps it was through this connection that we Scouts were recruited to help the 'war effort'. Well, was it really that or just a morale-boosting exercise? We assemble at the depot on a Saturday morning and are issued with a sack, for the purpose of scavenging off the ground with our bare hands (Health & Safety has yet to be invented), any scraps of metal we can find for recycling. Surprisingly, we find plenty of every description, including rusty nails, nuts and bolts, washers and also steel bands from wooden packing cases.

My family also shows its patriotism by weekly purchases of National Savings stamps from our door-to-door collector, Brenda Griffiths (a former fellow pupil at Round Hill Infants' School). From time to time, district National Savings Weeks are held with a target figure of thousands of pounds: enough to pay for a Spitfire. In this connection, I cycle to Woodside Road recreation ground to view a shot-down German bomber aircraft; a Heinkel 111K showing several bullet holes that is on display to advertise Savings Week.

Rationing of food and other commodities is imposed in stages from the beginning of the war.

Beeston Parish Church Magazine May 1944

To eke out a ration and make it go further is a skill acquired by most housewives. One of my mother's tricks is to skim the cream off the milk and whisk it to add to the butter ration. She

Clothing Coupons Book

also trades her clothing coupons: one of her sisters, Aunty Win, is quite a dresser; mother is thrifty. The conjunction of these two attributes leads to an arrangement whereby mother gives aunty her clothing coupons in a free exchange for aunty's still very wearable cast-offs. Early on in the war my mother responds to an appeal by giving up her aluminium pots and pans for melting down for use in aircraft construction. For next-door's fowls she saves the vegetable peelings, which the neighbours boil up and mix with a proprietary chicken feed. This is acknowledged from time to time by the gift of a few eggs, a welcome supplement to our wartime ration of dried egg that comes in brown, sealed, waxed cartons, bearing the Stars and Stripes denoting its country of origin — and making very tasty scrambled egg.

Watching someone doing a job is something I am often drawn to. In this case it is a team of men with oxyacetylene cutting equipment who are compulsorily taking down iron railings from the fronts of houses. These, we are told, are for melting down for making the armour plating for tanks. In later years I learn that they were piled up in scrap yards, unused and rusting.

During the war, between the ages of eleven and seventeen years, I am a pupil of the Henry Mellish County Secondary School (later, Grammar School) in Bulwell. The shortage of air raid shelters there in September 1939 imposes on us a regime of half-time attendance for part of our first year, with plenty of homework to do during the half-day at home. At 7.30am, as I begin my journey to school, I can see that the approaching bus has been fitted with masks to its headlights that have effectively reduced them to about half of their original diameter. Each mask looks as if it has been made out of a paint tin with three horizontal, rectangular slits cut into its circular base for the light to shine through. Above each slit, a shade projects to prevent the light shining upwards. As I board the bus, I can see outside only dimly through the blue translucent paint that has been applied to the window. These measures are all part of the air raid precautions for eliminating or dimming lights, known as the 'blackout'. It is the winter of 1940 and I am wearing a hand-knitted balaclava helmet with my school cap perched on top in compliance with school rules. On my way home, as the bus travels along University Boulevard, every 40 yards or so at the roadside I can see a steel-fabricated device belching out black smoke for hiding details on the ground from enemy aircraft. It comprises a cylindrical oil supply drum of 50cm diameter and 40cm height, resting on its base, above which is a burner and a one-metre high cylindrical chimney of about 20cm diameter. Resting on three spacers above the chimney is a cover shaped like a Chinese coolie hat. As the bus approaches Barton's Garage, Chilwell, I notice an advertising poster displaying these words: '*Coughs & Sneezes Spread Diseases — Trap the Germs in your Handkerchief!*' In other public places I have seen slogans such as '*Dig for Victory*' and '*BE LIKE DAD, KEEP MUM — Careless Talk Costs Lives*'. As I alight from the bus, I notice a six-inch standpipe with valve and control wheel for the supply of coal gas to those Barton's buses that are fitted on top with a frame containing a gas storage bag and have had their engines tuned to run on this alternative fuel.

The battery hand-torch I have in my pocket for seeing my way home in the blackout must comply with regulations. I've cut a one-inch diameter hole in a circular card that will fit behind the lens and applied a piece of tissue paper to shroud the bulb. On arriving home, it is getting dark and my first job is to put up the two blackout boards to cover the kitchen sash window above the brown salt-glazed sink, where curtains would be inappropriate. Of necessity, we have made these boards ourselves at the beginning of the war. They consist of a frame of wooden laths that would be normally used for making a lattice fence, on to which we have fixed with drawing pins a large sheet of thick black cartridge paper. I hold them in place with bradawls, from the toolbox, pushed into the window frame. The rest of the windows are fitted with curtains made from a heavy black material, specially manufactured for preventing the escape of light. Every night one of us draws them together with the utmost care and then goes outside to ensure that they are effective.

Another nightly ritual is the 9 o'clock news from the BBC, read by Alvar Liddell, preceded by the bass drumbeat of three dots and a dash — di di di dah — the Morse code for V for victory. I closely follow the progress of the war but always switch on at ten to nine to hear several national anthems of the allies, some of which tunes I find so stirring. After the news bulletin I listen to messages that are intended for the ears of members of resistance movements as they covertly listen to their concealed wireless receivers. Previously arranged between sender and recipient, each message has a secret meaning quite unconnected with its subject matter. So when I hear a message such as, *'The white rabbit has returned to the burrow'*, I catch the excitement of imagining my own involvement in the undercover action that it is intended to trigger.

NEW WESLEYAN CHAPEL

Chilwell Road Methodist Church during construction, 1901-02

For most of the war, through connections made at Chilwell Road Methodist Church, we make friends with local army personnel, stationed at the nearby Chilwell Central Ordnance Depot. They visit us at weekends for tea and spend the evening with us as a welcome break from being billeted in an army hut. Most of them have a musical talent: Leonard Brightmore is an accomplished pianist, as is Vic Ansell with whom we keep up our friendship for many years after the war. They are delighted to be able to find a piano to play. My favourite pieces played by Len and Vic are respectively *Rustle of Spring (Frülingsrauschen)* by Christian Sinding and *Wedding Day at Troldhaugen* by Edvard Grieg. Other musicians include: Dick Lowry who has a fine bass voice, cannot read music and has learned his repertoire from gramophone records; Eric Whitley (tenor) who later will go on to sing with the *Black & White Minstrel Show*. This exposure to classical music, not forgetting vocal Chilwell performances with piano accompaniment, is forming my musical tastes and creating a love of singing.

There exists a widespread camaraderie. One winter's night, dad comes in from work and has with him, complete with bell-bottomed trousers, a sailor whom he has found wandering and lost. He's called Eddie and is looking for his sweetheart, an ATS girl, stationed at 'the depot'. "Well, we'll give you some supper and find a bed for you, then you can find her in the morning". This brief encounter ends next morning, as we direct him on his way.

When at school, for much of the time I am not very aware that a war is raging. At about 12 years of age we are engaged in helping to feed the nation. I don't remember having any choice when Form 2A is recruited for a fortnight into a spud (potato) picking squad. We are told to come to school suitably clad, bringing a packed lunch and drinks, and are then transported by coach to a farm in Stragglethorpe, adjacent to the Nottingham to Grantham canal. Along the length of the field, we are assigned in pairs to a stint (section of a potato row) about the length of a cricket pitch. For collecting the potatoes, each of us is provided with a smaller version of a baby's tin (galvanized) bath. The tractor towing a rotating fork called a spinner drives down the length of the field, exposing the potatoes. We then have to work like mad to collect all of the spuds on our stint before the tractor returns along the next row, travelling in the opposite direction. In this we always succeed as we are patriotic and have the 'work ethic'. We are paid a pittance of 4d (four old pence) per hour. Thinking about this in later years, I believe that the farmers used us as sweated labour, making a packet out of us.

Sometime during the following year, many of the members of Form 3 volunteer to go away to a month's farming camp, run by several of the teachers. On the first Saturday, with all my gear in an army kitbag, I travel by train to Grantham, where we are picked up and transported about ten miles to the south to a small village called Boothby Pagnell. Here we are billeted in the disused village schoolroom, sleeping on the floor on straw-filled palliasses. The teachers provide us with a packed lunch, often of sandwiches containing haslet (pig's offal, cooked and compressed into a meat loaf, bound together with a cereal product). We call these sandwiches 'bread and bread'. Extra tea is mashed at breakfast time and our lunchtime drink is cold tea in a glass lemonade bottle. It is remarkably refreshing and from this experience I shall retain the taste for it for the rest of my life. On weekdays we are allocated to a farmer who picks us up and sets us on to various jobs. It is a hot summer, so whatever the job, it is made more tiring through coping with the blistering sun on one's back. These jobs include:

- Thistling: chopping off thistles in meadow land with a push hoe
- Sugar beet singling: first bending down and then resorting to crawling on hands and knees along rows of clumps of 3 or 4 young plants and removing all but the strongest
- Driving bullocks: the aim is to get them into a yard but because of my inexperience, I manage to scatter them over a wide area, much to the annoyance of the stockman
- Stooking or stowking: picking up two sheaves of wheat; bashing the corn heads together to form an upturned letter 'V'; then making a 'stook' out of four such pairs. Quite often the binder mechanism on the harvester fails to tie the twine around the sheaf. To remedy this I tie a half granny knot (left over right and under) and then do another left over right and under, so preventing the knot slipping as I tie the other half of the granny knot. I mention this detail, as I permanently adopt this method for tying my shoelaces

Corn Stooks

- Stacking (building a haystack): first, pitchforking hay sheaves from a flat, open dray to the stack builder at the base of the stack. As the stack increases in height the builder becomes out of reach, so an alcove called a 'stair-hole' is created in the side of the haystack, large enough for a man complete with pitchfork to stand within. A sheaf is then pitched up from the dray; the stair-hole man catches the sheaf on his own fork and pitches it up to the builder at the top of the stack. I am the one told to get into the stair-hole. I have never been so exhausted. I cannot stop for a breather, as I have to work as fast as those feeding me with sheaves from below.
- Kedlocking: proceeding in line with others across a cornfield and pulling out kedlocks (a local name for charlocks) by hand. The kedlock, a weed belonging to the mustard family, has a cluster of yellow flowers at its head and grows as high as the corn.
- Sheep dipping: I learn how to manhandle a reluctant sheep into a trough of bright yellow dip, without following it — and then to keep at a respectable distance as it emerges, belching and vigourously shaking itself.

Most of the farms that I visit have Italian prisoners of war as farm workers, who must be a low security risk, as they seem to move quite freely. Nevertheless, they wear dark brown trousers and a 'battle dress' tunic with a large colour-filled circle on the back. I do not know whether they are given any incentive to work but those I see appear somewhat indolent — but who can blame them?

It is during this time that my life in the country village is punctuated by reminders of the war. One night, I am sleeping soundly when the loud noise of a very low-flying aircraft awakens me, followed a few seconds later by a flash of light and the eruption of an explosion. The next day, some of my classmates, who have somehow managed to acquire bikes, discover the cause of this in the near vicinity: a Handley Page Hampden bomber has crashed with a full bomb load, killing the crew and scattering body parts.

In another incident, returning after a day's work, some of us stop by the side of a runway at Spittalgate bomber station, just to the south of Grantham. Coming in to land, close to the ground, is a Vickers Wellington twin-engine bomber. We are startled to see that its wheels are not down. In the nick of time, stepping out from a brick cabin near the beginning of the runway, a duty officer fires from a Verey (pronounced *veerie*) pistol, a red flare which rises in a low arc and falls to the ground, bouncing several times in front of the aircraft. The pilot sees it and opens up the engine throttles to climb away and circle to land safely.

It is around this time in 1942 that my brother, Ken, joins the local Home Guard. Along with other 17 year-olds he is assigned to the Mobile Squad. A chance to see some of the available armaments soon presents itself at a Home Guard publicity display on the Dovecote Lane recreation ground:

- An EY projector: a rifle modified for launching a hand grenade
- A PIAT anti-tank gun
- A spigot anti-tank mortar: it sat on four legs splayed flat to the ground

At home, one Sunday afternoon, I am pottering around in the back garden when I am startled by the sudden noise overhead of a low-flying aircraft — so low that I can see a member of the crew in the cabin — the closeness of the enemy is scary. Immediately, I recognize it as a Heinkel 111K from the distinctive shape of its tail. I later learn that this lone daylight raider, during an attempted attack on Stanton Ironworks (now Saint-Gobain Pipelines), has jettisoned a high explosive bomb, the crater of which I see later in a field just to the south of the future site of the Alderman White School.

In another incident, an aircraft used by the Royal Air Force Bomber Command in the earlier part of the war, a twin-engine Vickers Wellington, is repeatedly circling around this area for an unusually long time. I learn shortly afterwards that it has been previously captured by the Germans and is being covertly used for reconnaissance. However, this is discovered and the aircraft is shot down somewhere over Lincolnshire.

In the autumn of 1943 (or was it the spring of 1944?), I extend my experiences in farming, more motivated by the desire for pocket money than patriotism. To the right of the trees in Lime Tree Avenue approaching Wollaton Hall is a field of flax. There is no way of harvesting this successfully other than by pulling it up by hand. It is so dirty a job that my skin is firmly scaled with dust at the end of each day and the only way of removing it is a hard scrub in a hot bath. It is during my lunch breaks here that I go further into the park where an American Airborne Division is stationed, prior to taking part in the D-day landings. Standing across the other side of a wire fence, their brass band, complete with sousaphone, is playing '*American Patrol*' followed by '*Hawaiian War Chant*'.

For years, every Wednesday afternoon my mother and we three boys visit Grandma Drinkwater for tea. Returning from school in Bulwell, I alight from the Barton's bus at the Hop Pole and make my way towards Factory Lane, past the spot where earlier in the war my grandma had been knocked down in an accident involving an army motorcycle dispatch rider. She broke her femur and was treated in a wartime hospital at Selston. After tea, as I walk home up Factory Lane, I can see passing ahead from left to right along High Road, Chilwell, a convoy of army lorries. I reach the road junction but am quite unable to cross the road. One after another, a seemingly never-ending stream of brand new army lorries with camouflaged canvas tops passes across my vision — and then, after an interminable 20 minutes — they're gone. Perhaps they're going to be loaded with boxes of ammunition that, during a recent camp with some of my fellow scouts, I've seen stored in shelters on the grass verges of country lanes in Lincolnshire. These 40 feet long by 10 feet wide shelters are made from semi-circular sections of corrugated iron and are perhaps 50 feet apart along every lane where there's a verge — hundreds of them.

There is one occasion when at school that there are active signs of war. I am in the third form, that is, twelve going thirteen — and still in short trousers. It is during an afternoon lesson that the air raid siren wails and we can hear the sound of a heavy anti-aircraft gun barrage. At the repeated ringing of the electric end-of-lesson bells around the school we make our way to our allocated concrete air raid shelter on the games field. As we run across the large tarmac playground we are aware of the sound of a hail of shrapnel falling to the ground but amazingly this lethal shower hurts no one. However, there <u>are</u> continual reminders of the war: lady teachers now replace those male members of the teaching staff who have been called up for military service; during morning assembly Mr G F Houston, the Headmaster, announces all too often that A N Other who was a pupil or member of staff from (date) to (date) has been reported missing believed killed/killed in action. Mr Houston, strict but fair, demonstrably knows every boy in a school of 600 pupils, so I think this must be most distressing for him, but he betrays no emotion.

There is one occasion when such an event hits me very hard. In the last week of August 1944, Dennis (Den) Jones, a school friend of my elder brother, Ken, and with whom I too am well acquainted, visits us at home. He has just returned from training in Canada and the insignias on his sleeve and chest indicate that he is a Sergeant Navigator in the Royal Air Force. He sits comfortably in an armchair in the corner by the fireplace, looking a picture of health and tells us what a wonderful time he's been having abroad. He has been doing flying training as part of the aircrew of a Halifax bomber in a Pathfinder squadron whose job it is to mark out a target with flares prior to a bombing raid. As we see him off, he bids us cheerio and continues his visiting next door, where his aunt and uncle live. At the end of the first week in September we are shocked to hear the news that he is missing, believed killed. We later learn that his aircraft has been shot down over Essen on his first operational flight. He was only nineteen. In later years, I discover that his name is commemorated on the Runnymede Memorial, implying that he has no known grave. I always think of him on Remembrance Day.

A few months prior to this we are witnesses to the fact that our night bomber offensive is at its height. For the duration of most of the war, in order to give farmers effectively longer daylight hours, the clock has been advanced by one hour further than usual throughout the year. So, in winter, the time has been one hour ahead of GMT and in the summer, two hours ahead, which we call *Double Summer Time*. During these long summer evenings of 1944 we stand in the garden, looking upwards as the Beeston sky is filled with low-flying Lancaster bombers circling round as they group before setting off for their target.

Lockheed Hudson wartime aircraft

As is the case with many teenage boys, I am keen on aircraft recognition. One day, I spot a Lockheed Hudson, a twin-engined reconnaissance aircraft, circling Beeston and clearly in difficulty. I learn that the pilot has attempted a crash landing in the fields to the west of Bramcote Lane, Chilwell (later to become part of the Inham Nook estate). I get on my bike and go to investigate. Some of the crew had attempted to bale out but sadly they were too low for their parachutes to open and there are no survivors. I can see from the broken fronds, that the aircraft had passed through the topmost branches of the tall tree at the corner of Bramcote Avenue and Bramcote Lane. I do not know it at this time, but this tree is hardy enough to be still standing over 60 years later.

Now, at a distance of 66 years, I am fortunate in being able to recall with clarity the sights and sounds of my life as a schoolboy during World War Two.

MEMORIES OF THE SECOND WORLD WAR
By Peter Wright

When the war began I was a pupil at Meadow Lane School, Chilwell, but left shortly after when I became 14. Before I left we had to have air raid practice and that involved the children being dispersed to houses nearby. I had to go to a cottage in The Nook, opposite the school. I went a couple of times and crouched under the table in the front room. But I thought it would be better if I ran to my home in Woodland Grove because we had a proper air raid shelter, it wasn't very far and I could run quite fast. As there were no air raid warnings before I left Meadow Lane School, it didn't matter much anyway.

Early on in the war we all had to dig out and erect Anderson Shelters in our gardens and I remember helping Mr Cook, who lived two doors away, with his digging.

I found work with the Co-op No 25 Branch on Cator Lane, Chilwell, and one day when I loaded up the carrier bike with grocery orders for houses on Bramcote Lane I heard aircraft engines droning overhead. I looked up and saw two Heinkel 111s flying at about three to four thousand feet towards Stanton Iron Works (now Saint-Gobain Pipelines). I

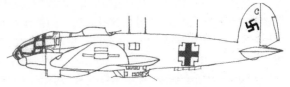

German Bomber – Heinkel 111

rushed back into the shop and reported it to the manager, Mr. Tomlinson. As the air raid siren was on the roof of the Co-op the raid had not apparently been seen by the authorities. By the time the siren went the bombers had dropped their load somewhere and were on their way back to Germany. The strange thing was no one took much notice until the siren sounded then everyone rushed home to their shelters.

One night bombs were dropped on Bramcote Lane, opposite Inham Road, and two homes had near misses. One shelter had a direct hit killing all the family including a young baby. The nurse escaped serious injury because she had returned to the bungalow to fetch the baby a feeding bottle. It was one of my delivery addresses and it made me very unhappy.

Dad and I had a fright one night when we were walking up the entry between our house and next door. CRASH! A bomb fell in Meadow Lane and the blast came up between the houses on Cator Lane and Woodland Grove, knocking dad and myself to the ground. Another time, incendiary bombs fell on Cator Lane Woods (now Clumber Avenue) setting fire to the trees. As dad was a Fire Warden he came back to the house for his tin hat, shovel and bucket. I wanted to help but he said it was too dangerous for me.

A bomb was dropped on Beeston Fields Golf Course one night, near the end of Cator Lane, luckily it didn't explode. It was about 14 feet deep in the ground and several streets on the Hillman Estate had to be evacuated until the bomb squad defused it and took it away.

In 1941 I went to work at JB Taps & Dies situated on Factory Lane behind Myford's. One night I was on fire-watch duty with the chargehand Albert Tuckwood. We slept on camp beds in the middle of the shop floor. In the night I heard banging outside, I roused Albert and he grabbed a coat and ran out to the back while I found a torch. I found Albert head first in an empty unwashed, night-soil bin that had been put to one side while the night-soil men emptied the other bins. What a mess! I had to sluice him down with a stirrup pump to get most of it off before he could go home for a bath and a change of clothes. He asked me not to tell anyone about the incident, which I didn't. The next day the council phoned the office to ask if the bloke who had fallen in the bin was alright. The boss knew nothing about it and asked the foreman who also didn't know anything. I don't know how the council knew. The news soon spread around the shop, much to everyone's amusement. I got it in the neck from Albert for letting the story get out when I had actually kept mum about the whole thing! That episode was still getting laughs at Albert's expense long after the war.

When I was 16 years old the Air Training Corps (ATC) was formed from the Air Defence Cadet Corps (ADCC) and a squadron was started in Beeston, in the school on Nether Street. This was No. 1359 Squadron. I joined in the first week of its organisation and was No 47 on the roll, being near the end of the alphabet. We went to camps around the area for our training.

BOMB ON 26 MONA STREET, BEESTON – 8th APRIL 1941 - 2.30a.m.
By George W Martin

The house shown in the photograph on the opposite page was No.26 Mona Street, Beeston, where I lived with my parents and younger brother. At the time I was nearly 13 years old and my brother was 11. The house was an Edwardian semi-detached and my mother's uncle lived in the adjoining house with his wife and daughter.

The Air Raid Warning siren had sounded early in the evening, as it often did at that time, and as there seemed to be no activity, we went to bed as usual. My brother and I slept in the downstairs front room instead of the bedroom we normally shared at the rear of the house, so that we could get out quickly in case of need.

I was woken by the sound of what seemed to be a low-flying aeroplane and the whistle of the bombs. Only half awake, I was not aware of the danger of the situation until the bombs struck. There was no recognisable explosion, just a tremendous roar as though an express train had hit the house, followed by a great cloud of dust, and then silence.

My brother was still asleep, and I woke him and tried to open the door into the hall, but it was jammed, and there was a huge crack in the wall. Then I heard my parents moving about and calling to us - I answered and my father forced open the door and took us all outside. My parents had been sleeping in the upstairs bedroom and when the bombs fell the ceiling and the attic floor fell down onto their bed. Fortunately it was an iron bedstead, which supported the weight, and they were able to creep out from underneath the debris without injury. The stairs and walls had disappeared, so they clambered down over the rubble in the dark, and my father fell and cut his hand quite badly.

We were in our night clothes, with bare feet, and the pavements and road were covered in shattered glass and debris. Neighbours came out and invited us indoors, providing us with shoes and coats so that we could walk down the street to my grandfather's house.

When he knew we were safe my father went back to put out incendiary bombs which were burning all around, and to search for Uncle Joe, Aunt Sal and Edna. They were in bed when the bomb fell and were buried in the rubble. Another bomb had fallen behind Uncle Joe's house, which was completely flattened. It was some time before they were rescued; Edna was injured, and Aunt Sal was very badly hurt and died the next day.

The bomb had struck the kitchens of the houses and under the stairs, and everything in the downstairs back room was smashed up against the fireplace; the contents of the kitchen were also totally destroyed. There was no sign of the gas cooker, the table wringer, or the sink. An incendiary bomb was burning in the roof and another in the wreckage at the rear of the house, which my father extinguished. The roof had been lifted up, turned through 90 degrees and dropped down again, overhanging the front of the house. The photograph shows the house after the wrecked roof had been removed.

Incendiary bombs were burning all around, from the rear of our house we could see several fires glowing in the attics of the houses on Windsor Street. The Fire Brigade arrived later and put out the fires which were still burning, saturating the ruin of the houses. All our possessions were either smashed or spoiled by the water.

Several bombs had fallen in the street, one on our houses and one in the garden, one in front of the house where the two Miss Sanders lived, which had damaged the front of the house and struck the gas main, causing a great roaring flame. One fell in front of the Harts' house, blowing Doris Hart into the crater, but amazingly she was unhurt. Another bomb fell on the Beeston Boiler Company Mess Room and one on the Beeston Boiler offices, demolishing the strongroom and hurling debris over my grandfather's house.

We spent the remainder of the next day at my grandfather's house and tried to salvage anything we could from the wreckage. We stayed with relatives for a month, until we were able to obtain the tenancy of another house and furnish a new home.

See page 38 for the official report of bombs dropped on Beeston 8 April 1941

Bomb damage to 26 Mona Street during a raid on the night of 7/8th April 1941

```
            INTERIM OPERATIONAL REPORT.


            Night: 7th/8th April 1941.


Beeston and Stapleford Urban District.

   Several small H.E.s and incendiary bombs fell at approximately
      2.15 hours at Mona Street, Beeston. Office of Beeston Boiler
      Company and two houses demolished. Several other houses
      damaged. Gas main caught fire. 2 serious casualties and
      1 slight casualty removed to General Hospital.

   1 H.E. fell at Acacia Walk. Slight damage caused to house.
      No casualties.

   Incendiary bombs also fell in Glebe Street, Middle Street,
      Windsor Street, Park Road and Dagmar Grove. Houses on fire.
      Fires soon extinguished.

   3 unexploded bombs in Station Road. Roads closed to traffic.
      No evacuation necessary.
```

Provisional report of Beeston bombings
(Park Road should have been recorded as Park Street)

Date. 8-4-41	Time reception completed 11.23	Telephonist's Name Hemingway

Message from,
   (Originator)   Subcontroller Beeston Urban.

Message Addressed to A.R.P. Control Notts. County.

Originator's Message Number. Clerk's B.S.U.12.	Time of origin 11.00	In Number I.C.31.

Text of Message.

    I report an Air Raid took place in this district at 02.15hrs today stop it consisted of High Explosive and Incendiary Bomb attacks stop this took place almost entirely on a straight line from the Beeston Boiler Company's Works to Glebe Street both at Beeston stop the works mentioned sustained a direct hit which has demolished the administrative block stop there was considerable damage to working class residential property in the immediate vicinity of these works about ten houses have been seriously damaged stop in Station Road close to the main road an U.X.B. has damaged Princes Works and another H.E. is believed to be in a shop on the opposite side of the road stop in addition to these a considerable number of I.B.'s were dropped and it is estimated by the Assistant Chief Warden that there may be as many as five hundred of these stop Resulting fires were quickly dealt with stop no deaths have been reported but three cases of injury were sent to the Nottingham General Hospital one of these having had preliminary treatment at the Dovecote Lane First Aid post stop two other cases were dealt with at that Post and afterwards sent home stop two further cases of minor injury were dealt with privately by Doctor and Nurse respectively stop the turnout of services was satisfactory as to personnel and transport and was amply sufficient for the calls which had to be made stop I am not aware of any difficulty in calling up of Personnel stop Wardens reports were satisfactory as a basis for action and the communications systems worked properly at all stages stop it was not necessary to use the Messenger Service stop the work of the services generally was satisfactory there being no appreciable delay in getting services to the spot and no more services were called out than appeared to be necessary at the time of call stop no difficulty was experienced on account of lack of co-ordination between services stop the Rescue Parties work is still proceeding and no points of special difficulty have yet been reported stop as to the Casualty Services everybody appeared to do his work adequately at the incident stop the Mobile Units was not engaged and its Doctor reported to Duty promptly stop with regard to the casualty brought to the post and afterwards sent to Hospital I understand that some relief was thereby rendered which might have been effected by a Doctor had he been on the scene stop a Rest Centre was opened at the Valley Mission, Queens Road, Beeston and five people were dealt with stop the Salvage of Property and removal of Debris is proceeding and suitable Billeting arrangements where necessary will be made stop the Officers of the Unemployment Assistant Board have arrived and are dealing with the appropriate cases stop as to Public Utility Services a Gas Main caught fire and was appropriately and promptly put out stop message ends.

MEMORIES OF THE WAR AND THE FLOODS
By Doris Wilson (née Hart)

I was a young teenager in April 1941 and lived at No. 42 Mona Street. In the early hours of 8th April I was woken by the sound of aircraft passing overhead. I got out of bed and saw the planes coming over. I walked down the stairs from my bedroom in the attic. There was a terrific explosion and all the front of the house was ripped off. A bomb had landed at the front and it made a big crater in the garden. The force of the blast blew me out of the house and I landed in the crater along with a lot of our furniture and possessions. Miraculously though I escaped without injury. I lost all my clothes and books and jewellery and lots of other things as well.

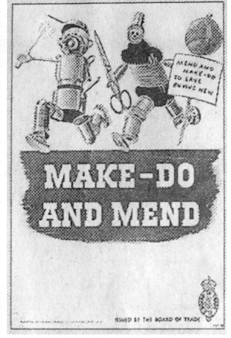

My family and I had to go and live with my aunt at No 34 Mona Street until after the war and then we moved to another house nearby.

I remember how tight things were during the war. The shortages of all everyday things and the rationing of food and clothes and how we had to 'make-do and mend' or go without. And nothing could be thrown away if it could possibly be used again.

And after the war ended rationing got even more stringent and bread could only be bought on ration. The winter of 1946/7 was very cold and we had a lot of snow. It wasn't easy to keep warm because coal was scarce, too. Eventually a thaw set in and the snow melted very quickly because the temperature rose suddenly. We had very bad floods and I remember the water coming up Mona Street, over Queens Road and up Dagmar Grove.

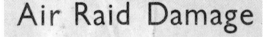

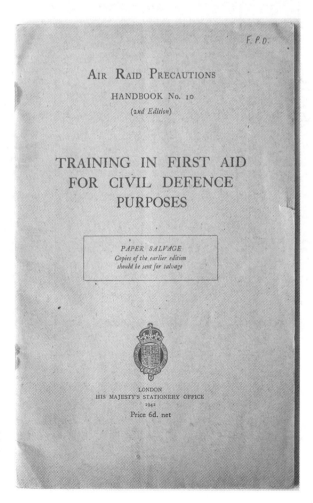

Air Raid Damage

Householders and Recovery of Furniture, etc.

The primary responsibility for recovering and protecting furniture and other removable goods and articles damaged by enemy action rests with their owner.

Local authorities will give assistance for the removal and local transport of goods or articles, or for their protection against loss or further damage, particularly where persons are rendered homeless.

Difficulty may arise, in some cases, in tracing the owner, for example where a furnished house has been left unoccupied, or the owner has become a casualty. In such cases, local authorities will take steps to protect furniture and other articles against loss or further damage due to exposure, until the owner is traced and can make his or her own arrangements.

All householders are, therefore, urged to see that every article they value is clearly marked with their name and address. The marking could be conveniently made by means of gummed labels affixed inside drawers or wardrobes or under tables and chairs, where it would not normally be seen. It would be helpful also if householders could add an address, in the same district, to which the furniture, etc., could be sent for storage, should the necessity arise.

Experience has shown that these precautions may be the means of saving from damage some cherished or valuable article.

Issued by the Beeston & Stapleford Urban District Council

F.P.O.

AIR RAID PRECAUTIONS

HANDBOOK No. 10

(2nd Edition)

TRAINING IN FIRST AID FOR CIVIL DEFENCE PURPOSES

PAPER SALVAGE
Copies of the earlier edition
should be sent for salvage

LONDON
HIS MAJESTY'S STATIONERY OFFICE
1942
Price 6d. net

1942

INCIDENT SHEET No.29. 09.00 hours 29th October 1940 to 09.00 hours 30th October 1940.

County District	Incident No.	Place	Time and date	Type and No. of bombs	Casualties	Damage	Remarks
Beeston Rural	186	Field Lane, Chilwell	Reported 11.44 hours. 29.10.40. Believed fell on night of 30/31st August 1940.	1 H.E.	none	no damage	Bomb unexploded.

INCIDENT SHEET No.33. 09.00 hours 5th November to 09.00 hours 6th November 1940.

County District	Incident No.	Place	Time and date	Type and No. of bombs	Casualties	Damage	Remarks
Beeston & Stapleford Urban	199	150 yds. inside field opposite house No.80 Brancote Lane, Chilwell.	Reported 18.25 hours. 5.11.40. Believed dropped on the night of 30/31st August.	1 H.E.	none	no damage	bomb unexploded

INCIDENT SHEET No.38. 09.00 hours 20th November to 09.00 hours 2nd November 1940.

County District	Incident No.	Place	Time and date	Type and No. of bombs	Casualties	Damage	Remarks
Beeston & Stapleford Urban	214	in front garden of 147 Brookhill Street, Stapleford.	during night of 19/20th November 1940.	Suspected unexploded A.A.Shell.	none	no damage.	

INCIDENT SHEET No.72. 09.00 hours 7th April 1941 to 09.00 hours 8th April 1941.

County District	Incident No.	Place	Time and date	Type and No. of bombs	Casualties	Damage	Remarks
Beeston & Stapleford U.D.	330	Globe Street, Mona Street, Windsor Street, Middle Street, Acacia walk, Dagmar Grove, Park Street, Beeston.	02.15 hours. 8.4.41.	several I.B. 7 H.E. 3 UXB.	2 women seriously wounded. 1 child & 3 women slightly injured.	Offices of Beeston Boiler Co. demolished. 2 houses demolished & several other houses damaged.	Two UXBs at No.217 & one at Princess Works, Station Road, Beeston. High Street & Station Road blocked. Rest centre opened.

Four extracts from Incident Sheets logging bombs dropped in the Beeston area 1940-1941

Beeston Toreadors' Carnival Band raising money for War Weapons' Week 24-31 May 1941, on Broadgate Recreation Ground, Beeston. The houses in the background are on The City.

BEESTON & STAPLEFORD URBAN DISTRICT COUNCIL.

Fire Guard Headquarters,
123 High Road, BEESTON.

December 1942.

Dear Sir,

Following the Registration of women for Civil Defence Duties, a number of women living in your immediate locality have become liable for fire prevention duty in Street Parties. These persons have been enrolled and directed to report to you as the Fire Guard Leader, in order that you may include them on the appropriate duty rota for the Street Party. Arrangements for their training will be made as soon as possible. I shall be obliged therefore, if you will make arrangements for the inclusion of these persons in a rota (nearest to their residence, if possible), and instruct them as to their duty. Steel Helmets and Armbands will be issued in due course. Please make a list of these persons with their addresses, and the Unit they have joined, for reference by your Senior Fire Guard. A copy of the Notice of Direction which is being sent to these persons, is enclosed for your information. They should keep their own direction notice after producing for your inspection.

Yours faithfully,

GEO. H. KEEBLE.

Fire Guard Staff Officer.

Mrs A Shirley 8 HG.
Miss Bessie Wiseman 1 HG
Mrs J M Leggett 7 HG
Mrs A S Chambers 24 HG

STAND FIRM

1. What do I do if fighting breaks out in my neighbourhood?

Keep indoors or in your shelter until the battle is over. If you can have a trench ready in your garden or field, so much the better. You may want to use it for protection if your house is damaged. But if you are at work, or if you have special orders, carry on as long as possible and only take cover when danger approaches. If you are on your way to work, finish your journey if you can.

If you see an enemy tank, or a few enemy soldiers, do not assume that the enemy are in control of the area. What you have seen may be a party sent on in advance, or stragglers from the main body who can easily be rounded up.

CARRY ON

2. What do I do in areas which are some way from the fighting?

Stay in your district and carry on. Go to work whether in shop, field, factory or office. Do your shopping, send your children to school until you are told not to. Do not try to go and live somewhere else. Do not use the roads for any unnecessary journey; they must be left free for troop movements even a long way from the district where actual fighting is taking place.

3. Will certain roads and railways be reserved for the use of the Military, even in areas far from the scene of action?

Yes, certain roads will have to be reserved for important troop movements; but such reservations should be only temporary. As far as possible, bus companies and railways will try to maintain essential public services, though it may be necessary to cut these down. Bicyclists and pedestrians may use the roads for journeys to work, unless instructed not to do so.

ADVICE AND ORDERS

4. Whom shall I ask for advice?

The police and A.R.P. wardens.

5. From whom shall I take orders?

In most cases from the police and A.R.P. wardens. But there may be times when you will have to take orders from the military and the Home Guard in uniform.

6. Is there any means by which I can tell that an order is a true order and not faked?

You will generally know your policeman and your A.R.P. wardens by sight, and can trust them. With a bit of common sense you can tell if a soldier is really British or only pretending to be so. If in doubt ask a policeman, or ask a soldier whom you know personally.

INSTRUCTIONS

7. What does it mean when the church bells are rung?

It is a warning to the local garrison that troops have been seen landing from the air in the neighbourhood of the church in question. Church bells will *not* be rung all over the country as a general warning that invasion has taken place. The ringing of church bells in one place will not be taken up in neighbouring churches.

8. Will instructions be given over the wireless?

Yes; so far as possible. But remember that the enemy can overhear any wireless message, so that the wireless cannot be used for instructions which might give him valuable information.

9. In what other ways will instructions be given?

Through the Press; by loudspeaker vans; and perhaps by leaflets and posters. But remember that genuine Government leaflets will be given to you only by the policeman, your A.R.P. warden or your postman; while genuine posters and instructions will be put up only on Ministry of Information notice boards and official sites, such as police stations, post offices, A.R.P. posts, town halls and schools.

FOOD

10. Should I try to lay in extra food?

No. If you have already laid in a stock of food, keep it for a real emergency; but do not add to it. The Government has made arrangements for food supplies.

NEWS

11. Will normal news services continue?

Yes. Careful plans have been made to enable newspapers and wireless broadcasts to carry on, and in case of need there are emergency measures which will bring you the news. But if there should be some temporary breakdown in news supply, it is very important that you should not listen to rumours nor pass them on, but should wait till real news comes through again. Do not use the telephones or send telegrams if you can possibly avoid it.

MOTOR-CARS

12. Should I put my car, lorry or motor-bicycle out of action?

Yes, when you are told to do so by the police, A.R.P. wardens or military; or when it is obvious that there is an immediate risk of its being seized by the enemy—then disable and hide your bicycle and destroy your maps.

13. How should it be put out of action?

Remove distributor head and leads and either empty the tank or remove the carburettor. If you don't know how to do this, find out now from your nearest garage. In the case of diesel engines remove the injection pump and connection. The parts removed must be hidden well away from the vehicle.

THE ENEMY

14. Should I defend myself against the enemy?

The enemy is not likely to turn aside to attack separate houses. If small parties are going about threatening persons and property in an area not under enemy control and come your way, you have the right of every man and woman to do what you can to protect yourself, your family and your home.

GIVE ALL THE HELP YOU CAN TO OUR TROOPS

Do not tell the enemy anything

Do not give him anything

Do not help him in any way

(55061) Wt. 46281/T1009 14,050,800 (2 kds.) 5/41 Hw. G.51

Issued by The Ministry of Information, the War Office and the Ministry of Home Security, May 1941

42

THE NIGHT WAR BROKE OUT IN BEESTON
By Evelyn Martin

3rd September 1939

I was a member of the St John Ambulance Brigade and at the outbreak of war we had not got around to organising any kind of shift system for air raid warnings, a few Boy Scouts were given lists of names to call people out to man the Fire Station, ARP Posts or the Dovecote Lane Clinic for casualties, etc., but all volunteers were expected at their allotted posts complete with tin hats and gas masks which were given to us the previous day.

The air raid sirens blew about 9.00p.m and as I had not yet gone to bed, I hurried into my full armour i.e. tin hat and gas mask, one powder compact and one prayer book. I kissed my husband and baby daughter a fond farewell and rushed out to do battle, not knowing if I would ever see them again or what the immediate future held for me. (I actually got back home about 7.30 the following morning!)

As I was rushing along the street, which had been newly gravelled, I met a lady at the junction, arms outstretched, mouth open, screaming "*Where's me mam? I want me mam*". And she pushed me to the ground in her panic. She did not stop but ran off still shouting so I picked myself up, examined my bloodied kneecaps and decided to carry on to the First Aid Post at the old ambulance station on Queens Road (now a retail outlet for motorcycles) where I believed they had some medical supplies that could help me.

I did not get a hero's welcome, the lady in charge gave me a large slab of cotton wool and told me to sit in a corner out of the way. Everybody was running around filling every available utensil and bucket with water in case the water supplies were bombed and asking questions such as where was the raid and had any bombs dropped in the locality? We were all nervous and apprehensive.

The all clear sounded at about 6.30 in the morning and somebody had, at last, the time to clean up my knees and put large bandages around them. You could not go off duty until your replacement arrived so I continued to sit there, feeling silly with a tin helmet on, bandages on my legs, a huge service mask over my shoulder and a yellow silk minidress covered in blood at the front with summer sandals on my feet. On my way back home I heard comments such as "*look, they are coming back from the front already*" and I received wolf whistles from a nearby building site. I had a few hours of glory in our street from the neighbours as I was Beeston's first war casualty. I never got a medal. But I still have the scars!

HURTS CROFT, CHILWELL, BOMBED
By Bessie Frame

We lived in The Close, Hurts Croft, Chilwell, and one night in 1941 when my father was out on fire-watching duty, we had an air raid. There had been a bomb alert and we waited.............

A bomber came over and dropped a stick of bombs, one of which nearly demolished two houses. Shrapnel landed in one of our bedrooms via the window frame.

The second fell on a spare plot of land nearly wiping out a pear tree. The debris scattered widely and a little piece of it flew at an angle through a leaded light and came to rest in our standard lamp, which I had for years bearing the marks, proudly standing in my sitting room.

It was thought the third bomb fell on Gregory's Nursery behind Scrivelsby Gardens. As a result, all the residents had to get out and spend the night at the Wesleyan Chapel on Chilwell Road.

We were told there was an unexploded bomb near Hurts Croft and as a consequence we were all prevented from going back home for at least a week.

At that time my husband was in the army and on duty on the ack-ack gun site just outside Nottingham. He plotted the bomber and to his horror found where it was heading. It was thought to be making for Chilwell Depot.

Course No. 88   Certificate No. 254

NOTTINGHAMSHIRE.

CERTIFICATE TO INSTRUCTOR (L.A.G.C.)

THIS IS TO CERTIFY that Thomas L.V.White,

of 24 Park Road, Chilwell, Notts.
    L.A.R.P.
has attended a course of instruction to become an Instructor (L.A.G.C.) in Anti-Gas Measures, conducted under the authority of the Nottinghamshire County Council in accordance with the scheme approved by the Home Office, and has passed an examination of proficiency entitling him to carry out LOCAL ANTI-GAS TRAINING in accordance with that Scheme, as the Home Office may from time to time lay down, in (a) anti-gas measures (b) elementary methods of protection against high explosive bombs, (c) incendiary bomb control.
Shire Hall,
    Nottingham.

Date 4th August, 1942.   Tweedale Westby
                                    Clerk of the County Council.

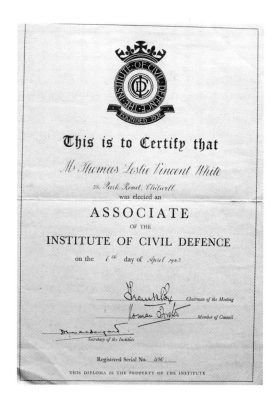

This is to Certify that

Mr Thomas Leslie Vincent White

24 Park Road, Chilwell

was elected an

ASSOCIATE

OF THE

INSTITUTE OF CIVIL DEFENCE

on the *4th* day of *April 1943*

                        Chairman of the Meeting

                        Member of Council

        Secretary of the Institute

Registered Serial No. 456

THIS DIPLOMA IS THE PROPERTY OF THE INSTITUTE

This Card is presented to

Mr T. L. V. White

in acknowledgment of services rendered to the Fire Guard as a *Assistant Fire Guard Officer* during the Test Exercise, specified by the Regional Commissioner, which took place on Dec. 13th, 1943.

                    F. W. LITCHFIELD (Chairman),
                    Fire Prevention Committee
                    Beeston & Stapleford Urban District Council.

SECTOR No. :   AREA CAPTAIN :

Mr T L V White was a local councillor and Chairman of the Beeston and Stapleford Urban District Council in 1949

NORTH MIDLAND CIVIL DEFENCE REGIONAL SCHOOL

Certificate No. NMR/32   28th July 1943

BADGE ISSUED. 21·6·44

L·F·G·I

Nominating Authority Beeston & Stapleford U.D.C

This is to Certify that Mr L. White

has attended a course of instruction, to become an Instructor (L.F.G.I.), conducted under the authority of THE NORTH MIDLAND CIVIL DEFENCE REGION, in accordance with the scheme approved by the Ministry of Home Security, and has passed an examination of proficiency entitling him/her to give instruction in methods of conducting FIRE

GUARD TACTICAL TRAINING

J. C. Webster   C. T. Bragg
Regional Fire Prevention Training Officer.   Clerk to the Nominating Authority.

HIGH ON THE HILL AT CHILWELL: MY MEMORIES OF SERVICE IN THE ATS/WRAC
By Maisie Waggott ex Newbery née Robinson

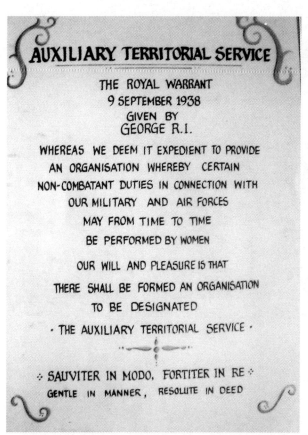

AUXILIARY TERRITORIAL SERVICE

THE ROYAL WARRANT
9 SEPTEMBER 1938
GIVEN BY
GEORGE R.I.

WHEREAS WE DEEM IT EXPEDIENT TO PROVIDE
AN ORGANISATION WHEREBY CERTAIN
NON-COMBATANT DUTIES IN CONNECTION WITH
OUR MILITARY AND AIR FORCES
MAY FROM TIME TO TIME
BE PERFORMED BY WOMEN

OUR WILL AND PLEASURE IS THAT

THERE SHALL BE FORMED AN ORGANISATION

TO BE DESIGNATED

· THE AUXILIARY TERRITORIAL SERVICE ·

❖ SAUVITER IN MODO. FORTITER IN RE ❖
GENTLE IN MANNER, RESOLUTE IN DEED

I was aged 23 when I volunteered to join the ATS at the Recruiting Office in Trinity Square, Nottingham on 12 September 1940. A week later I was embodied at Neville's Cross Reception Depot, County Durham on 20 September.

After three weeks training, and kitted out in uniform, I was posted to COD (Central Ordnance Depot) Chilwell, Nottingham, as a Storewoman, on 11 October 1940, which was fortunate as my family lived Beeston. The ATS were billeted in a camp of brick-built huts high on the hill overlooking the Depot buildings. I was allocated to C Company, Platoon 4, Hut 48, and each hut housed 24 girls. Every morning we cleaned our own particular bed space and barracked the bedding for inspection before parading down the hill to our place of work. My work was in the huge building, No 157 MT Stores (Mechanical Transport), for the RAOC (Royal Army Ordnance Corps).

The stores would arrive by rail and road from suppliers all around the country and we were responsible for packing the stores destined for the war zones worldwide. Vehicles of every description passed through Chilwell and the MT spares had to be supplied and packed for all destinations to reach them safely. We were Trade Tested and had to learn all about the stores we were handling, and on passing a Trade Test, we were eligible for an increase in our pay. In our enthusiasm we worked hard for the war effort and it meant that promotion was a goal to reach for in gaining stripes. During 1942/43 I was fortunate to have several promotions. First of all I was Lance Corporal followed by Corporal, Sergeant and Staff Sergeant. Then finally, Warrant Officer Class II in 1945.

Trade Testing gave us a foresight into the stores we would be handling in the course of our work, particularly the areas due to receive them in all parts of the world, such as the North Africa Campaign, the North Atlantic (Murmansk) and the Japanese Far East. Stores were specially treated for the climatic conditions they would be used in. For example, tank sealing (arcticisation) for Russia, and wax dipping for the South East Asia Command, for the humidity. We had a Russian representative stationed in the Depot to oversee the arcticisation of tanks and vehicle spares going to Russia.

Night shift was introduced the war intensified, and so bunk beds were provided to accommodate more ATS girls, with up to 5,000 in the camp at Chilwell from all over the country and British Empire. A new accommodation block was built halfway up the hill called the *Sandhurst Building*, later renamed *Williams Barracks*, after Major General Leslie Williams, Controller of Ordnance Services. It housed several hundred girls and had its own cookhouse, NAAFI (Navy, Army, Air Force Institute) baths, showers and lecture rooms, and it was centrally heated. The building was likened to a modern ocean-going liner of the day in the Queen Mary class when it was lit up. I well remember this building being cause for concern for the Duty Officer and NCO at the time of 'blackout' days on account of the large windows.

Welding and tyre re-treading were specialist jobs done by the ATS, as were many other trades including Clerks, Cooks, Typists, Telephonists, Orderlies, Administration, Drivers, Storewomen etc.,

↓ Maisie

Maisie supervising ATS girls packing Mechanical Transport spares in Building 157 for all the war zones around the world

Staff Sergeant Maisie Newbery photographed in 1942

Queen Elizabeth on a visit to Chilwell Depot, March 1943, Brigadier Readman looking on

Once a week we had early morning drill, or a route march, and we were allowed to start work half an hour later than usual on those days. We carried hurricane lamps at front and rear, as we paraded up and down the hill when we were on night shift, marching to and from work. The land surrounding some huts in the camp was eventually put under agricultural use, and the work did disturb us at times when on night shift, as we tried to sleep during the days.

Discipline in Camp was extremely strict. Rotas were made for all the work to be done around the huts, both inside and outside, for cleanliness. Points would be awarded to each company. They were in competition with each other and the results were published in the

Company Office. We were confined to barracks one night each week (CB night), this was the time we had kit inspections and current affairs talks, we changed worn clothes at the Quarter Master Stores, and performed various other duties in keeping the camp tidy.

Military Law was authorised for the ATS by the Army Council in 1941, and during that year HRH Princess Mary visited Chilwell as Commandant in Chief. The Guard of Honour was inspected, and I was proud to be chosen and photographed. Our second Royal visit to the Depot was by King George VI and Queen Elizabeth (the late Queen Mother) in 1943. They toured various departments, including Central Packing which was my department. Our Camp was officially named *Queen Elizabeth Camp* that day by the Queen.

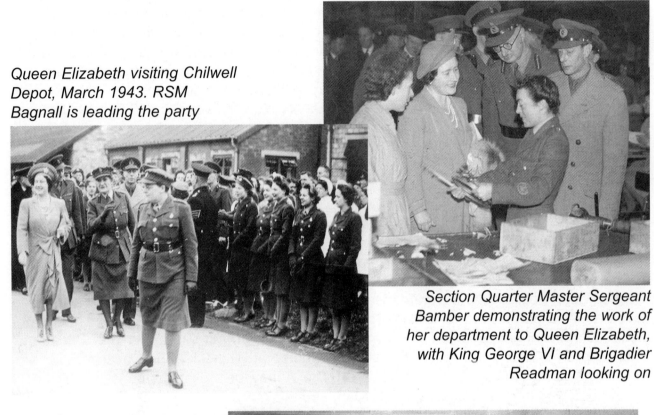

Queen Elizabeth visiting Chilwell Depot, March 1943. RSM Bagnall is leading the party

Section Quarter Master Sergeant Bamber demonstrating the work of her department to Queen Elizabeth, with King George VI and Brigadier Readman looking on

Warrant Officers' and Sergeants' Mess, Central Ordnance Depot, Chilwell

↓ Maisie

Warrant Officer Class II Maisie Newbery, front left, April 1946

Comfort Fund parcels arrived at various times from schools and local authorities; they would contain hand-knitted articles and toiletries. I remember my parcel contained a khaki woollen scarf and grey mittens which I still have in my collection of memorabilia. The name and address of the school girl was enclosed and I wrote to thank her. We also received a consignment of patchwork quilts from the Canadian Red Cross which, when opened, were for double beds. This meant we had to cut them and divide each one between two girls. I have since gifted mine to the ATS/WRAC Museum Headquarters in Winchester.

Entertainment in Chilwell Depot was extremely good with Dances and Concerts, Christmas Pantomimes as well as the famous *Blue Rockets Dance Band*. The camp hospital gave the best of medical attention and helped many girls during time of sickness to full recovery, in pleasant surroundings. Church Parades were held regularly in Chilwell Depot.

The day of the D-Day landings in Normandy on the 6 June 1944 will live in my memory. I remember parading up the hill after our night shift in the Depot and we could hear the drone of aeroplanes returning to their air bases, and then hearing the news over the wireless as we had breakfast. VE-Day (Victory in Europe) 8 May 1945, was to follow, and we continued with the pressure of work until we finally reached VJ-Day (Victory in Japan) on 15 August 1945 and the war was over at last. After hostilities ceased we still had much work to do in dealing with returned vehicles and spares.

Also on 15 August, I attended a presentation at the Officers' Mess, Headquarters, Highfield House, Chilwell, and was awarded a Certificate of Good Service on behalf of the Quarter Master General of the Forces. This certificate is proudly kept in my album of ATS memorabilia.

I was an overseas volunteer during the whole of my service at Chilwell. This meant being medically examined to be ready in case I was selected for overseas duties. However, I was destined to stay in the Central Packing Department sending MT spares to every theatre of war worldwide.

I had been approached several times by Heads of Department - military and civilian, to have my name put forward for Officer Training but I declined. Eventually the subject of de-mobilisation became uppermost in our minds as we awaited our Group number. During this time I applied to attend a respite Rehabilitation Course at Welbeck Abbey, near Nottingham, which was partly annexed for military use. (The Abbey being the home of the Duke of Portland). I was there for two months in 1946, and this gave me time to decide that I wanted to stay in the ATS and extend my service by applying for a Commission. On 14 March 1947, I re-enrolled for extended Service with the following Testimonial from Chilwell Depot.

Testimonial: *A very efficient Warrant Officer with a sound knowledge of Mechanical Stores*
Military Conduct: *Exemplary.*

On 30 September 1947 I attended the War Office Selection Board at Hobbs Barracks, Lingfield, Surrey and on 14 October commenced at the Officer Cadet Training Unit at Guildford, transferring to Imperial Service College, Windsor, on 30 December. On 18 March

Warrant Officer Class II Maisie Newbery, 8 April 1947, in the centre

1948 I was appointed ATS Subaltern and served at Old Dalby, Leicestershire. The ATS became the Women's Royal Army Corps on 1 February 1949 and on the 1 May of that year I was promoted to Lieutenant. I resigned my commission on 15 March 1951 in order to get married.

I enjoyed my wartime service in the ATS and will always remember my time 'high on the hill at Chilwell'.

Mrs Maisie Waggott is now in her 90th year and lives in County Durham. Pictures from Mrs Waggott's collection.

During the War women's clothes were designed to make the most of a limited amount of fabric.

When rationing ended skirts became full again and designs reflected the availability of new materials.

THE BOMBING OF BEESTON
By Mary Glenn

On reflection I consider that despite the highly industrial area of Beeston South, we were either lucky, or the enemy was not very clever, because we were not subjected to a great deal of damage. An enemy plane jettisoned a load of incendiary bombs and high explosive bombs on the Queens Road area, between Station Road and Humber Road in 1940. These were quickly put out by the Air Raid Wardens and residents.

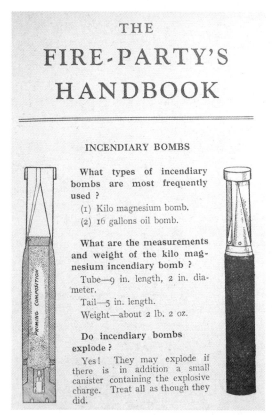

THE FIRE-PARTY'S HANDBOOK

INCENDIARY BOMBS

What types of incendiary bombs are most frequently used ?
(1) Kilo magnesium bomb.
(2) 16 gallons oil bomb.

What are the measurements and weight of the kilo magnesium incendiary bomb ?
Tube—9 in. length, 2 in. diameter.
Tail—5 in. length.
Weight—about 2 lb. 2 oz.

Do incendiary bombs explode ?
Yes! They may explode if there is in addition a small canister containing the explosive charge. Treat all as though they did.

There were wooden poles at the bottom of the garden that supported the wireless aerials. One of the incendiaries landed on ours but was put out before little damage was done. On a sadder note, a high explosive bomb fell on a house in Mona Street on 8th April 1941 and a lady was killed, but a young girl was blown out of a bedroom and landed on the road unharmed.

A further bomb fell on a pair of houses on Beech Avenue, Beeston Rylands. These were demolished and replaced by a detached house after the war. A lot of damage was done on the night of 8/9th May 1941 on what I believe was the only attack on Nottingham.

I gave up sitting in an air-raid shelter and went to bed; I needed my sleep because I was working at Ericsson's, wiring portable telephones, 'Tele Ls' for the army and 'Fullerphones' for the navy. I was woken by a terrific explosion and I don't think my feet touched the stairs on my way down. I dived under the table with my father and then we heard the whistle of another bomb but there was no explosion. When daylight came we went out to survey the damage, there was a huge crater in the middle of Queens Road outside the Queens Hotel with burst gas and water mains, and it was a frightening sight. The windows of our house had gone with the blast and lumps of tarmac from the road had come through the roof. The traffic was diverted up King Street, but later on an unexploded bomb was found to have entered diagonally through a house in King Street, so that pair of houses had to be demolished and rebuilding took place after the war.

Another bomb fell on a boat house at the side of the river and the resulting crater was left to fill with water in which the children fished for tadpoles. I am told that there was also a crater at the top of Station Road outside Victor Oade's shop, now a mobile phone shop, but I have no memory of that.

The worst tragedy was when a bomb made a direct hit on an Anderson Shelter in the garden of a bungalow on Bramcote Lane and several people were killed. So perhaps the enemy were looking for the factories, but thankfully they were unable to find them.

I have another vivid memory of a night spent at the pictures when we heard what we thought was a thunderstorm, but when we came out there was a terrible red glow in the western sky and that turned out to be the bombing of Coventry.

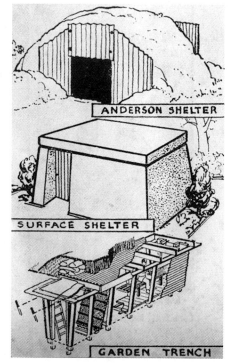

ANDERSON SHELTER

SURFACE SHELTER

GARDEN TRENCH

URBAN DISTRICT OF BEESTON AND STAPLEFORD.

CONFIDENTIAL.

INVASION COMMITTEE.

At the first meeting of this Committee held at the Town Hall, Beeston, on Monday, the 23rd day of February 1942, there were present:-

Mr. V.H. Oade, J.P.	Chairman.
" L.W.A. White.	Deputy Chairman.
" J. Heard.	representing the U.D.C.
Lt.-Col. N. Lloyd Dexter.	Sector Commander.
" J.E. Marshall.	representing 3rd Notts. Home Guard.
Mr. W.V. Potts.	Civil Defence Sub-Controller.
Inspector W.A. Fletcher.	Senior Police Officer.
Mr. F.M. Sainsbury.	Food Executive Officer.
" E.B. Harrington.	Divisional Officer, N.F.S.
" C.H. Wragg.	Clerk to the U.D.C.
Major Simmonds.	Asst. County A.R.P. Officer.

In attendance:-

Capt. C. Clegg.	Sector Staff Officer.
Dr. C.H. Warner.	Medical Officer of Health.
Mr. G.C. Hardy.	Surveyor to the U.D.C. and Assistant Director of Works Services.
" A.R. Baldwin.	Assistant Chief Warden.
" W.R. Brownhill.	Sanitary Inspector.
" G.H. Keeble.	Fire Prevention Officer.
" H. Britton.	District Welfare Officer.

The Chairman referred to the Memorandum issued by the County Controller (copies of which had been circulated), in which it is stated that the Committee had been established at the instance of the Regional Commissioner on instructions conveyed through the medium of the County Council, with the object of ensuring co-ordinated action by the various branches of the civil administration within the community to meet the situation which will arise if the district is cut off from the outside world, and to form a channel through which the Military Commander can issue his orders for the operation of civilian services to assist in his plan of defence.

Extract from the minutes of the first meeting of the Invasion Committee, 23 February 1942

MESSERSCHMIT - 109 Single-seat fighter
World War Two German aeroplane

CHILDHOOD MEMORIES
By Alan F Oxley

When the media shows the tragedies of war, there is always a sharp reminder of my own childhood, being brought up under severe rationing, but I only remember that time as being as good as any. If you are contented, you need no more from life. I was two and half years old when the World War II broke out, and the few memories during those formative years, although now distant, are quite distinct.

During 1941 my father joined the REME (Royal Electrical & Mechanical Engineers) to serve King and country, in the then far off North Africa and Italy. Mum, I am sure found times difficult, but neither my sister Joy nor I ever went without. Our table was always full, but thinking back I am certain that Mum went without, to make sure our growing bodies received the nourishment required. We lived across the fields from the Chilwell Depot (Central Ordnance Depot or COD) which was the largest ordnance depot in the British Army and eventually housed the REME workshops and thousands of troops, including the ladies of the ATS (Auxiliary Territorial Service). Looking from my parents' bedroom window on Attenborough Lane, there could be seen a training ground and huge warehouses in the distance, yet I had little idea of what was happening within the complex.

Surprisingly we came under very little bombardment, although on one occasion my mother was slow responding to the sirens. Ironically, she was always in the habit of tidying before leaving the house, just in case we had visitors! For our own safety we were usually deposited under the stairs, or sometimes it was under either the thrall in the larder or in the bath (baths were cast iron and open sided) while she carried out her chores. By the time we were ready the German bombers were flying overhead and I distinctly remember running down Attenborough Lane to the air raid shelter on the corner of Bye Pass Road, with the whole area illuminated by searchlights, flak, and as I was to find out later, bombs! Although, as a four-year-old, no one told me that Chilwell High Road had a direct hit, destroying the water main, which flooded air raid shelters on Heathfield Grove, that then had to be evacuated. A building in the Long Eaton Fabric factory complex on the Bye Pass Road was also hit, but fortunately no one was injured. Further bombs fell that night in Attenborough including the top of Elm Avenue, Allen's Farm and Clarence Road. The Clarence Road site which was known as 'the bomb crater' filled with water providing a play area for the children, particularly for collecting frog spawn. Fortunately none of the bombs made their intended target of the well-camouflaged Ordnance Depot itself.

It is amazing how secret these matters were kept when compared with today's openness on all matters. Typical of this was when I walked down Stoneshill - a footpath from Field Lane to the brickwork's entrance on School Lane which followed the backs of the houses - and discovered that military vehicles were stored in part of Chilwell brickyard, which was also the site of a rifle range. On another occasion my sister and I were of the very few fortunate enough to see the King and Queen pass by on their way from the Chilwell Ordnance Depot, but that's another story. I understand signposts were removed to foil the enemy, although I distinctly remember one at the corner of Bye Pass Road and Attenborough Lane reading Ashby-de-la-Zouch 16 miles and Birmingham 44 miles. Having said that, it is difficult to date and may have been after the war.

The old National Shell Filling Factory, which became an ordnance depot in 1919, was revitalised during 1935 when work started on turning it into modern premises for the supply of army vehicles and parts. There was a population explosion just prior to the outbreak of the war when civilian workers arrived with their families from all parts of the UK, many of them moving into the empty property in the area around Depot Corner. Such was the increase in population my sister had to travel to the Chetwynd Road School at Toton for a year, until extra room (two wooden-hutted classrooms built in the garden of the headmaster's house) was provided at Meadow Lane. When I started school in 1942 Chilwell Meadow Lane School was catering for children up to the age of fourteen and the primary years had to be accommodated in the Christ

Church Hall. Whilst I was there I remember the wrought iron fencing on Elm Avenue, Chilwell being removed, using acetylene torches, from the top of the brick walls as part of the war effort.

The COD employed people from a wide area and in the evening a queue of Barton's buses stretched from Depot Corner to Charles Avenue awaiting passengers, and the Attenborough station's long platforms were filled to capacity as they had been in the Great War. After the war security was relaxed and civilian workers were taken into the site by road and rail.

I was not partial to school dinners that were served in a temporary dining room set up in the Memorial Institute, just around the corner from the school. I think everything was steamed, and the potato substitute POM was a ghastly powder formula, which the cooks could not improve upon. So most days we would go directly home for lunch, usually by bus (the 5X, known to us as *The Draycott Flyer* which ran directly along Queens Road and Bye Pass Road), and walk the one and half miles straight back to school.

After school my friends and I would take various devious routes. On one occasion we went as far as the Hillman Estate, (between Cator Lane and Bramcote Lane) to see a Lockheed Hudson aircraft, which had failed to make it home and had crash-landed in a field next to what was then known as Simms' shop on Bramcote Lane, now the Bramcote Lane Stores. There were so many ways home, across fields, through the golf course, beside streams and brooks, all of which provided diversions along the way to our intended destination. In those days the clear water was full of tiddlers and watercress. However, one stream which crossed Attenborough Lane and Bye Pass Road, now culverted, became very black and polluted with oil and waste from the Ordnance Depot. If we walked through Old Chilwell a stop would be made at a little shop next to the old blacksmith's at the bottom of Hallams Lane. There was a large green parrot at the end of the counter which greeted everyone upon entry. I am not certain that there wasn't something rude in what it said, although the way we were brought up I would not have understood it anyway. I suppose it was our bus fare we spent on 'chewing wood', a bonus as sweets were rationed. I think it was two ounces of sweets per person per week. 'Chewing wood' was not the sort of delight today's youngsters would enjoy, I am not sure that I did really! It was a little twig with a liquorice taste which rapidly disappeared, leaving a masticated piece of wood, that would have best been dispatched to the waste bin, but most of us kept in the mouth until it eventually disappeared.

Tweentowns, the area around what is now known as Chilwell Meadows (to the east of the comprehensive school) was very marshy, with fresh water springs. It was here that we watched in disbelief as Billy Hollingsworth's horse was

Stapleford & Sandiacre News

SATURDAY, FEBRUARY 16, 1946

WEST GATE, LONG EATON
TELEPHONE 140

WE have received a statement of accounts showing that the Attenborough Model Railway had another successful year. The collection boxes raised £36, in comparison with £51 in 1944, but this was owing to it not being possible to open the railway more often, due to domestic reasons. However, on Easter Sunday and Monday, April 1 and 2, the attendance was 731, and the amount raised £23. At Whitsuntide, on Sunday, May 21, and Monday, May 22, the attendance was 638. This was in spite of very heavy rain, and the sum collected was £13. Once more, a number of appointments were made, including parties. The illuminations, approximately 100 pea lamps lit after darkness set in, were the chief attraction, and it is hoped that there will be more illuminations in time for next Easter. As the war is now over, various comforts funds have ceased to operate, but in spite of this, it has been decided that the railway will carry on as usual, and will support the comforts funds that have not yet closed, also various charities. During the war years, starting in August, 1941, over 7,000 persons visited the railway, and the various war comforts funds received the benefit of £200. "I am indebted to the 'Long Eaton Advertiser' and the 'Beeston Gazette and Echo'," says Mr. J. H. Gibbons, "for their continued support in connection with advertisements and announcements."

shot with a humane killer and carted off to the knacker's yard. I also remember being chased away by one of the servants, the cook I think, from the bottom corner of the Manor House field, for drinking from a spring or was it because we were trespassing?

Sunday School was held in the Village Institute on Back Lane (now The Strand), Attenborough, which was shared with the Attenborough Preparatory School. Originally this was built for the Sunday School (shown on maps of the period) and village activities. During the Great War (WWI) women of the village met there on a Wednesday afternoon to knit comforts for the troops, so when the school was transferred the children had the Wednesday afternoon off. After Sunday School most would go along the lane to Mrs. Tryner's sweet shop to make their purchases. Prior to the war the Tryner family, on Sunday afternoons during the summer, erected a tent on the footpath (now the site of the old Nature Reserve car park off The Strand) to the river for the sale of drinks and confectionery. However, the real highlight was the rare occasions Mr Gibbons opened to the public the wonderful and enchanting model railway. This was housed in a garden shed on what is now Shady Lane. Some years later Mr Gibbons opened Attenborough Model Railway shop on Arkwright Street, Nottingham.

Although as a youngster I did not know anything other than the life we led, I suppose my sister who is five years older, would have known better times, but to me they are still wonderful memories.

BEESTON IN WORLD WAR TWO
By Edith Green (née Ryde)

We - the Ryde family - mum and dad, sister Gwen aged 18, brother David 11 and myself Frances Edith aged 16 were living in a cul-de-sac off Leyton Crescent in Beeston Rylands during World War Two. My elder brother, Ken, was away serving in the army under Montgomery. Behind the house, which was a semi, was a field which backed on to the railway line.

On the night of 8 May 1941 we had fortunately gone into the air raid shelter when the bombs came down (we did not always use the shelter). Our house took a direct hit and was completely wrecked. The house adjoining, where the Evisons lived, was still partly standing but of course, later, had to be pulled down. All our belongings had gone and we had only the scant clothes we stood up in.

Kind neighbours - the Woodwards - took my sister and me into their home for the remainder of the night. Mum and dad and David went off to Aunt Edith who lived on Trevor Road and they stayed there the night. In the morning we joined them. As we had only the few clothes we were wearing we had to go to a building off Wollaton Road which as far as I remember was a red-brick building near the rear of Hallam's greengrocery shop, to pick some more from the store which was kept there for such an eventuality. I believe these clothes came from people in America. There were probably stores like it all round the country.

When we returned to Aunt Edith's we had a real shock because grandma and grandad walked in. They had also been bombed. Their house was (or rather had been) on Moreland Street off Meadow Lane in Nottingham not far from the Co-op Bakery which of course received a direct hit that night tragically killing so many.

We were now in a bit of a dilemma as aunt's house had only two rooms upstairs and two downstairs and there were nine people living in it. I had to sleep in a chair in the living room.

Eventually we were offered a house on Georgina Road, Beeston, by a lady who was going to live with her mother for a while. However, after a time she wanted the house back and we had to get out. Fortunately there were rooms available at the back of an empty shop in the Rylands next to the chip shop on Lilac Crescent and we were able to move there. The empty shop I seem to remember was used by the ARP.

THE WOMEN'S LAND ARMY TIMBER CORPS

It became impossible to import timber during the Second World War and so we needed to be self-reliant and produce all the timber that was badly needed for the war effort ourselves.

About 6,000 young women joined the Women's Land Army Timber Corps and worked in the forests of Great Britain to harvest timber and prepare it for use as ship's masts, telegraph poles, railway sleepers, pit props, ladders and newsprint etc., doing the work previously only done by men. Great stamina was needed by these girls who worked ten hours a day operating sawmills, wielding six-pound axes to fell trees, working with horses, driving tractors, loading etc., whatever the weather and far from home and family. Most of the girls were from towns and not accustomed to the woods and the open air life.

The uniform was the same as the Land Girls' but included a green beret, and the badge featured a fir tree instead of a wheat sheaf. They were known as lumberjills and after the war those with the requisite skills were sent to Germany to salvage equipment from abandoned sawmills.

*Nottingham Evening Post
3 September 1939*

Do It Now

Have you filled in the prepaid postcard indicating the address of alternative accommodation in the event of becoming homeless, and returned it to the A.R.P. authorities? If not, do it now.

The matter is urgent. In your own interests, and to facilitate the work of the departments responsible for your welfare, it is essential that this information should be available immediately. So far only half the cards have been returned.

If you are unable to make any arrangements write word "None," and return the card.

*Nottingham Evening Post
17 March 1941*

PAPER RESTRICTIONS

Reductions In Force This Week

As already announced the consumption of newsprint used by the papers of the country is being substantially reduced this week at the request of the Government. This will necessitate smaller newspapers.

To-day and Friday, therefore, the "Nottingham Guardian" is reduced to 4 pages, and the usual 6 pages will be retained on the other days. The "Evening Post" is of 4-page size to-day, and will be so on Saturday, and 6-page the rest of the week.

To make sure of getting the papers readers should place an order with their newsagent for them to be reserved and delivered regularly. They should also aid the industry and the country generally by carefully saving all waste paper and disposing of it as requested in the national interest.

*Nottingham Evening Post
17 March 1941*

BEESTON AND STAPLEFORD URBAN
DISTRICT COUNCIL

IMPORTANT NOTICE TO ALL FIREWATCHERS

The rumour that relaxation of fire-watching has come into operation is untrue, and it should be emphasised that all conditions existing at the moment in relation to fire watching remain in force.

The matter is under consideration by the Council.

C. H. WRAGG.

Clerk to the Council.

Beeston Gazette & Echo, 13 November 1943

ROYAL VISITS TO CHILWELL
By Alan F Oxley

The death of the Queen Mother on Saturday the 30th March 2002, revived memories of an incident, almost sixty years earlier, when King George VI and Queen Elizabeth passed through Chilwell and Beeston.

It was the 3rd March 1943 when they visited the Chilwell Ordnance Depot and during part of their tour of the whole of the Depot they named the ATS (Auxiliary Territorial Service) Camp on the hill the 'Queen Elizabeth Camp'. *The Chilwell Story (VC Factory and Ordnance Depot)* by Captain M J Haslam RAOC, covers The Royal Visit, and mentions Beatrice Clulee hearing the Queen saying afterwards "*Here I am at last, my own camp.*" It is rather interesting and not mentioned in the book that whilst she was there the Queen planted a tree that was commemorated with a plaque. Regrettably, the tree was removed when topsoil was cleared from the site for one of the housing developments within the old Depot grounds. However, the developer decided that the nameplate should remain, but within a short time some vandal removed this, and I suppose it is now lost forever.

On that particular afternoon my sister and I decided to walk home from Meadow Lane School, along the High Road through Old Chilwell. Just past the Charlton Arms a group of ladies leaning on the garden gates, informed us that there were special visitors at the Depot. A couple of hundred yards later, outside Thompson's house, as we made to cross the road, a large khaki car approached, complete with outriders, and there in front of us for one fleeting moment were the royal couple. Funnily enough, I always see the Queen Mother in my mind dressed in powder blue with a grey fur collar, and this is exactly how she was described in *The Chilwell Story*. They acknowledged us with a fleeting smile and a wave, and two delighted youngsters, sped home to tell everyone. Remember, this was the time of utmost secrecy, and quite frankly the response we received was somewhat muted, even though the local papers covered the story, for security reasons the name of Chilwell was never mentioned, stating vaguely that they had visited a camp in the North Midlands. Our joy was short lived, but the memory has stayed vividly with both of us ever since.

They were not the only royal visitors to Chilwell, as it is known Charles I crossed the river at Barton Ferry, where it is said he gave a royal charter to the ferryman. King George V visited the National Shell Filling Factory (it became the Ordnance Depot in 1919) at Chilwell on the 15th December 1916, most probably by train directly into the works. Queen Elizabeth II (the then Princess Elizabeth) and the Duke of Edinburgh spent an evening in the Royal Train when it was kept in the secure sidings of Chilwell Depot in June 1949, during Nottingham's Quincentenary celebrations.

King George VI and Queen Elizabeth at Chilwell Depot, 3 March 1943

July, August and October 1939

Items on this page are from the collection of Mr F Rayment, a Fire Guard during the War on Hampden Grove, Beeston and donated to the Beeston & District Local History Society by his daughter Betty.

1942 - 1943

WARTIME 1939-1946
By Jean Mellors née Robinson

I was 14 years old in 1941, the Second World War had been ongoing since September 1939 and all families had been given Anderson air-raid shelters to position in the garden. This entailed a huge hole to be dug about three feet deep and 6ft x 4ft wide. The shelter was made of corrugated iron sections slotted into the ground space and then a bowed section fitted together to form a roof, so that the shelter was half buried in the ground. We then piled soil over the roof section with turf covering, made a makeshift door for the small opening and three wooden steps to take us down to our refuge in the event of enemy bombings. We made our shelter comfy with benches to sit or lie on with blankets and pillows and our father fitted an electric light extension.

During the winter of 1940/41 we spent many an hour in the shelter when the air raid warning sounded. We dreaded the awful wail in the middle of the night but our parents insisted we take cover until the all-clear siren sounded. We even made siren suits for the younger members of the family, home-made all-in-one jump suits with feet and a hood, quick to jump into and made from blankets, so they were very warm.

On the night of April 7/8th 1941 we were woken by the air raid siren and told by dad to get to the shelter quickly, as already the enemy planes were overhead and gun fire could be heard. By the time we; my mother and sister had pulled on slacks, jumpers and grabbed coats, the loud explosions of bombs was rocking the ground and the area round the terrace houses was one of chaos and pandemonium. We were now ordered to run down the street to the large council air raid shelter, more robustly built of concrete and therefore a safer bet, but on reaching the street we were met with a most amazing sight. Our street had been bombed with a basket of incendiary fire bombs. There were dozens of these fire bombs on fire the length of the street; many folk had them on their roofs. Air raid wardens were dashing about with stirrup pumps putting out small fires. I, along with my mother and sister made our way through the frightening glare of fire and horrendous noise. Most noise came from the next street, Mona Street, where high explosive bombs had devastated several houses with loss of life. On reaching the large municipal shelter we joined about 50 other neighbours all hoping we would be safe together.

We were then oblivious of the mayhem being caused by the German war planes, and it was only on emerging after seemingly hours of seclusion in our underground shelter that we began to see the extent of damage to property and the help needed by injured people.

Our next door neighbours who were still in bed when the incendiaries dropped, had the misfortune to get one of these bombs crashing through the slate roof to land above the pillows of two sleeping brothers. They escaped with only singed hair and the small fire was quickly extinguished.

Many stories were told in the succeeding days, it was certainly a night to be remembered. Much more damage happened in Nottingham with many lives lost only a month later.

It makes me smile now as of course the next day we all went to work as usual. We were very tired but carried on with everyday things; the war had to be won!

I attended Nether Street Girls' School in 1941 and when we heard the air raid siren I had to go to Mrs Keeling's house on King Street to use her Anderson shelter as the shelters at school hadn't been completed. Each time I turned up however, she gave me a cup of tea and biscuits in the house because she didn't like going in the shelter. This turned out very lucky for her as one night her shelter had a direct hit. The house had an unexploded bomb down the chimney that came to rest at the back of the settee in the living room. Although the house was badly damaged, Mrs Keeling was unhurt.

The offices of the grocery and provisions companies Allied Suppliers, Meadow Dairy, Home and Colonial, Lipton's and Maypole were evacuated from London because of the Blitz. They used The Grange in Beeston, now the Police Headquarters on Chilwell Road, and had further premises at the corner of Meadow Lane and Queens Road West, Chilwell, where the Beekeeper pub is now. I went to work at the Chilwell site after leaving school at the age of fourteen. I had a job in Data Processing which was a new thing in those days. Before I worked there a bomb had dropped very close, I think it was on premises near Meadow Lane School.

When war was declared in September 1939 one of the government's provisions in case of invasion was to stockpile coal. They took over a small field belonging to St. John's football team, situated alongside the railway at Beeston and between Windsor Street and Station Road to the west. Lorries arrived regularly loaded with coal which was distributed over the entire field and piled to a great height. The mountain of coal remained untouched until the war ended and then the whole procedure was reversed; lorries and bulldozers worked continuously until the field was entirely cleared. This left the ground in a black gungy mess but what local families found embedded in the soil after they had gone was five years of coal nuggets which could easily be extracted with a little digging. Small children were sent over the back garden fences of Windsor Street and Alexandra Crescent with buckets and trowels and then they crept back home with their plunder. A little devious but very rewarding as even coal was rationed after the end of hostilities, just one amusing episode of post-war Beeston.

*****

Facsimile Birthday Card sent to a young boy in Toton from his father in Egypt, in June 1942

YOUR BED

BY FAR THE BEST bedding for any shelter is a properly made sleeping bag. Nothing else can give so much warmth. Here is a simple way of making a sleeping bag from the blankets you already have, which does not spoil them in any way. Or you can use old woollen skirts, parts of old blankets, and so on.

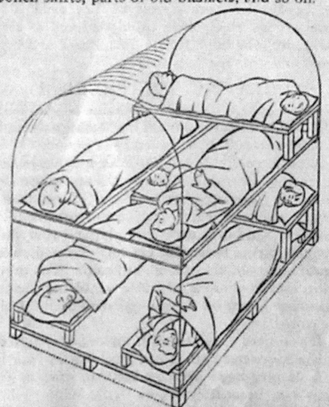

Take any Army or similar thick blanket about 7 ft. long and 6½ ft. wide (or pieces of old blankets could, of course, be joined together). Line with muslin or cotton material to within a short distance of the top. Sew straight across both blanket and lining horizontally at intervals of about a foot, making pockets which should be well stuffed with folded newspaper. The newspaper stuffing should be changed every month.

Fold the two sides of the blanket towards the centre and sew together to within about 2 ft. of the top. Sew together at the bottom. Sew tapes on the open sides of the bag at the top so that they can be tied together when the person is inside

A PERSONAL APPEAL TO THE
CITIZENS OF BEESTON AND DISTRICT

THIS appeal is mainly directed to our residents whose gardens are laid down to flower beds and lawns. Are you one of these? If so, do please consider now, whether you could utilise a substantial part or all of your garden for the growing of more vegetables.

"Fresh winter vegetables are essential - we must have them, And we must grow them ourselves" should be the watchword of every household. This YOU can do if you are prepared to sacrifice beauty for utility.

There is no guarantee that adequate supplies will be available during the winter months, and it is well to bear in mind the Minister of Agriculture's new slogan, which applies both to gardeners and allotment-holders - "Grow for winter as well as summer."

The Council will not be content until we obtain 100 per cent. from our resources, and if you have no garden, or not enough, and wish to pull your weight, will you please apply to the Town Hall for an allotment.

We are confident that you can be relied upon to make this effort for the nation and yourself, and so maintain the high reputation of our district.

DIG FOR VICTORY

V. H. OADE,
Chairman of the Council.

Beeston Gazette & Echo, 18 October 1941

RATIONING

Rationing was introduced in 1939 and the availability of goods was restricted by the government. Petrol was rationed immediately, some basic foodstuffs in January 1940, meat in March and other items added throughout the year. The weekly allowance per person was:

2 ounces of tea
2 ounces of butter
4 ounces of margarine
2 ounces of sweets
4 ounces of cooking fats
8 ounces of sugar
4 ounces of bacon and ham
1s 2d (6p) worth of meat
2 ounces of cheese
3 pints of milk
1 fresh egg or 1 packet of dried egg every four weeks
1lb of jam every 2 months

In December 1941 'points' rationing was introduced for tinned meat, fish and vegetables and other unrationed goods. Each person was given a number of points and a range of foods had a points value. The individual could choose how to spend their points. Items such as oranges, lemons, bananas and salmon were not rationed, but were unavailable. The 'National Loaf' was introduced which used more grain than white bread and produced a nutritious brown loaf.

Before the war a quarter of the population was undernourished. By the end of the war everyone was fitter due to their healthier wartime diet.

EMERGENCY DISTRIBUTION OF MILK IN NOTTINGHAM AND DISTRICT

(1) As from SUNDAY, SEPT. 3rd. there will be one delivery of Milk per day, during the hours of Daylight

(2) Customers are requested to RETURN BOTTLES DAILY to ensure supplies

Ll. FEBER, General Manager Nottingham Co-op. Society

A. E. GARNER, Nottingham Branch National Dairymen's Association

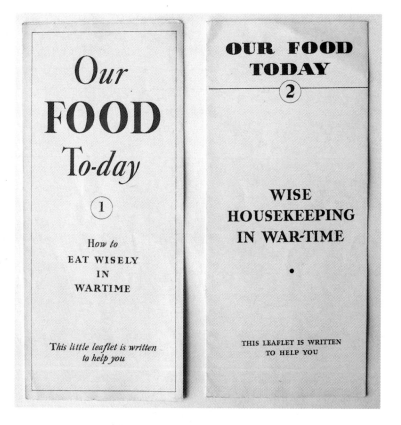

Sunday, 3 September 1939
Nottingham Evening Post

Rhubarb joined the war effort in 1939 and its price was controlled at 7½d (3p) per pound. This resulted in a black market but despite Hitler's worst efforts all trains carrying rhubarb to the main market in London arrived unscathed!

Shortages of food in wartime meant that people had to eat differently. Less eggs, sugar, fats and meat were consumed than previously. This applied to everyone so that those who had a poor diet before now had the same rations as everyone else. Thus the overall health of the nation improved, infant mortality was reduced and people lived longer.

The government introduced an advertising campaign featuring the characters Potato Pete and Dr. Carrot to impress upon people the nutritional value of vegetables and the population was encouraged to eat such things as Woolton pie, named after the Minister of Food, Lord Woolton, because it didn't contain meat. It was made from seasonal vegetables, which were in plentiful supply, topped with potato and a small amount of cheese. Spam – tinned luncheon meat from America – also helped to supplement the wartime diet.

Even bath water was rationed and a limit of five inches was imposed. Clothes rationing, introduced in June 1941, changed the fashions of the day and women wore their skirts shorter and straighter to economise on fabric. Men's trousers were made without turn-ups. Garments, and furniture also, carried the 'utility' symbol to show they were basic but good value. Nylon and silk stockings were unavailable except at highly inflated prices on the black market. So for a night out young ladies would colour their legs, often with gravy browning, and get a friend to draw a seam up the middle, as stockings had in those days, with an eyebrow pencil and hope it didn't rain!

CANNED FOODS (From 'ABC of ARP' 1939)

Early in the war people were urged to keep a stock of tinned foods so that meals could be produced if fresh food was hard to come by, but in 1941 canned meat, vegetables and fish were included in the points rationing scheme. In 1939 *The Canned Foods Advisory Bureau* in London issued a useful Bulletin giving practical advice on Food Storage as follows:

'Most Canned Foods will keep indefinitely. This particularly applies to meats, fish and soups. Others, such as fruits, vegetables and milk, should not be stored for excessively long periods. FRUITS are best used within nine to twelve months; otherwise they tend to lose their attractive appearance.

VEGETABLES may suffer in the same way if stored for more than two years.

SWEETENED FULL CREAM MILK is best used within six to nine months, otherwise it might become sugary.

UNSWEETENED MILK can be stored for a much longer period - two to three years.'

A Week's Supply for a Family of Four

The following suggestion assumes:

(1)   That due to temporary dislocation of transport, the only supplies available are FLOUR, TEA, SUGAR and CEREALS.

(2)   That meals of a standard comparable with normal times are desired.

(3)   That supplies are needed for a family of four (two adults and two children).

(4)   That sufficient food is required to provide three full meals a day for a period of seven days.

In these circumstances the following quantities should be ample:

SOUPS
6 Cans Thick Soups (large).

FISH
2 Cans Herrings, large (or 4 small) or Kippers.
1 Can Herring or Cods' Roes or 1 can Sausages
2 Cans Sardines or Brisling (small).
1 Can Salmon (1 lb.).

VEGETABLES
2 Cans Baked Beans in Sauce (large size).
2 Cans Spaghetti in Sauce.
3 Cans Peas (medium).
2 Cans Spinach (medium).
6 Cans Potatoes (medium).
2 Cans Carrots (medium).
2 Cans Tomatoes (medium).
1 Can Macedoine of Vegetables (medium).

FRUITS
1 Can Plums or Apricots (large).
2 Cans Blackcurrants (medium).
2 Cans Prunes (16 oz.).

MEAT
Can Meat Roll or Galantine (16 oz.).
Can Tongue (1 lb.).
Can Corned Beef (12 oz.).
Can Stewed Steak (1½ lb.).
Can Bacon or Ham (1 lb.).

OTHER FOODS
4 Cans Milk Pudding.
1 Can Steamed Sponge Pudding.
8 Cans Evaporated Milk (large, unsweetened).
2 Cans Cream (medium size).
1 Can Coffee or Cafe au Lait.
2 Cans Jam or Marmalade.
2 Cans Butter (1 lb.).
1 Can Cheese (1 lb.).
1 Can Suet or Dripping (1 lb.).
Also Biscuits; Tea or Cocoa.

ON THE MENU, SHEEP'S HEART, JUST LIKE RUBBER
By Gwen Price
(And Wartime Cookery Hints)

I was a secretary working at Stanton Ironworks, now Saint-Gobain Pipelines, and was expected to work on Saturday mornings, so I made six difficult journeys a week, walking from my new home in north-west Beeston to where the Nurseryman pub is now, on Derby Road, where a bus picked up workers at 8.10 every morning, if you missed it, then you had to walk and I've done that a few times too. A good three and a half miles, but it was wartime and a lack of public transport was something else the hard-pressed British people had to put up with.

> ### Every Crumb Counts
> Never throw away stale bread. Use it as breadcrumbs in savoury or sweet puddings. Bake strips of bread for rusks. Use crisped bread-crumbs as a breakfast cereal, or crush them for coatings. Soak, squeeze and beat up with a fork for sweet and savoury puddings etc.

I remember my 32nd birthday very well as it was a working day and when I opened my office desk there in front of me were two new laid eggs, a present from a workmate and I was thrilled, I took them to my mother and we had a boiled egg each for tea, a trivial gift by modern standards, but in wartime with its shortages of all food, a very welcome one. We had two ounces of margarine, three ounces each of butter and lard, three ounces of bacon, two ounces of cheese and eight ounces of sugar. And that was the basic ration, I seemed to survive on beetroot sandwiches, and then in 1946 bread was rationed. From then on we had B.U.s - bread units - in our ration books, covering bread, flour and confectionery. If you wanted cake, you couldn't have bread, and vice versa.

> ### Rules for Using Dried Egg.
> Store in a cool, dry place, and replace the lid of the tin after use. To turn a dried egg into a fresh one, mix one level tablespoon of the powder with two tablespoons of water. This mixture equals one fresh egg. Now treat the egg as you would a fresh one. Don't make up more egg than necessary for the dish you are making. Beat as usual before adding to other ingredients.

After the war things were worse. We had beaten Germany but we now had to feed them as well as ourselves and other people too, like the Dutch; we had heard terrible stories about how the Dutch had been reduced to eating flower bulbs. But people took it all for what it was, and got on with it, you accepted the position, that was that.

Sometimes you heard that one shop or another had a bit extra in, and queues would start forming but working as I did I never had time to join shopping queues, nor did I have time to turn the garden into an allotment, although I did what I could. Beeston people grew what they could, but it was an advantage if you knew someone who lived in the country who could help.

> ### Carrot Sandwiches for a Change
> Add two parts of grated raw carrot to one part of finely shredded white-heart of cabbage, and bind with chutney or sweet pickle, pepper and salt to taste. Bind some grated raw carrot with mustard sauce, flavoured with a dash of vinegar. Cook diced carrot in a curry sauce until tender enough to spread easily with a knife. All these fillings taste their best with wholemeal bread.

> ### Dig for your Dinner
> When salvage is all that remains of the joint
> And there isn't a tin and you haven't a point
> Instead of creating a dance and a ballad
> Just raid the allotment and dig up a salad!

My husband was serving in India and although he wasn't able to send me food parcels very often, he was able to send some occasionally. Notably tea - then on ration and items such as elastic - which was extremely difficult to replace when in short supply and the population is making-do and mending such clothes as they have.

There was an advantage in working at Stanton though not always a particularly great one - the works canteen, and although they were frequently hit by food shortages, they served food outside the range of rationed goods. A typical meal was sheep's heart with cabbage and mashed potato, but like the worst sort of school meal imaginable this contained all the perils and pitfalls that assaulted the wartime palate. The cabbage leaves served up to the workers were cut from the base of the vegetable, and were the hardest and the least easily digested. The mashed potato was powdered and the sheep's heart was like eating rubber. There was also a club at Stanton for executives, with different dining facilities from the staff canteen. We went there too sometimes, and we might have liver or a little fish, and of course there were Spam fritters!

One evening I remember going for a walk along Chilwell Road, outside the Hop Pole pub was a sign which read 'No Beer'. Can you imagine that now? A pub with no beer! However, word had done the rounds that the Chequers almost opposite was expecting a delivery of beer and there were queues waiting.

One of the worst problems of the wartime winters was the cold. Coal was

> **The Wise Housewife**
> 1 Shops early
> 2 Carries her own parcels and takes her own wrapping
> 3 Saves fuel, light and time.
> 4 Keeps her family healthy by giving them at least one uncooked, and one correctly cooked vegetable every day.
> 5 Uses vegetable water for cooking

rationed and most public buildings were unheated. If you went to the cinema in winter you took a hot water bottle and kept it on your lap. When I arrived home from work I would make a little fire with sticks and a bit of coal and would arrange a clothes horse around the fire with clothes on it to screen me from the cold, and build a sort of igloo, the best I could do to keep warm. Food and fuel shortages also created a new code of behaviour, new manners if you

> The Queen of Hearts said "No" to tarts,
> There's Wheatmeal Bread for tea.
> Each cream-gold slice is oh,
> so nice and better far for me

like - if you went out to tea, you'd have a basket with you containing at least one lump of coal. You couldn't expect someone to use all their fuel keeping you warm.

The restrictions and lack of goods were bad enough, yet the populace came through, their belts tightened and certainly a few pounds lighter in weight. The experience, however, wasn't all horrible, despite the German dive bombers and the food queues, there was more camaraderie than there is now, everyone looked after their neighbour. It was tough - but then it was tough for everyone.

"LISTEN TO THE KITCHEN FRONT AT 8.15 A.M. EVERY MORNING"

The Radio Doctor Says:
"If I were only allowed to say three things on the Kitchen Front, I should say eat some raw green vegetables every day. I should praise milk and more milk, and I should preach the virtues of food which contains so much nutriment - cheese."

Wartime Britain living on an adequate but meagre diet was constantly concerned about its health and that was the reason it listened to the Radio Doctor. (Dr Charles Hill, secretary of the British Medical Association who was not identified until after the war ended). His patients, numbering six million and on some occasions up to 14 million, listened not only because his advice was sensible, (don't give father extra butter, mother, that's your ration), but because in his slow, fruity, compassionate voice he spoke in down-to-earth language like nobody else. Hill 'got away' with many things on the air such as using the word 'belly', and stressing the need for regular bowel movements. He praised "that humble black-coated worker, the prune". He once asked *How's your stomach today? Is it firm and steady or somewhat warm, or a little wobbly and windy?"* One wartime Christmas when he was talking about the possible causes of a hangover, he remarked *"It may even be due to too much drink, though if it was I'd like to know where you got it"*. He later became chairman of the Independent Television Authority before taking the same role at the B.B.C.

BEESTON CIVIC RESTAURANT
By Steve Voce

In 1940 the Beeston and Stapleford Urban District Council received a government circular which recommended that, because of the war situation, communal feeding stations should be set up. Before the end of February 1941 the first of these opened at the Station Road School and Mr. F M Sainsbury was appointed the first Emergency Feeding Officer. Twelve months later the council set up a committee to control feeding stations.

The Civic Restaurant started out as a public feeding station and served meals in the Beeston Lads' Club. The Council's Restaurant Committee began to consider the possibility of a purpose built facility and a site was chosen just south of the Station Road and Nether Street junction which covered some 3,355 square yards (about half the size of a football pitch).

Fronting on to it was 'Cheapside', which may be remembered as a series of pokey-fronted shops, such as Cheapside Radio Services; Rose Render's ladies' hairdresser; Bill Jones the cycle dealer; Lacey's the cobblers; Lockwood's grocery shop; Mrs. Elsie Walker's confectionery shop and A & A Hayes' furniture store.

The properties were demolished and in 1948 the erection of the restaurant commenced to the design of architect Mr. T Newman. Interestingly, the council was not allowed to construct it of brick or stone as perhaps they would have preferred. Due to post-war building restrictions, the government Ministry Of Works department approved for use their standard hutting construction with brick in-filling. The cost was estimated at £15,000 which included a wooden block floor to be installed for formal events and dances. The building was equipped with a 250 seat self-service section and a waitress area capable of seating 50.

The restaurant was surrounded by gardens designed and maintained by the Parks Committee of the local

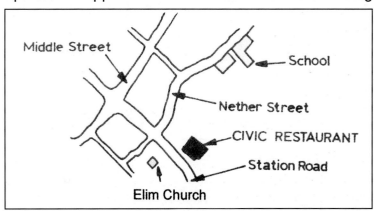

council and offered a car park to the north of the site. Members of the District Council and its Chairman, Mr. W Ireland, were present at the opening ceremony at noon on Tuesday the 19th of April 1948. A huge crowd gathered to listen to the Chairman of the Restaurant Committee, Mrs. N Curtis, who described the event as a very pleasing duty, marking another step in the progress of the Urban District Council. She received a gilt key from Mr. Newman, the architect, with which she performed the official opening.

Interested visitors were given a guided tour of the premises and the opportunity to enjoy a meal. The first person to buy a ticket was nine year old Paul Middleton of Woodland Grove, Chilwell, who queued in place of his father. The first menu reads:-

Soup 2d. Main Meal Is Id. Sweet 4d. Tea 2d. Coffee 2d. Ices 4d.

Which meant a three-course meal with tea or coffee could be had for 9p in today's money!

The self-service dining room was open from Monday to Saturday, 12 noon until 2pm. The café opened from 10am to 10pm, every day but Sunday, offering lunches, teas, suppers and snacks.

Forty bookings were received during the first week, one of them being a formal dinner on Wednesday the 20th of April at which civic leaders enjoyed a meal and had glowing words of praise for the project. It was pointed out that the Civic Restaurant scheme in the district had, to date, raised over £140,000, leaving £850 to benefit the rates. Following dinner the party was entertained by mezzo-soprano, Elsie Bebbington; elocutionist Audrey Vowels; baritone, Mr. W. Brown with Mr. W Turgoose at the piano.

Eventually the need for a Civic Restaurant dwindled and the building was sold to local electrical dealer Alex Owen who established his administrative headquarters at the premises where it remained for a number of years until the business changed hands in the 1970s. These days the building is used for hairdressing.

BEESTON AND STAPLEFORD URBAN DISTRICT COUNCIL

COMMUNAL FEEDING CENTRE

Station   Road   Schools,   Beeston

OPEN   ON

WEDNESDAY,   FEBRUARY   19,   1941
at   12.30 p.m.

And each day thereafter (excluding Sundays) from 12 Noon until 2 p.m. for the provision of a

MID-DAY MEAL

PRICES:	
SOUP	**1d.** AND **2d.**
MEAT & 2 VEG.	**6d.**
(Children 14 and under, 4d.)	
SWEET	**2d.**
TEA or **COFFEE**	**1d.**

This Centre is under the management of your Local Council in conjunction with the Ministry of Food

Beeston Gazette & Echo, 15 February 1941

FASHION AND CLOTHING IN WORLD WAR TWO
By Anna Church

All aspects of life had to change in the Second World War and fashion and clothing was no exception. Raw materials were in short supply and a decrease in factory output forced the cost of clothing to rise rapidly between 1939 and 1941 which prompted the Board of Trade to introduce regulations to control the supply of cloth, clothing and footwear. Rationing began on 1 June 1941 and the *Utility Scheme* which controlled the quality and price of cloth and clothing was introduced towards the end of the year. In spring 1942 the *Civilian Clothing (Restriction) Orders* imposed stringent austerity to oversee the construction of most items of clothing in both factories and couture houses. The aim was to make the most appropriate and economical use of insufficient raw materials and to ensure fair shares of clothing for all. People were also encouraged to *Make-Do and Mend.*

Rationing

It was almost impossible to import fabric and other materials necessary for making clothes. Also, manufacturers in Britain had more important items to make for the war effort such as parachutes and uniforms. Every type of cloth was in short supply and had to be severely rationed which had the effect of reducing manufacture and making thousands of workers available for the production of munitions. Strict rationing that operated on a coupon system (coupons and cash would be exchanged for goods) commenced on 1 July 1941. The national and local press contained all the details. In the beginning adults were allowed 66 coupons each per year which would only have allowed a woman to buy one new outfit. As the war progressed the number of coupons reduced, falling to 48 in the middle of the war and by 1945 were as low as 36 a year. The clothes rationing scheme lasted until 1949.
In the early part of the scheme a black market

CLOTHING NOW RATIONED

Surprise Scheme in Operation To-day: Footwear Included

66 COUPONS FOR A YEAR'S NEEDS

One Suit Takes 26: Concessions For Children

By OUR POLITICAL CORRESPONDENT

Beginning to-day, clothing, cloth, footwear, and knitting wool will be rationed, and coupons will be necessary for purchases.

Each person will have sixty-six coupons for a year. No special issue is ready, but there is a spare page in existing ration books, and this page, containing twenty-six margarine coupons, will be used for the articles newly rationed. Clothing cards with forty coupons more should be available in August.

Sunday Times, 1 June 1941

developed in coupons and a large number of books became lost or stolen. To overcome this, the government issued new rules which meant that coupons had to be stamped in the book and detached only at the point of sale. A small number of items could be bought without coupons such as overalls, boiler suits, ribbons, shoe laces, clogs, hats, scarves, items for babies under four months old and blackout material. Headscarves printed with patriotic symbols and slogans were very popular and coupon-free hats allowed self-indulgence in a limited wardrobe and boosted morale.

Utility Scheme

The Utility Mark, 'Civilian Clothing 1941' appeared on all utility items.

As there was a shortage of cotton, wool and leather etc., utility clothing was introduced to control the supply and on 11 September 1941 the *Utility Apparel (Maximum Prices) Order* came into force. Clothing prices had to be stabilised so that people could afford good quality clothing, therefore the range of garments using the utility symbol had to be controlled. The government supervised the manufacture of raw materials and supplied cloth to the garment industry. The aim was to avoid shortages as this would dramatically increase prices and put the garments out of reach of most of the population and would be bad for morale. Also, poor quality clothing would be a waste of scant resources and ration coupons. Manufacturers had to adopt more efficient working practices as much of the skilled workforce had left to join the armed forces. Efficiency was increased but choice was reduced.

The scarcity of fabric meant economies in design had to be made. In 1942 under *The Civilian Clothing Order* the government introduced regulations that made it illegal and unpatriotic to embellish clothing for sale. No trimmings, unnecessary pleats, tucks, pockets and buttons could be used on utility clothing and austerity regulations restricted the amount of fabric that could be used. The Board of Trade commissioned the expertise of London-based couturiers to design clothes that would dispel the idea that this would lead to standardisation. To comply *The Incorporated Society of London Fashion Designers,* which included Norman Hartnell and Hardy Amies, leading designers of the day, created 34 smart but practical Utility Clothing designs. They fulfilled the Board's criteria that the clothes should be desirable but not so stylish that they created demand. Utility designs followed existing styles of square shoulders and short skirts whilst meeting the strict regulations for minimum cloth usage and were restricted to a maximum of four buttons, four pleats and two pockets. Garments were made with rip-proof seams and reinforced shoulders to be hard wearing and durable. The strict controls created a precedent for manufacturing standards and clothing quality in post-war British factories. A Utility Scheme for furniture was implemented in 1943.

Make-Do and Mend

Everyone was encouraged to *Make-Do and Mend,* women in particular. A cartoon character, *Mrs Sew and Sew,* featured in women's magazines etc., to introduce ideas for remodelling cast off clothing and worn household textiles. Many women had always done this and

NEW OFFICIAL LIST of COUPONS NEEDED for CLOTHING and FOOTWEAR 1st JULY 1941

Here is your new reference list. Cut it out. It is the *official* record of the correct number of coupons for each rationed article, and it takes the place of earlier lists.

Garments not listed take the coupon rating of nearest like garment	Man	Woman	Child*
Single texture mackintosh, raincoat overcoat, cape, cloak—unlined or saddle lined—other than woollen, leather or fur	9	9	7
Mackintosh, cape, raincoat—other than those above	16	15	11
Overcoat lining (detached)	7	7	4
Jacket, blazer, bolero blouse-type jacket—if lined and woollen, leather or fur	13	12	8
Jacket (including blouse, type), blazer—if unlined and not woollen, leather or fur	6	6	4
Jacket (including blouse type), blazer—other than those in the two categories above	10	10	6
Cardigan, sweater, jersey, jumper, pullover, waist-coat—with long sleeves, and woollen, leather or fur	8	8	5
Waistcoat, jumper, jersey, sweater, cardigan—other than those in previous item	5	5	3
Shirt†—if woollen	7		6
Shirt†—other than woollen; boys' woollen blouse	5		4
Blouse, shirt-blouse, shawl—if woollen		6	4
Blouse, shirt-blouse, shawl—other than woollen		4	3
Trousers, slacks, over-trousers, breeches—if woollen	8	8	6
Trousers, slacks, over-trousers, breeches—other than woollen	5	5	4
Shorts—if woollen	5	5	3
Shorts—other than woollen	3	3	2
Skirt, divided skirt—if woollen		6	4
Skirt, divided skirt—other than woollen		4	3
One-piece shelter suit,—if woollen	11	11	8
Men and boys' overall—other than woollen	6		4
Dressing- or bathing-gown—if woollen	8	8	6
Dressing- or bathing-gown—other than wool	6	6	5
Pyjama Suit, nightshirt	8	8	6
Nightdress		6	5
Combinations—if woollen	7		4
Combinations—other than woollen	5		3
Woollen vest; non-woollen vest with sleeves; woollen pants or trunks; non-woollen pants (long legs); cotton football jersey; bathing costume	4		2
Undergarment not elsewhere listed; athlete's vest	3		2
Pair of stockings, socks, bathing trunks—if woollen	3		1
Pair of socks—other than woollen; cotton swimming drawers	1		1
Collar, shirt-front†, pair of cuffs or sleeves, tie	1	1	1
4 handkerchiefs (each of area less than 1 sq. ft.)	1	1	1
2 *other* handkerchiefs (less than 2 ft. in length or breadth)	1	1	1
Scarf, pair of gloves or mittens	2	2	2
Pair of slippers, goloshes, rubber overshoes, plimsolls, football boots, and certain specialist sport shoes	4	4	2
Pair of rubber boots or overboots, sandals, rubber-soled canvas tennis shoes	5		2
Pair of boots, shoes, overboots—other than those in previous two categories	7		2
Pair of leggings, gaiters or spats	3	3	2
Dress, gown, frock—if woollen		11	8
Dress, gown, frock—other than woollen		7	5
Gym tunic, girl's skirt or bodice		8	6

*Sizes exempt from Purchase Tax.
†With or without collars attached

ISSUED BY THE BOARD OF TRADE

found it somewhat patronising. Wedding dresses would be passed on from bride to bride. Pillowcases could be made into blouses or baby clothes and various other things. Men's trousers could be become women's skirts and children's clothes and most cast off clothing would be converted one way or another. Ration-free trims could be added to extend or personalise a limited wardrobe. As

fabric was difficult to obtain blackout material was often used to make garments, also synthetic parachute silk when available. Blankets could be turned into coats and old knitwear was taken apart and the wool reknitted into other garments. The Women's Voluntary Service set up knitting circles and took part in the *Knitting for Britain* campaign. The WVS also set up and ran Swap Shops where people could take their clothes and change them for something different. Swap Shops were very popular, especially with people who had growing children.

After the War and the 'New Look'

The public became resentful after the war when rationing wasn't relaxed on clothing. Garments were being manufactured but exported in an effort to rebuild the British wool and textile industries. Paris fashion houses were producing wonderful clothes and America was making simple, classic styles.

In 1947 Christian Dior introduced the 'New Look'. It was very controversial as the new design used lots of expensive natural fabric, the absolute antithesis of Utility Clothing and could be thought unpatriotic. With very full skirts and nipped-in waists the new look was reminiscent of an earlier, more feminine age and after their wartime emancipation women wanted to be feminine again. Manufacturers responded to the public demand for newness and change and made replicas of the new fashion and the boxy, uniform wartime clothes were soon a thing of the past. Democratic fashion had come to an end.

The two outfits on the left are typical of a 1946 fashion plate that would be seen in a fashion trade magazine providing current style information and trends. This is pre 'New Look' (by one year). It was a while before the new look filtered through to accessible fashion. It is characteristic of the styles reflecting the shortage of fabrics and the exporting of wool and materials in an effort to rebuild the British economy.

Late 1940s dress. A feminine style completely different from the wartime fashions.

Illustrations from Anna Church's collection. Sketches by Anna Church.

WARTIME MEMORIES
By Neville Bostock

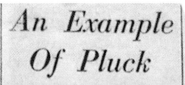

An Example Of Pluck

BEESTON SOLDIER AT NIJMEGEN

Pte. Bostock

SEATED in the living room at 45, Grenville - road, Beeston, with her 4½-year-old son, Neville John, Mrs. E. Bostock read to-day of the heroic work of her husband, Pte. Walter George Bostock, of the R.A.M.C., who, for the last three weeks, has been working day and night in a military hospital at Nijmegen, Holland.

It was the first information she had received as to his whereabouts since Sunday, 24 September, when he left home to rejoin his unit after a few hours' stay.

"We didn't even know what he was doing," Mrs. Bostock told an "Evening News" reporter, who called to-day with the news of her husband's whereabouts.

On 24 September he walked unexpectedly — accompanied by an Army friend, Derek Dumaurier — into his father's house in Park-street, Beeston, where he knew he would find his wife. It was a great surprise, but shortlived. Pte. Bostock and his companion left a few hours later—destination unknown.

PLUCK AND ENDURANCE

News of his presence in Holland came to-day from Reuter's correspondent, Desmond Tighe, in the following dispatch to the "Evening News":

"Two R.A.M.C. orderlies of the British First Airborne Division, George Bostock and Derek Dumaurier, have given an example of pluck and endurance.

"When I saw them they had been carrying out their duties for the last three weeks in a shelled hospital near Nijmegen working day and night while German heavy artillery plugged shells into neighbouring woods, but they dismissed their job as nothing.

"It was pretty uncomfortable, but it is our job," said Dumaurier.

"We arrived with the airborne reinforcements, otherwise we should have been with our pals inside the Arnhem pocket."

So, through the war correspondent and the "Evening News," Mrs. Bostock knows the whereabouts of her husband and that he is safe.

As I was born during the early months of the Second World War my memories of the effects that that conflict had on everyday life are rather sketchy. However, I do vaguely recall that from time to time a strange man wearing a uniform came and stayed at our house for a few days. My mother said that he was my father. I think I was rather jealous, because when he was there my mother devoted a lot of time to him and not as much to me as she usually did, the effect being that on one occasion I asked out point blank *"When's that man going away?"* On another occasion I was caught going through his kit bag and when asked what I was doing my reply was *"I am looking for my baby sister"*. I had obviously said that I wanted a baby sister and my mother had replied that I might get one when daddy comes back from the war. Daddy had come home and I expected him to have brought a baby sister for me - in his kit bag!

One Sunday afternoon in September 1944 we were at my grandparents' house when, out of the blue, my father and an army friend walked in. It was only a flying visit because a few hours later they left - destination unknown. For about a month we didn't know where he was or what he was doing and then one day a newspaper reporter from the old *Nottingham Evening News* came to our house with news of his whereabouts. Reproduced here is his report. (From my collection of memorabilia.)

AT EL ALAMEIN

Pte. Bostock was called up a fortnight after the outbreak of war as a mobile member of the Red Cross.

After working in this country in hospitals he was sent abroad to the Middle East in July, 1942.

He arrived there just in time for the big British break through at El Alamein and was with the Eighth Army right up to their invasion of Sicily.

After this he returned to this country, and was transferred to the British First Airborne Division a few weeks ago.

Pte. Bostock worked as a press operator at Ericssons Telephone Co., Ltd., Beeston before joining the Army.

75

THE NORTH AFRICAN CAMPAIGN

The North African Campaign was fought during 1940-3 between Axis troops – a combination of German and Italian Forces – and Britain and her allies along the Egypt-Libya coastal area for control of the Suez Canal and the Mediterranean. It began when Italy invaded Egypt. The Italian Forces were driven back into Libya and German Forces under Rommel – the specially trained Afrika Korps – were sent to reinforce Italian military strength. Tobruk in Libya was taken by the Australians in January 1941 then changed hands several times until finally taken by the British late in 1942. The German advance was halted on the Egyptian Mediterranean coast by a British victory under the commander of the Eighth Army (Desert Rats), General, later Field Marshall Montgomery, at El Alamein. The Germans retreated into Tunisia and attacked US troops. They were finally driven back and along with Italian troops were caught in a pincer movement by the Allied Forces to whom they surrendered in May 1943.

Beeston Gazette & Echo, 6 May 1944

VERY YOUNG WOMEN AT WAR
By Margaret Scothern

In the early 1940s I was a member of the 78th Nottingham Girl Guides. As you may know, Girl Guides and Boy Scouts work for badges and one of the badges we could earn was for 'war work'. Obviously at the tender age of 12 we could not undertake anything very serious or dangerous, so my father suggested my friend and I might like to pack parcels for local people serving in H.M. Forces overseas.

The scheme was organised by the British Legion and many of the volunteer packers were colleagues of my father from Ericsson Telephones. So my friend Joyce and I went off to the British Legion on Hall Croft, Beeston to do our bit for the war effort. I can't quite remember how we got there, as the blackout was no place for young girls to be wandering about on their own, although it was probably safer than 12 year old girls going about their business today in daylight! I can only assume we were escorted as we walked there and back; cars and petrol being in short supply.

The brown cardboard boxes, about the size of a shoe box, were arranged on a large table and we set to work packing cigarettes and items such as gloves, balaclava helmets and scarves, which had been knitted by the nimble fingers of the ladies of Beeston. We also sent toiletries, courtesy of the Boots Company, and anything else available at the time. I think we did the packing on a monthly basis and I remember one evening when Joyce's father's name appeared on the list, he was serving in France at the time, and it caused us great excitement to know that a parcel was about to go on its way to him. Rationing made it difficult to get many luxuries to the brave people serving overseas but at least they knew they were remembered and appreciated by the people of Beeston. Yes, we did get our 'war work' badges!

* * * * *

Lessons proceeding as normal at Church Street School in 1942

URBAN DISTRICTS
of
Arnold, Beeston and Stapleford, Carlton, Long Eaton and West Bridgford.

FIRE PREVENTION (BUSINESS PREMISES) ORDER, 1941.

APPEAL TO MEN BETWEEN 18 AND 60 YEARS OF AGE

In all cases where occupiers of premises are unable to make arrangements for fire watching of their premises because of the lack of employees, your Local Authority has to provide the personnel to assist the occupier to deal with fires.

Returns which have been made by occupiers of premises have been examined and reveal that a considerable number of persons will have to be provided.

It is VITAL in the interests of the safety of your Urban District that these men should be available to deal with outbreaks of fires resulting from enemy action.

An appeal is now made to all men between the ages of 18 and 60 (inclusive) who are not at present members of any Civil Defence Service to offer their services for this work.

Volunteers will not be expected to do more than 48 hours duty in any one month, and the hours of duty will be kept as low as possible. Volunteers should send their names, ages and addresses to the Clerk to their Local Authority at the address given below, or call personally and enrol as soon as possible, as the need is urgent.

A. H. JAMES,
PUBLIC OFFICES, ARNOT HILL
HOUSE, ARNOLD.
Clerk to Arnold U.D.C.

A. E. F. WALKER,
COUNCIL HOUSE, BURTON RD.,
CARLTON.
Clerk to Carlton U.D.C.

C. H. WRAGG,
TOWN HALL, BEESTON
Clerk to Beeston and Stapleford U.D.C.
W. E. STANLEY,
TOWN HALL, LONG EATON.
Clerk to Long Eaton U.D.C.
E. WRAGG
THE HALL, WEST BRIDGFORD
Clerk to West Bridgford U.D.C.

Nottingham Evening Post, 20 February 1941

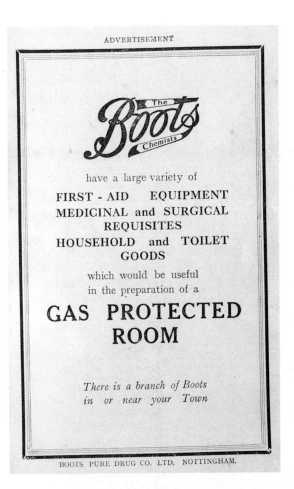

From 'Personal Protection Against Gas' 1938

HITLER WILL SEND
NO
WARNING

PRACTISE PUTTING ON YOUR GAS MASK

1. Hold your breath. (*To breathe in gas may be fatal.*) 2. Hold mask in front of face, thumbs inside straps. 3. Thrust chin well forward into mask. Pull straps as far over head as they will go. 4. Run finger round face-piece taking care head-straps are not twisted

MAKE SURE IT FITS

See that the rubber fits snugly at sides of jaw and under chin. The head-straps should be adjusted to hold the mask firmly. To test for fit, hold a piece of paper to end of mask and breathe in. The paper should stick.

Arrows indicate points needing particular attention

From 'The Fire Guards' Handbook' 1942

KEEP YOUR SHELTER
Ideal for mushroom growing after the war.

Grow them also in your cellar, shed, garage, barn, greenhouse, or open garden, all the year round. Our New Cropost Method Requires No Manure. We show you how and buy your crops—any quantity at a guaranteed price. Start now. Area 10ft. x 10ft. yields up to 200lbs. worth 5/- to 10/- per lb. Send 2½d. for "Mushroom Growing for Profit."

British Mushroom Industry Ltd.,
Dept. S.E.14.
Covent Garden
Market. W.C.2

Sunday Express, 6 May 1945

BEESTON & STAPLEFORD
(including Trowell)

SALUTE THE SOLDIER WEEK
MAY 13 to MAY 20

Target £300,000

to maintain the eighth army for one day

First go the Sappers, feeling their way over the fields where death lurks ... behind them the tanks and infantry ... behind them all the savers at home. Show them that YOU are backing them.

PULL YOUR WEIGHT

by investing Every Penny in 3% Savings Bonds, 2½ % National War Bonds 3% Defence Bonds, National Savings Certificates and Stamps.... Post Office and Trustee Savings Banks

Beeston Gazette & Echo, 6 May 1944

BEESTON AND STAPLEFORD

(including Trowell)

"SALUTE THE SOLDIER" WEEK, MAY 13 to 20, 1944

PROGRAMME

For Beeston, Chilwell, Attenborough and Toton

FRIDAY, MAY 12

CIVIC RECEPTION at the Town Hall, Beeston.

SATURDAY, MAY 13

FLAG DAY.

GRAND OPENING CEREMONY. Parade assemble Dovecote Lane Recreation Ground at 2.0 p.m., and move off at 2.15. Taking part:—No. 8 Central Workshop R.E.M.E. Pipers Band, the No. 2 Coy. Army Cadet Corps Band, the 17th Nottingham. (Beeston) Boys' Brigade Band, the Attenborough and Long Eaton Sea Cadets Corps Band, Military, A.T.S., No. 2 Coy. Army Cadets, the 3rd Notts. Battalion (C. Coy) Home Guard, 1st Battalion Mobile Platoon Notts. Home Guard, N.F.S., Civil Defence, Pre-Service Units, W.V.S., British Red Cross, St. John Ambulance Brigade, Boys' Brigade, Sea Scouts, Air Scouts, Guides, Rangers, etc., etc., via Queens Road, Station Road, The Square, Chilwell Road, Devonshire Avenue, Bramcote Road, Park Street, Wollaton Road, High Road to Broadgate Recreation Ground, where the OPENING CEREMONY will be performed by BRIGADIER E. P. READMAN, C.B.E., T.D. The Salute will be taken in the Square.

7.15 p.m. — OPENING OF THE MODEL EXHIBITION at the Church Institute, Station Road, Beeston.

7.45 p.m. — OPENING OF THE ARMY EXHIBITION at the Lads' Club, Station Road, Beeston.

SUNDAY, MAY 14

7.0 p.m. — GRAND "SALUTE THE SOLDIER" CELEBRITY CONCERT at the Palace Cinema, High Road, Beeston. "Stars" include:- Ruth Packer, Tudor Davies, Lawrence Clay, Frank Britton.

MONDAY, MAY 15

1.0 p.m. — LADIES' INVESTMENT LUNCHEON, at Hands' Café, Beeston.

3.0 p.m. — THE MAIN INDICATOR in the Square will be changed.

7.30 p.m. — DANCING TO THE FAMOUS "BLUE ROCKETS" BAND at Station Road Schools.

TUESDAY, MAY 16

1.0 p.m. — BEESTON ROTARY CLUB INVESTMENT LUNCHEON at Hands' Café.

3.0 p.m. — THE MAIN INDICATOR in the Square will be changed.

6.30 p.m. — POPULAR CONCERT by the Pupils of the Combined Schools of Beeston, Chilwell and Toton, at Station Road Schools.

6.45 p.m. — SALUTE TO THE MOTHERS OF SOLDIERS EVENING at the Memorial Institute, Chilwell. For Mothers of Soldiers and A.T.S. in the districts of Chilwell, Attenborough and Toton.

WEDNESDAY, MAY 17

3.0 p.m. — THE MAIN INDICATOR in the Square will be changed.

7.30 p.m. — "LISTEN TO THE BAND. "Military Band Concert by the No. 4 Coy. Army Cadets Silver Band, at Broadgate Recreation Ground.

THURSDAY, MAY 18

3.0 p.m. — CHILDREN'S DAY. Grand Fancy Dress Parade and Competitions on Broadgate Recreation Ground. The famous SHERWOOD FORESTERS BAND will play selections.

3.0 p.m. — WHIST DRIVE at Beeston British Legion Headquarters, Hall Croft, organised by the British Legion.

4.0 p.m. — THE MAIN INDICATOR in the Square will be changed by a local scholar.

7.50 p.m. — GRAND EXHIBITION AND DEMONSTRATION of Home Guard Weapons, and demonstration of BATTLE TRAINING by "C" Coy. 3rd Notts. Battalion Home Guard on Dovecote Lane Recreation Ground and the Lads' Club Ground, Beeston.

7.0 p.m. — WHIST DRIVE at Beeston British Legion Headquarters, Hall Croft, organised by the British Legion.

7.30 p.m. — FILM SHOW at Messrs. Chambers' Canteen, Toton, to be given by the Film Unit of the Ministry of Information.

FRIDAY, MAY 19

3.0 p.m. — THE MAIN INDICATOR in the Square will be changed.

7.30 p.m. — "ACK-ACK CIRCUS" DISPLAY, to be given by permission of Ack-Ack Command.

7.0 p.m. — THE "BARWIN" "SALUTE THE SOLDIER" DANCE at Station Road Schools.

SATURDAY, MAY 20

3.30 p.m. — THE MAIN INDICATOR in the Square will be changed.

MONDAY, MAY 22

3.0 p.m. — THE FINAL TOTAL FOR "SALUTE THE SOLDIER" WEEK will be announced at the MAIN INDICATOR.

EXHIBITIONS YOU MUST SEE

The ARMY EXHIBITION at the Lads' Club, Station Road, Beeston. Open each evening from May 13th to May 19th.

The MODEL EXHIBITION at the Institute, Station Road, Beeston (opposite Station Road Schools.). Open from May 13th to 20th.

The BOOK EXHIBITION at the LIBRARY, Foster Avenue, Beeston.

The THREE CRUSADER TANKS, fitted ready for going into battle.

WARTIME EXPERIENCES IN THE LOCAL DEFENCE VOLUNTEERS, THE HOME GUARD AND THE AIR RAID PRECAUTIONS FIRST AID SERVICE
By Edward Smedley

Part 1 The Local Defence Volunteers and the Home Guard

The so-called 'Phoney War' having been brought to a sudden end by Hitler's 'blitzkrieg' advance through Denmark into Norway and through Holland and Belgium into Northern France, there came into being the Local Defence Volunteers, later to become the Home Guard.

Having had experience of the River Trent, I and other members of the 2nd Beeston or the 1st Notts Sea Scouts, together with many others with river experience or other relevant skills, immediately joined the newly formed River Patrol of the LDV.

As far as I now recall, the leaders were Messrs Mathieson, Thurlby, Davis and Laurenson (ranks unknown), and some other original members were alphabetically, Messrs Bagshaw, Barnsdale, Chapman, Fleeman, Grummitt, Lambert, Stevens, Thraves (Douglas and Fred), Tomkins and Warburton (spelling not guaranteed in all cases).

Mitchell's Boating Station on the River Trent, Beeston Lock in the background

Our first parade was a meeting in a shed at Mitchell's Boat Yard (now Beeston Marina) when we were addressed by a young army officer who outlined the 'blitzkrieg' technique of the German army and in particular the ruthless efficiency of the German paratroops whom we would probably encounter first in the event of an invasion. Basic training by a Sergeant from Chilwell Ordnance Depot then followed.

Had it come to the crunch, I don't think that we, inexperienced in combat and with little training, armed only with old rifles, could have done much against experienced German parachute troops, armed with automatic weapons and stick grenades!

We were armed with Ross 0.3 inch bore sniper rifles which were very long, accurate and powerful. Their power was clearly demonstrated when one of our team at Barton Ferry accidentally discharged a shot in the farm shed where the rifles were stored. The bullet went diagonally through the thick wooden top of a work bench, knocked a piece out of an old cast-iron cooking pot, went through the blade of a large knife (used for cutting hay from a stack) and badly chipped the walls. The man escaped unharmed but somewhat shaken.

Target practice took place across the river just downstream of the bend below Clifton Hall (later to become a school) where the steep cliff on the far bank provided an excellent stopper for the bullets. The target, on the strip of low ground at the foot of the cliff, consisted of a full-size hardboard cut-out of a paratrooper, the bulls-eye being over his heart.

My first posting was to a position at the mouth of the River Erewash near Barton Ferry where there was a sand-bagged strong point protected by barbed wire and a nearby hut in which the off-duty men could rest. Such was the shortage of gear that we had at first to share uniforms (which were only denims) that were kept in the hut. We cycled there in our ordinary clothes, grabbed a uniform and arm band in the hut and went on guard. As there was a wide range of height and girth amongst the various shifts which worked at this post, the fit of the uniform was somewhat approximate.

The importance of this position (and of a similar one near Thrumpton Ferry) was considered to be the suitability of the extensive meadows around the river as a landing place for paratroops or saboteurs targeting Chilwell Depot or the local railway systems.

At night, the area around the river patrolled by the LDV was an exclusion zone which meant that anyone seen there at night would be treated with suspicion. This exclusion zone gave us problems with courting couples in the summer when the clocks were set at double summer time so that sunset was very late. These couples had to come out into the country late at night to get some privacy.

My first experience of nearby bombing was here on a night when there had been much activity, with

Barton Ferry at the mouth of the River Erewash at Attenborough, about 1910

heavy anti-aircraft fire some considerable distance away to the south west. A single German aircraft flew fairly low over our post and released one bomb which made a large crater in a field between us and the railway. Although the enemy plane was low, we could not see it in the dark.

Thrumpton Ferry, 1905

My next posting was to similar duties near to Thrumpton Ferry and the downstream end of the Cranfleet Canal. Here instead of a hut, the off-duty men slept in an old Royal National Lifeboat Institution rowing and sailing lifeboat, under a tarpaulin spread over the framework of an unfinished superstructure. This lifeboat had been bought from the RNLI before the war by a Mr Chapman (who was one of the initial members of the River Patrol of the LDV) with the intention of converting it into a cabin cruiser. This conversion was only partly finished when the war started. Mr Chapman was a familiar figure on the river and a man of many skills, being a good skater and marksman and a quite outstanding small-boat sailor.

When I last saw this lifeboat it was moored alongside the riverside bungalow of his old friend Mr Bunt Warburton, but its ultimate fate I do not know. Both Messrs Chapman and Warburton are regrettably no longer with us. I never knew Mr Warburton's real Christian names. The name 'Bunt' was widely used by his friends and appears on his gravestone in Beeston Cemetery but I do not know how it originated. At work, he was known as 'Charles' but I do not think that this was his real name.

Up to the autumn of 1940, Fred Thraves and I, having studied first aid in the Sea Scouts and done further study later, had been doing regular night shifts at the Air Raid Precautions First Aid Post at the school on Meadow Lane, Chilwell as well as a shift on another night on the River Patrol. As enemy activity had then increased locally by that time, the Air Raid Precautions authorities wanted us to be available for duty whenever there was an air raid alarm at night. As we had been attached to the first aid post before the formation of the LDV River Patrol we had to leave the latter.

Fred joined the Royal Navy early in 1941 but I remained with the First Aid Service throughout the war with the exception of my temporary duty in the navy in 1944.

Part 2   The Air Raid Precautions First Aid Service

The first serious enemy activity affecting the First Aid Post at Meadow Lane School occurred in the late summer of 1940 when there was a raid involving both high explosive and incendiary bombs on Beeston, Chilwell and Attenborough.

A report was received of a wounded man having been taken into an air raid shelter at the junction of Attenborough Lane and Barratt Lane. A squad led by Mr Sid Simpson (a highly skilled first aider) together with Mr Albert Coombes (a veteran of the battle of Jutland), Fred Thraves and myself was sent to attend to the casualty who was fortunately not very seriously injured.

On the way to this incident, we passed the factory of the Long Eaton Fabric Company on the Chilwell Bye Pass Road which had been hit and was burning furiously. The Fire Brigade was already tackling the blaze valiantly, in spite of the danger that further bombs might have been aimed at the fire.

As we arrived at the shelter, several incendiary bombs were burning on the road nearby and the characteristic whirring sound of more of these bombs falling could be heard. No fires were started by them whilst we were there.

These incendiary bombs (the so-called Kilo Magnesiums) often fell in groups as they were usually released from canisters containing several bombs.

The whirring sound when they were falling was probably caused by the dome-shaped 'cowling' with a hole in the centre, which was fitted to the end of the tail fins, presumably to act as an air brake to limit the rate of descent.

At this stage of the war, burning incendiary bombs which had not fallen onto any building or other vulnerable target could have been ignored. Later, the Germans put a small explosive charge in these bombs, mainly to discourage attempts to extinguish them or to stop the spread of fire by stirrup pumps or hoses. (Early in the war we had been trained to tackle these bombs with a stirrup pump and to escape from a burning building without external aid.)

During the raid a number of the high explosive bombs fell elsewhere in the district, but I did not discover all of the locations. One fell in the residential area between Hallams Lane and School Lane, Chilwell, at or near Hurts Croft, which damaged some houses. (See page 43) Some also fell harmlessly near the river, upstream of the Marina, one of which fell on the edge of the water and formed a 'gulf' which filled with water.

The day after this raid some young fellows attached to the 2nd Beeston Sea Scouts went to the river to examine the bomb craters there. They then crossed over to the River Training Base (which was then on the site now occupied by the Beeston Sailing Club) where they met the owner of a houseboat moored near to their base. He said that a bomb had fallen into the river only two yards from the end of the floating landing stage alongside his houseboat and (very fortunately for him) had failed to explode. Being naturally very worried about this he persuaded two of the young men to don their bathing trunks and dive down to the position he had indicated.

Not surprisingly, in view of the reasoning outlined below, they found nothing (otherwise they would probably not have been so ready to dive down). It was thought very unlikely that the object which this man had seen fall into the river could have been a High Explosive bomb. Such a heavy object, falling at high speed from the air into seven or eight feet of water would have produced a great spout of water and high speed waves even though it did not explode. This violent disturbance so close by would almost certainly have swamped or seriously damaged the landing stage.

It was thought more likely that a piece of rock or earth had been thrown across the river by the bomb which had made the 'gulf' on the other side and it was this that the man had seen to fall nearby.

There were a number of minor incidents during the period from the summer of 1940 until the night of 8th May 1941 when Beeston and district came within the outer edge of a major attack on Nottingham. This night was also memorable as the date on which Rudolf Hess (Hitler's deputy) parachuted from a Messerschmitt 110 over Scotland in what was generally thought to have been an attempt to do some sort of a deal with Britain before Hitler invaded Russia, which he did only a few weeks later.

It also marked a change in Hitler's policy, as he stopped the practice of 'saturation bombing' of major British cities around this time. The main reason for this was, no doubt, the need to concentrate as much as possible of the Luftwaffe for his assault on Russia.

Around this time also, the RAF had begun to achieve greater success against night raiders, following the introduction into service of specialised night-fighters, heavily armed and equipped with Radar.

Many HE bombs were dropped. Those I can remember fell in Meadow Lane, Chilwell, Beeston Rylands, Mona Street and the Queen's Hotel and in the King Street/Lower Regent Street area.

I was on duty at the Meadow Lane School First Aid Post and was outside at the front of the building (to get some relief from the stuffy atmosphere in the blacked-out interior) when the bombs fell nearby. At least one bomb exploded in front of the premises of the Nottingham Transport Company, the supply depot for the Meadow Dairy Group (on the site now occupied by The Beekeeper Public House). A man and his wife nearby were injured, the husband seriously and the wife superficially. He was rushed to the hospital (which was heavily engaged with the casualties from the city), but I don't think he survived. His wife was treated inside the First Aid Post. Although I cannot recall any damage to the building, the blast from the bomb sent a rush of air down the chimney which blew smoke, soot and ashes into the Control Room. Those inside thought at first that an incendiary bomb had come down the chimney.

Just before this incident, the night sky over Nottingham was, for a few seconds, brilliantly illuminated by a great burst of fire. This I later learned had been caused by a direct hit on a gas-holder in the Sneinton area.

More bombs fell farther down Meadow Lane near to the Golf Club premises but they did not explode. Until the Bomb Disposal Squad had dealt with them notices were posted and this section of the road was roped off.

A bomb on the King Street/Lower Regent Street area also failed to explode. When the Bomb Disposal Squad had dealt with this, a man had the good idea of passing a hat round among the grateful residents and giving the collection to the soldiers involved.

I was later transferred to a new Post in the environs of the Chilwell Grange (at the bottom of Cator Lane, the site now forming part of the school playing field). By this time things had quietened on the air raid side although we did do gas training while I was there.

My final posting was to the Ambulance Depot on Villa Street, Beeston, where I experienced no military activity. Intensive exercises were still carried out including co-operation with the Home Guard when they were doing realistic exercises (which produced one minor casualty). The work gradually developed into more of a civilian ambulance service, dealing with accidents, illness, maternity cases, etc., which continued for a few years after the war, until replaced by the modern highly organised and efficient Ambulance Service.

In conclusion, local government records showed that seventy HE bombs, one oil bomb and an unknown number of incendiaries fell on the district during the war. I expected that there would have been a map showing where the bombs fell in Beeston and district. In my search I was most courteously and efficiently helped by a lady at the Broxtowe Borough Council offices who checked the possible existence of a map, but no evidence of it was found.

RADAR
By Helen Jenkins

This long-range antenna (approx 40m in diameter) rotates on a track to observe activities near the horizon.

Radar is a system or technique for detecting the position, movement and nature of a remote object by means of radio waves reflected from its surface. The term RADAR is derived from the phrase 'Radio Detection and Ranging', and Allied forces used this name during World War II for a variety of devices concerned with radio detection and position finding. Such devices not only indicate the presence and range of an object (the target) but also determine its position in space, its size and shape and its velocity and direction of motion. Although originally developed as an instrument of war, radar today is used extensively in many peacetime pursuits, such as navigation for aeroplanes and marine vessels; controlling air traffic; detecting weather patterns; tracking spacecraft and 'spotting' speeding vehicles.

The oldest radar system was developed millions of years ago and is still used worldwide – it is the ultrasonic sensor of a bat! Bats emit a short cry from their noses, receiving the echo with a set of two antennae (ears). The working principle is the same as that of modern radar.

The oldest radar-warning device was also developed millions of years ago. Tiger moths (which are on bats' menus), are equipped with ears, which can detect and jam the ultrasonic signal of a bat and they have also developed tactics to evade a bat's attack.

The basic concepts of radar are based on the laws of radio-wave reflection. In 1864, James Clark Maxwell, a British physicist, developed equations governing the behaviour of electromagnetic waves. These principles were first demonstrated and developed in 1886 in experiments by the German physicist, Heinrich Hertz. He calculated that an electric current swinging rapidly backwards and forwards in a conducting wire (the antenna) would radiate electromagnetic waves into the surrounding space. With such a wire, he created and detected such oscillations in his laboratory; using an electric spark, in which the current oscillated rapidly – (that is how lightning creates its characteristic crackling noise on the radio). Today we call these waves radio waves. At first, they were called 'Hertzian waves' – we honour their discoverer by measuring frequencies in Hertz (Hz) oscillations per second and at radio frequencies, in megahertz (MHz).

In 1904 the German inventor Christian Hulsmeyer received a patent for the Telemobiloskop or Remote Object Viewing Device. This achieved ranges of 3000m against ships, even before amplifier tubes were invented. It was offered as an application to prevent ship collisions but didn't attract customer interest and fell into oblivion. So radar was invented before sonar (the acoustic equivalent used in seafaring), which was developed in the aftermath of the Titanic catastrophe of 1912.

The first successful radio range-finding experiment occurred in 1924, when the British physicist Sir Edward Appleton used radio echoes to determine the height of the ionosphere, an ionised layer of the upper atmosphere which reflects longer radio waves.

The first practical radar system was produced in 1935 by the British physicist, Sir Robert Watson-Watt.

He was asked by the Air Ministry to investigate the possibility of creating a 'death-ray' weapon using radio waves. At the time, Watson-Watt was working at the National Physics Laboratory in Slough. He did not create a 'death-ray' weapon but he did find that his radio

Sir Robert Watson-Watt

transmitters could create an echo from a plane which was more than 200 miles away. Such a distance would give the RAF an early warning of an attack.

As a result of this success, Watson-Watt was appointed superintendent of a newly formed establishment controlled by the Air Ministry, Bawdsey Research Station, near Felixstowe in Suffolk. The work done by the team at Bawdsey led to the creation of a chain of radar stations throughout the east and south coasts of England, by 1938. This system, known as Chain Home and Chain Home Low, was a vital part of the defence of Great Britain. Incidentally, Bawdsey was featured recently in the BBC *Restoration* programme as being in need of conservation in recognition of the vital part it played in the defence of Great Britain in World War Two.

In 1939 two British scientists were responsible for the most important advance made in the technology of radar during World War Two. The physicist Henry Boot and biophysicist John T Randall invented an electron tube called the resonant-cavity magnetron. This type of tube is capable of generating high-frequency radio pulses with large amounts of power, thus permitting the development of microwave radar, which operates in the very shortwave band of less than 1 cm. using lasers. (Microwave radar, also called LIDAR; light detection and ranging; is used today for communications and to measure atmospheric pollution. Also, magnetrons are used as the source of heat in microwave ovens).

HQ	Group Headquarters
Ŧ	Chain Home RDF
Ŧ	Chain Home Low RDF
✕	Fighter Airfield
✕	Sector Airfield

RDF = Radar Direction Finding

The advanced radar systems developed in the 1930s played an essential role in the Battle of Britain in 1940, in which the Luftwaffe (Hitler's Air force) failed to win control of British skies. Although the Germans had their own radar systems; throughout the rest of the war, the British and Americans were able to maintain technical superiority.

In 1941, history could have been changed because of radar, but, because of human error, it wasn't. A British radar unit operator reported the largest group of aircraft he had ever seen on his screen on the island of Hawaii, close to Pearl Harbour. The duty officer at Pearl Harbour told the radio operator not to worry about it. If the radar report had been taken seriously, the fleet at Pearl Harbour would have had more than half an hour to prepare for an attack by the Japanese bombers.

At the end of World War Two, most of today's technologies had already been put to use, relying on contemporary means. There was chirp radar in production, (it would sound like a bird if it could be heard), the monopulse principle was invented – even synthetic aperture radar (SAR) existed. This works by collecting the echo returns from many radar pulses and processing them into a single radar image.

Chain Home was used to detect the V2 rockets (the world's first ballistic missiles) after they left their launch sites so it can also be called the world's first Anti-Ballistic-Missile radar system. The V2 rockets carried a ton of explosive and were used near the end of the war to bombard London. They were unstoppable by gun or aircraft. Among ideas which were 'born' after 1945 are Phased

Chain Home transmitter aerial towers with wooden receiver towers to the right

Array antenna technology and the concept of multistatic radar.

Germany was ejected from the radar business after losing the War. Until 1950 any research in the field of radar was forbidden, so many researchers emigrated, including engineer Wernher Von Braun (who had been prominent in the development of the German ballistic missile programme).

Radar was kept highly secret throughout the War. Only in 1946 was it announced that an American device had successfully measured the distance to the moon; starting Radar Astronomy. Later, it became known that a Hungarian device had already measured the same distance in 1944.

The increasing hostility primarily between the USA and the USSR – the Cold War - renewed military interest in radar improvements. After the Soviets detonated their first atomic bomb in 1949, interest in radar development, especially air defence, increased. Major programmes included the installation of the DEW (Distant Early Warning) network of long-range radar across northern North America to warn against bomber attacks. As the potential threat of Inter-Continental Ballistic Missiles increased, UK, Greenland and Alaska installed the Ballistic Missile Early Warning System.

Radar found many applications in civilian and military life, becoming more specialised and sophisticated. The use of radar in Air traffic Control grew quickly during the Cold War, especially with the increase in air traffic which occurred in the 1960s. Today nearly all commercial and private aircraft have transponders. These send out radar signals encoded with information about an aircraft and its flight which other aircraft and Air Traffic Controllers can use. American traffic engineer John Barker, discovered in 1947 that moving vehicles would reflect radar waves, which could be analysed to determine the vehicle's speed. Police began using traffic radar in the 1950s and its accuracy has greatly increased since the 1980s.

Doppler radar came into use in the 1960s and was first used by weather forecasters in the 1970s. In the 1990s in the USA there was a nationwide network of more than 130 Doppler radar stations to help meteorologists track weather patterns.

As radar continues to improve, so does technology for evading it. Stealth technology is used mostly on stealth aircraft and ships, in order to make them less visible (ideally <u>invisible</u>) to radar. This was most notably used during the Gulf War (1991). Radar absorbing coatings and deceptive shapes are used. Drivers may know radar only as an invisible threat when speeding, as police radars are used as a means to enforce law. Radar is also on its way to being used to a driver's advantage, as automotive radars are now entering the market. They are used to automatically keep a set distance from the vehicle in front, and to warn the driver when obstacles are encountered in his lane.

Flight controllers use radar to keep track of dozens of aircraft, which are circling in the waiting loop, and to schedule them for landing. This is only made apparent to us when radar is defective and many flights are cancelled or redirected to other airports and local accommodation is fully booked!

*****

"AYE, AYE, SIR!"

Lord Mottistone relates that when a British trawler shot down a dive-bomber, someone was sent from the Admiralty to inquire from the captain how it was they were so successful in the encounter.

The captain, pointing to George, his gunner, replied: "I sez, 'George.' He sez, 'Aye, aye, sir. Then I sez, 'Aeroplane reported.' He sez, 'Aye, aye, sir.' Then I sez, 'Shoot the blighter.' He sez. 'Aye, aye sir,' then shoots him."

Empire News, 25 May 1941

Major General John Seely, 1st Barron Mottistone, was MP for Ilkeston 1910-1922 and Secretary of State for War in the years leading up to World War Two. He was a member of a Nottinghamshire family of wealthy colliery owners.

THE BATTLE OF BRITAIN

Daily Telegraph, 15 August 1945

In the summer of 1940 the German Luftwaffe (air force) began an aerial offensive in an attempt to destroy the Royal Air Force as a prelude to the invasion of Great Britain. They tried by air combat and the bombing of vital airfields in the south of the country but met with stubborn British resistance. British radar technology was superior to the Germans' and we were able to direct RAF Spitfire fighters and Hurricane fighter-bombers onto the oncoming bomber streams (see pages 86-88). This resulted in the Luftwaffe switching their offensive to attacks on British cities (the Blitz) and losing the chance of gaining air superiority. From the beginning of July to the end of October the Germans lost twice as many planes as the RAF.

RADAR cover for the Battle of Britain in 1940. By this time low-flying raiders could be picked up across the Straits of Dover

Daily Telegraph, 15 August 1945

I REMEMBER THE BLACKOUT
By Avis McDermott

I remember sitting at home one night in the winter when someone knocked on the door or window and shouted "PUT THAT LIGHT OUT!" It meant the wardens were on their rounds again making sure there wasn't a chink of light visible anywhere.

On dark nights pedestrians groped along black pavements without the benefit of street lights. In the winters when we had the dreaded pea-souper fogs it was almost impossible to see the pavement as the fog swirled about. People bumped into lamp-posts and fellow-beings in the dark.

But what about the big tin chimneys? The dreaded oil-filled smoke screens were situated on the edge of the pavements in various parts of Nottingham. They were lit when an air raid was imminent and the sirens sounded. Black smoke puthered out. It was supposed to confuse the enemy aircraft as the pall of acrid, black, sooty, fog-like smoke filled the air. It was not uncommon to hear a clanging sound followed by cursing as some hapless person collided with these five-foot tall metal monsters which took up most of the darkened pavement.

How many people alighted from a bus when it stopped, only to land in a heap on the road? It was almost impossible to see the bus stops and thinking the bus had arrived, passengers would alight, only to find they were a good fifty yards away from the stop. The bus was still moving slowly farther up the road............

* * * * *

On 1st September 1939, blackout was introduced under the Defence regulations. At night all lights had to be excluded to prevent the location of towns by enemy aircraft. Blackout material was used and Air Raid Wardens (ARPs) were empowered to check for visible lights. The Beeston area had 529 wardens. The blackout lasted for 2,061 consecutive nights.

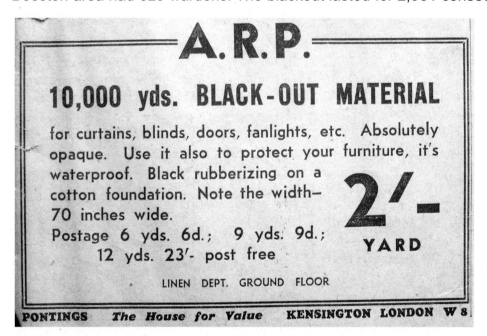

Daily Express,
2 September 1939

What do I do to improve my blackout? (Wartime advice)

I inspect it at night from outside my house at least once a week. I make sure that the curtains cannot flap, and that any roof lights are perfectly screened. I see that the blackout is in place before turning on the light.
I remember that the blackout is just as important in the morning, and I therefore find out the blackout times each day.
If I have been burning refuse in the garden I see that the fire is properly extinguished before dark.
Doing these things helps to ensure the safety of the district as well as my own home.

THE WOMEN'S VOLUNTARY SERVICE

When war threatened in 1938 volunteers were needed for Air Raid Precautions. The Home Secretary had the idea of setting up a women's organization to help with the work in Civil Defence and in May of that year the *Women's Voluntary Service for Air Raid Precautions* was founded. Every woman had the opportunity to help with the defence of the country against attacks by the enemy, and when war was declared on 3 September 1939 over 150,000 women had joined the WVS. They included the young, the elderly, the housebound, those unable to join the forces, those with dependants and those unable to carry out essential war work. The name was changed to *WVS for Civil Defence* after a short while when the work became more varied.

The women helped with the evacuation of children to the country from the cities. They carried out welfare work for the troops and staffed hostels and communal feeding centres. They provided food and clothing for refugees and organized rest centres for those made homeless in air raids. The *Make-Do and Mend* scheme was one of the campaigns organized by the WVS. They contacted the Red Cross in America to ask for help with clothing for people who had lost their possessions in air raids. Accordingly, clothing bundles were sent to us, which along with clothing from commonwealth countries were kept in stores all over the country ready for when the need arose. Beeston had one such store off Wollaton Road, (see page 54). Help and advice was also given to those who had lost personal papers in the raids. Numerous other indispensable tasks were undertaken by the WVS in wartime.

In 1945 after the war ended the Home Office decided the WVS should carry on with work of a social nature for 'possibly two years more'. They continued with their hard work and in the post-war years set up Darby and Joan clubs for older people and helped those affected by the harsh winters and coal shortages. In 1947 they set up the *Meals on Wheels* service in Welwyn Garden City and later ran it nationwide. The Queen agreed to become Patron when she ascended the throne and awarded the honour of adding *Royal* to the title in 1966.

Today, over 60 years on the now WRVS are still working to help people cope in difficult circumstances. Amongst other things they provide non-nursing services in hospitals and help local communities in emergencies such as the Kegworth air disaster and Hillsborough football stadium tragedy when they helped and supported the injured and their families.

*****

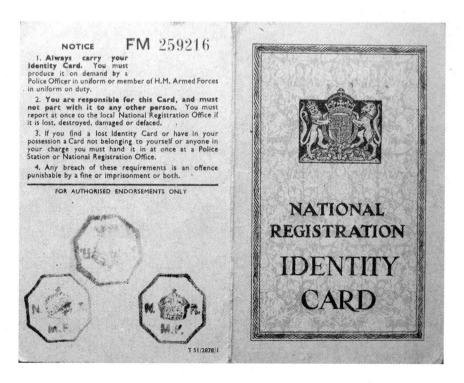

SOME MEMORIES OF THE WAR YEARS
By Carole White

I can remember going to the sweet shop with coupons from my ration book. When my coupons ran out my parents let me have theirs.

Everyone had to allocate a certain shop in which to get their groceries, although we lived on Trafalgar Road in Beeston Rylands, ours was the Home and Colonial at 24, High Road, Beeston, we got our fats, bacon, eggs, sugar and cheese from there and we were registered at A. Elliott's (Butcher) 47, High Road, for our meat.

Coal was rationed and everyone had an open fire in those days. After a delivery the Coal Merchant would come every Saturday morning for something off the bill.

My Uncle Fred – Trooper Frederick Smith of the 14/20 Hussars, Nottinghamshire Yeomanry – was killed in action in Egypt in October 1942. He was the brother of my father, Alf Smith, a founder member of the Beeston & District Local History Society. He left a wife, Mary, and a young son, Peter, and they lived in Dagmar Grove. Fred was one of nine children but the only one to be killed or injured in the war.

I remember my parents telling me about an incendiary bomb that landed on a house in the Queens Road area of Beeston. It burnt through the roof and then descended and burnt through the kitchen table. And at that time some people used to take shelter under their kitchen tables when the air raid sirens sounded.

My mum told me that when they heard the air raid sirens the family went to my grandmother's house near the corner of Trafalgar Road and Lily Grove to sit in the cellar until the 'all clear'. My baby brother had to wear a large gas mask that covered his head and shoulders and air had to be pumped in so that he could breathe. He remembers as a toddler going with mum to granny's house at the bottom of the street and being laid in a bed of some sort down in the cellar, on a slab, during an air raid. He also recalls mum quickly taking him in from the garden if a low-flying plane came over.

Some years later bullets were discovered in the roof of our next-door neighbour's house when they had their roof repaired.

Dad had an allotment on the Golden Drop, near where Longlands Road is today and he used to grow all our vegetables. The Council allowed people to keep a number of chickens for the fresh eggs according to the size of their gardens. Our garden was only small so we could only have four. Dad also bred rabbits for us to eat. The houses on Prince of Wales Terrace had large gardens and so they were allowed to keep pigs as well. So with the vegetables, rabbits, chickens and eggs, we never went hungry!

During the war dad was a fireman at Chilwell Depot and one day when enemy planes were overhead, a bomb was dropped close by and everyone rushed for the air raid shelters. Dad could feel someone pushing him hard in the back and he turned round to tell them off only to find he was the last one in and the pushing sensation was the force of the blast.

We were all told to make-do and mend, which meant nothing could be thrown away.

Instead everything possible had to be mended to be used again, and items of clothing had to be patched, darned and repaired. I remember the milk bottles had cardboard lids with a removable centre and we used to pop the middles out and wind wool through the middle and round the edges to make pom-poms etc. Raffia would be used also and the circles we made were joined up to make bags or mats. Mum always saved shiny paper from chocolates, etc. in a special tin and then in December we wrapped the pieces around cotton wool balls to hang on the Christmas tree. Margarine and butter wrappers were always well-scraped and then the paper would be put over a cake during baking or used to cover other food. We got into the habit of saving pieces of string and brown paper too. Nothing was thrown away if it could possibly be used again. My family laugh at me when I wash plastic bags to reuse, obviously 'Waste not, Want not' was instilled into me at an early age. Knitting, sewing and making pegged rugs was not only essential but also something to do to take your mind off what was happening overseas.

HOME OFFICE
AIR RAID PRECAUTIONS DEPARTMENT
ANTI-GAS PROTECTION
OF BABIES AND
YOUNG CHILDREN
Crown Copyright Reserved

LONDON: HIS MAJESTY'S STATIONERY OFFICE: 1939

CONTENTS

	Page
GENERAL MEMORANDUM	1
Description of the Small Child's Respirator ...	1
Description of the Baby's Protective Helmet ...	3
The Choice of the right Protective Device ...	4
INSTRUCTIONS FOR USE OF BABY'S PROTECTIVE HELMET	6
INSTRUCTIONS FOR USE OF SMALL CHILD'S RESPIRATOR	7

July 1939

My aunt, who was also from the Rylands, joined the Land Army and was billeted on a farm in Wiltshire. She thoroughly enjoyed her time working outdoors and when she came home she had muscles that didn't exist before she went away! The family she was billeted with corresponded with her for many years after the war ended.

I can remember seeing tanks coming along Queens Road. They used to scare me because they were so big and so very noisy and they left their track marks all over the road surface. They would be going to or coming from Chilwell Depot. It must have been terrifying for the people who lived on Queens Road to regularly having several tanks thundering by their front doors.

Mum had waited five long years to have a baby. My brother was born in 1940, which being in wartime wasn't an ideal time to have a baby. Apparently there were second-hand clothes shops where a good item of children's clothing could be exchanged for a larger size. Maybe paying a small charge or a few clothing coupons.

As dad was a joiner by trade he was often asked by people living near us to make them a new wooden front gate or fence which he could only do when wood was available.

Just after the war I remember walking down the street with my mum and looking at people's small front garden walls and asking what the little black square things were on the tops of the walls. I was told that was all that was left after the wrought-iron gates and iron railings had been cut off and sent away to be melted down for the war effort along with old saucepans and any other old metal items, to be turned into tanks, planes and other armaments.

I recall playing with two gas masks after the war that mum kept in the sideboard. And I still have my Identity Card and Ration Book!

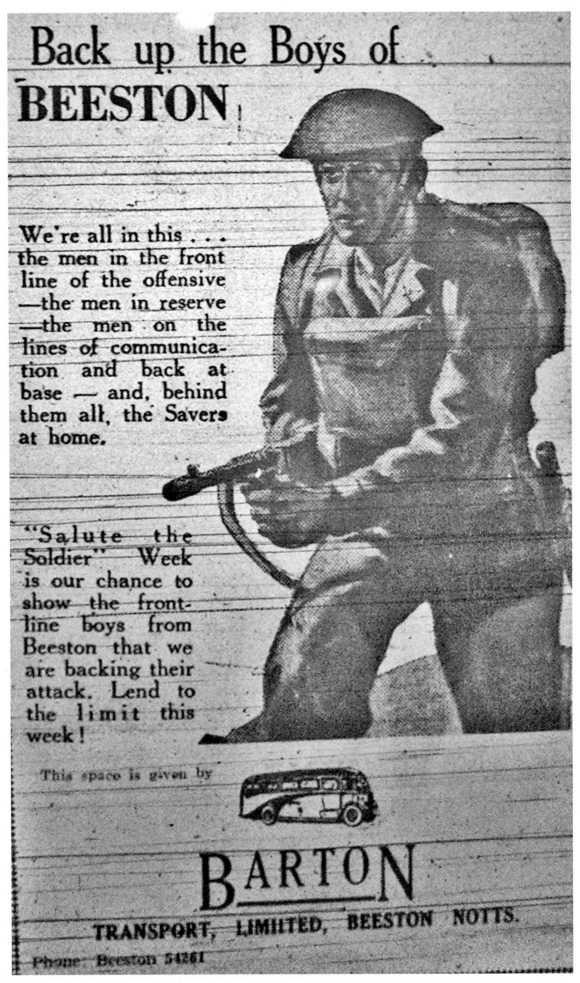

Back up the Boys of BEESTON

We're all in this . . . the men in the front line of the offensive —the men in reserve —the men on the lines of communication and back at base — and, behind them all, the Savers at home.

"Salute the Soldier" Week is our chance to show the front-line boys from Beeston that we are backing their attack. Lend to the limit this week!

This space is given by

BARTON
TRANSPORT, LIMITED, BEESTON NOTTS.
Phone Beeston 54261

Beeston Gazette & Echo, April 1944

94

GASBAGS HELP THE NATIONAL EFFORT
By Alan F Oxley

*Barton's bus in World War Two
with a Gasbag on the roof*

During October 1939 motor fuel was rationed and mileage of motor bus operators was cut by 30 per cent, involving the reduction of bus services accordingly. This obviously affected Barton Transport Ltd., of Chilwell, one of the largest independent stage carriage operators in Western Europe, providing buses in a major part of the East Midlands.

Having overcome this problem in World War One, the company decided to re-introduce buses converted to run on town gas, using basically the same principles. Originally T.H. Barton (Tom senior) had patented the idea and developed this on his own vehicles and also sold 'Gasbags' to other businesses. The gas was carried in large rubberised canvas bags - with stitched joints - on the roof, with a six-inch board fixed to brackets to hold it in place. The gas was taken directly from the mains, by hose, and fed from the gasbag to the engine. Initial starting was made with petrol, switching over to gas once the engine was warm. One of the improvements to the original was a frame fitted to the roof which was covered in plywood to retain the gasbag, as there had been problems with the bags drooping down the side of the vehicle on the earlier examples.

Twenty-eight single-deck buses, two Wolseley cars and two 10cwt vans were so converted. A little later a gasbag trailer was built and fitted firstly to a single-deck bus then heightened to fit behind a double-decker. However, this was very short-lived, as the trailer was very unstable, particularly in high winds. The gas undertaking provided metered points for fuelling, these being situated at the Chilwell headquarters; Dorothy Avenue, Sandiacre; Melton Mowbray and Station Street, Nottingham. By January 1944 gasbag buses had travelled 893,000 miles making a saving of 162,000 gallons of petrol (based on figures quoted by the company, I have calculated that 54,000,000 cubic feet of gas was consumed).

Although Barton Transport Ltd., had successfully run vehicles on town gas, the Ministry of War Transport Department informed them and other large operators they had to convert ten per cent of their fleet to producer gas trailer operation. The method of propulsion involved the heating of anthracite and water to produce a gas which ran for up to eighty miles before refuelling with anthracite was needed. Barton Transport Ltd., were supplied with their quota but they proved to be a dismal failure. Mr Barton did build his own improved model, but the results of his efforts have never been produced, so we can only assume this was also a failure.

Among the local names included in the King's Birthday Honours List in June 1943 was that of Thomas Henry Barton who was appointed Officer of the most Excellent Order of the British Empire, for services to the passenger transport industry. To commemorate this the Company employees commissioned a portrait of T.H. Barton in oils by Norman Hepple. This was presented to him, on the 27th January 1944, when 150 people attended a dinner at the British Restaurant in the Chilwell Memorial Institute. A fitting tribute to an ingenious and brilliant engineer.

*Oil painting of
T.H. Barton O.B.E.
by Norman Hepple*

THE BEVIN BOYS
By Leslie Milton, written by Nicola Wright

Leslie Milton, a former Bevin Boy, spoke at a Local History Society Meeting in April 2000 and the following are his recollections.

In 1942 Ernest Bevin, the Minister of Labour and National Service, made an appeal to young men leaving school to join the coal industry. He stated that there was a call for coal on which the country depended. In 1940 and 1941 36,000 miners had moved to war work, and there was a need for 40,000 new recruits. By March 1943 the appeal had only produced 2,300 new miners. Further appeals brought the same lack of response.

From 2 December 1943 a system of co-opting men into the industry was introduced. National Insurance Numbers were used, and those whose number ended in the chosen number were automatically sent into mining. In December 1943 and January 1944 two numbers were chosen, and then one each month after that.

Leslie Milton was called up on 6 March 1944, and was allocated lodgings in a private house in Mansfield. Many others went to hostels which catered for between 150 and 200 Bevin Boys. Leslie went to Cresswell Colliery where there was a designated seam on which the Boys could train, which they did for four weeks. He then moved to New Hucknall Colliery working on the screens where coal was sorted from stones, and emptying ash wagons. Because he wore glasses at the time, he was not allowed to work underground and so worked at the surface with the older men. Very few Bevin Boys worked at the coal face. And absenteeism was an acute problem. Five hundred were prosecuted, and more than a hundred were jailed for a short term.

As the Timekeeper needed some help and as Leslie had previously worked in the Post Office he was invited to take the job as Timekeeper's assistant. When the Timekeeper retired, he took over the job and when a new colliery manager arrived, he persuaded Leslie to be his secretary.

In October, 1945 Parliament discussed what to do with the Bevin Boys now that the war was over. Should they be kept on in the industry, or should they be allowed to leave? The final decision was that they should be demobbed in the same way as men in the forces, i.e. by number. Leslie stayed until October 31st and handed over to another Bevin Boy before moving on to Mansfield Woodhouse.

After the war the Bevin Boys were not very well treated compared with people from the forces. They were not given a demob suit, they received no gratuity and those injured received no compensation. Many considered them to be the forgotten army, and the first official post-war recognition of their service to the country came from John Major and his associates in Parliament many years later.

In February 1997 RJB Mining invited the Bevin Boys to Selby Coalfield to inspect their two-mile seam. One of the more noticeable changes from the wartime was that the pit ponies had been replaced by diesel locomotives.

BEESTON AND STAPLEFORD URBAN DISTRICT COUNCIL

INFLUENZA

HELP YOUR NEIGHBOUR

An earnest appeal is made to **YOU** to render such service as is possible to anyone in your immediate neighbourhood suffering from influenza and needing **YOUR** help.

Beeston Gazette & Echo, 18 and 25 December 1943

THE RADIO SECURITY SERVICE IN WORLD WAR TWO
By Judith Church

In the summer of 1939 Lord Sandhurst of MI5, a radio amateur, asked the President of the Radio Society of Great Britain if other radio amateurs would take part in a listening watch. It was hoped that enemy agents might be detected by short wave listeners. Although radio amateurs had their transmitters confiscated when war broke out, they were allowed to keep their receivers and most were adept at reading weak Morse code signals. Also, the type of equipment they used helped to ensure an accurate knowledge of the frequency being used for transmission and reception in the frequency bands used by amateurs. The Post Office set up Intercept Stations and many radio amateurs all over the country took part. The whole organisation became MI8I known as the Radio Security Service (RSS).

To begin with the RSS operated from a cell inside Wormwood Scrubs prison, London, but because of air raids and the increase in size of the organisation the HQ was moved in late 1940 to Barnet, Hertfordshire, known by its postal address, Box 25 Barnet.

The background and nationality of potential recruits was thoroughly checked by the police and when accepted the radio amateur signed the Official Secrets Act, was provided with log sheets, postage stamps and addressed envelopes, given a number and allocated a frequency band on which to search for signals. They were called Voluntary Interceptors (VIs). Most already had full time jobs and therefore had to listen in the evenings and if possible, during the night.

By 1944 the RSS were employing more than 1500 people most of whom were radio amateurs. More than half were Interceptors and many others worked on the investigation of numerous radio networks which were being constantly extended and altered by the Germans.

It was thought by the enemy that the material they were sending was indecipherable and so they were quite frank in what they said. Through this, complete knowledge was gained of the structure and daily working of the whole German Secret Service. This enabled us to capture each German spy as soon as he arrived in England. It was also of great value in deception and made it possible for false information to be fed into the German General Staff through their Secret Service.

After a while some VIs moved to HQ and produced a chart plotting the movement of the operators they had identified from their Morse styles and other clues. This was also of great help in understanding the development and intentions of the enemy's Secret Service.

The skill of the VIs listening for long hours to weak Morse signals that were often confused with ear-splitting noise helped the RSS to play its part in breaking German codes and revealing the innermost dealings of their Secret Service. There is no doubt that the information obtained helped to save lives and shorten the war.

The need for secrecy was so important and impressed so strongly upon the VIs that thirty-four years later when the BBC broadcast a television programme called *The Secret Listeners* it was realised they had still not discussed the work with anyone, not even with each other.

Local History Society member Mr Gordon Treece was a VI and had not previously talked about his work, but he was finally persuaded to put pen to paper in 1996 and in the following article tells us about the part he played in the Radio Security Service.

SECRET MESSAGES IN BEESTON
By Gordon Treece

It is surprising how many memories the VE Celebrations have revived, like many others the wife and I were soon involved. Having one of our light vans commandeered by the Fire Service and fitted with a tow-bar it fell to me to jump out of bed when the phone rang and the wife shouted 'yellow'. She mostly answered the phone while I put my trousers on! So out I went up Stoney Street, hitched up a fire pump and went off to some point in Beeston or Chilwell, but like many more times in the early part of the war there was no action. This happened so many times, out at 11pm back at midnight, back to bed then the phone goes again – yellow warning and out we go again. This yellow warning was given every time an enemy plane had just crossed the coast. This began to get everyone down – losing sleep for nothing, so they changed the warning to 'purple' which meant that enemy planes were very near. This did not happen very often in 1940 so everyone's sleep was not disturbed so much.

One other thing we had to endure was the blackout, I don't think that anyone who didn't experience it can imagine what it was like, crawling about in total darkness especially on moonless nights – cars with no lights except headlights shining through little slits on metal covers over the lights. I remember one night the police were checking motorists at the top of City Road, one car failed to stop so another PC fifty yards on threw his torch at his windscreen which quickly did the trick.

There was always the lighter side to the gloom of the blackout. Living on business premises we had the use of the telephone, originally 'Beeston 81', it would often ring about 10pm and a voice would say, "*This is the Beeston Police Station, outside your shop is Police Officer So and So, could we speak to him a minute?*" (No radio on the police in those days). So out went the wife with torch and in the gloom had the job of finding the officer, this was the one job she didn't mind doing. We got to know one or two of them quite well and one used to borrow my cycle to visit his parents – he said it was the best bike he had ever ridden – I purchased it second hand from Tom Bennett, on Beeston High Road, for £1 and it rode like a Rolls.

The blackout was a further trouble to us. We were in the laundry trade and very busy doing work for Chilwell Depot and ATS girls, so as soon as it became dark all the windows had to be closed and sealed off with blinds, these kept the light in all right and also kept the heat in and the fresh air out – we often worked overtime. I don't know how those poor girls put up with it, but they did. One thing that amused us at the time, we laundered some 200 sheets a week for the ATS girls and they started with brand new sheets, hard unbleached cotton, so stiff they almost stood on end, it took ten washes or so before turning them into a reasonably soft sheet. In those days there were fifteen laundries in Nottingham, one each in Beeston, Bramcote and Long Eaton, but now they have all closed.

I continued to serve in the AFS (Auxiliary Fire Service) until one morning in February 1940 I received a surprise letter, it said that my name had been vetted by the police and would I be interested in doing some work with my short-wave receiver for the Secret Service. At this stage I must say that I was a radio amateur and I am still licensed today, so I will go back two years to 1938 when I obtained my transmitting licence and to do that I had to learn Morse code. It took several months practising only in my spare time, so after climbing the stairs to the top of the Post Office building in Queen Street, Nottingham, I was relieved to pass OK. I had just one year on the air with my transmitter when war was declared and we were quickly silenced, so quick that a Post office van took away my transmitting gear on the day war was declared – but they didn't want the receiver and that's what I had in February 1940 when the letter arrived. I couldn't reply quickly enough to say yes. They asked for a passport photo, so off I went down to Church Street to Miss Moore's hut, I am sure many will remember that. When I look at that photo now after 66 years, no wonder Miss Moore said "*smile please*" – I was full of apprehension. I was soon supplied with a pass with a photo in and it said that this person was not to be questioned under any circumstances.

They also supplied log books, message pads, envelopes and labels with a secret address on – Box 25 Barnet, Herts., – and a station to look for on 8000 kilocycles per second at 8pm. I soon found him, a strong signal and he obliged with two messages which were promptly sent off to Box 25, and in return I received a letter of thanks and a request for more please, that's how I got started. Each night this station sent two or three messages which went on for about three weeks and then to my disappointment HQ said this station is now identified and covered. They soon gave me another enemy station to follow and for the next three years I sent dozens of messages all in groups of five-letter cipher. Some stations were very weak and difficult to follow and often letters and groups were missing, but HQ said what you miss the fellow in another town will get so don't worry – no tape recorders in those days! There were some 1500 VIs spread all over the country. By this time HQ had supplied me with the best receiver the USA was producing, the AR88, it weighed over 1/2cwt and I used this until about 1952, it was and still is, a very popular receiver. Between 1940 and 1943 many stations were followed that came up every night at the same time. Sometimes they had no traffic (messages) but other nights, several, and they had to be taken sometimes up until midnight. I also did a watch in the mornings whenever possible between 0600 and 0800. By this time I had been released from the AFS. By 1943 HQ had built two or three new Intercept Stations. The largest one at Hanslope near Northampton was manned by many radio amateurs who had gone in full-time. They had all the best equipment and large directive antennae so they took over from all the part-time volunteers like myself because they could deal with it much better than we could. They asked us to concentrate on general search to find new enemy stations. We were disappointed to be relieved from taking messages but knew it was the right thing.

We were each given a small band of frequencies to cover and I still remember mine, 5500-5700kcs. So up and down I went, all the time I could give, and soon got to know all the stations that were unwanted, anything new and suspicious was soon pounced upon and followed up each day or night until HQ said thanks very much this is now identified and covered, so please find more suspects, and so it went on. Lots of stations did everything to avoid detection, some used to change the call signs, for example a different one for each day of the month, and some times they didn't use one at all! But that didn't fox us; we could recognise the sound of these transmitters and the sound of their 'fist' (method of keying). They were very careful not to give any details away. I remember one station when asked by the other for his initials would say "*Sorry Bill, good night*" and then he closed down. Sometimes a station would appear and never make contact; one such was given us to follow at 4am each morning. I volunteered to do two mornings a week so I slept in the air-raid shelter down stairs so as not to disturb the XYL (wife) and youngster. This indoor shelter was the size of a bed, a steel top supported on four stout angle irons; it was designed to withstand the house falling on it. We couldn't have an Anderson shelter outside because of the danger of the boiler and tank with 300 gallons of petrol in it. I set the alarm and was on watch for 4am. This station came up every morning at the same time for the next six weeks without fail, called for 15 minutes but never made contact. He suddenly stopped and although we kept watch for a further three weeks he was never heard again. HQ said the station he was trying to contact, perhaps someone with a small transmitter was caught and either shot or imprisoned. We kept on searching and supplying new material until the late 1950s.

There were about twelve members in the Nottingham group, eight were radio amateurs and the others just volunteers who could read the Morse code, there was one other operator in Beeston beside myself. He was Bob Tunney who did his work from Meadow Road, sadly Bob is no longer with us. At one time we were enrolled in the Royal Observer Corps for cover and could wear the uniform if we wanted just in case there were any 'white feathers' floating about, some liked wearing uniform but I didn't so I never had one.

There were not many spies with transmitters in this country but one or two were caught but were not shot or imprisoned. They were allowed to continue to send back information which was faulty and misleading and just to make sure they did they had a gun in their backs whilst transmitting.

When VE-Day arrived the urgency of the work declined. Some of us had given all our spare time to the cause, in my case about 4000 hours on the receiver during the period 1940-1945. I found it a great substitute for the loss of amateur radio and wouldn't have missed it for anything. The work continued until 1957 when GCHQ at Cheltenham finally closed us down. It remained on the secret list for over thirty years and took years more to be brought out into the open.

Gordon Treece was the proprietor of the Shaftesbury Laundry which was situated on Beeston High Road on the western corner of Derby Street.

BLETCHLEY PARK, STATION X, THE SECRET WAR
By Henry Balen, written by Nicola Wright

Or, *"What did you do in the War Daddy?"* This was the alternative title Henry Balen gave to the Local History Society at the beginning of his talk in 2002.

He said that this question had been difficult to answer as he had to sign the Official Secrets Act which forbade any talk about what he did. He was in the Royal Artillery and was transferred to the Intelligence Corps as a Lance Corporal and took courses in cryptography, codes and cipher writing before moving to Bletchley Park.

Codes have been used throughout history and two examples are Julius Caesar's use of a cipher which substituted other letters for the ones on the original message. It worked by substituting each letter with the one that stood four places further along in the alphabet so that A = D, B = E, C = F and so on. It is known that a soldier of the Spartan army wrote a message on his shaved head so that when his hair grew the message was concealed.

An ingenious cipher was invented by Thomas Jefferson, later US President, in the early 1790s. It used a log cut into 26 discs each with the letters of the alphabet inscribed around the edge; they were mounted on a spindle in a random order. By turning these wheels words could be scrambled and unscrambled. The number of ways this system could be used was practically boundless. This became known as the Jefferson Wheel.

Bletchley Park in Buckinghamshire is a Gothic mansion which housed the British code-breaking organisation before the war and employed about 12 people monitoring friendly nations. With the advent of war they began recruiting university professors, dons, graduates, chess champions etc., and probably amassed the finest collection of brains in the country. From 1943 to 1946 nine thousand people were employed from all branches of the armed forces including American personnel, some lodged in Bedford and were brought in each day by bus. A military camp was also built. But the secret of its success was the fact that no one knew what the next section was doing, even though they all met socially.

At Kedleston Hall, Derbyshire; Beaumanor near Loughborough and Chicksands near Bedford, Radio Listening Stations were manned by ATS girls who developed great skills in taking down unintelligible messages in Morse. They became very adept at recognising German operators by their style of Morse and their rhythm and speed.

The Germans sent formal text about the weather every day as a test and every message was numbered and if not understood by the receiver then an operator would ask for a repeat of message number so and so, thus the listeners could work out what text was being used on a particular day. The enigma machine had several codes for each branch of the German forces. It was an easy text if you knew the key being used. But it was changed every 12 hours. The Germans broke our Naval code which caused havoc on the North Atlantic run and enabled them to assemble submarines to wait for our convoys. When we broke their code they recalled the submarines. The Germans intercepted radio telephone calls and listened to Churchill and Roosevelt. The Allies found typescripts after they arrived in Berlin.

Henry worked on Japanese Diplomatic Codes and therefore was unaware of the existence of the Enigma Machine. Field Marshall Montgomery later said *"Cracking the enigma code was the major force which helped us to win the war"*.

THE SECRET WAR

A great number of ATS, WAAF and WRNS personnel were engaged in the essential work of intercepting and recording details of the enemy's signals traffic. These are details penned from my personal knowledge of events at that time.

As operators in the field of intercepting German Morse code traffic, we too signed the Official Secrets Act and only in recent years can speak of what we did and where. Yes, there were Radio Listening Stations, the largest being Beaumanor which in 1944 had over 1,000 operators, half of whom were ATS. Other Stations in the Midlands and North included Kedleston Hall and Forest Moor, near Harrogate. In the spring of 1945 Kedleston Hall was to be used as a training centre for ATS personnel who had volunteered for service in India. The Hall having previously been used for training Operators to use the Japanese Morse code. However, with the ending of hostilities in the Far East, the ATS were not required to ship to India.

Forest Moor opened in 1943. After four months training on the Isle of Man, I and about 80 other ATS girls were posted to our Radio Listening Stations. Forest Moor was my destination, and our group travelled in canvas-covered lorries from our accommodation in a requisitioned boarding school for girls, to the wireless station on the Moor. We worked in four watches of about 120 operators in each, enabling the various German frequencies to be constantly intercepted. All the messages were sent to what we only knew as Station X, but now know as Bletchley Park, the home of the famous Enigma Machine.

After the war ended, interception of other traffic continued, and early in 1946 I was posted to Beaumanor where intercept operations were still in progress by the ATS.

Later in 1946 I was commissioned and then I left the army in 1950 to be married. I was still constrained by the Official Secrets Act and neither my husband nor my father, a regular army officer, knew what I or hundreds of my 'Y' Signals companions in the ATS did during or after the war.

It was not until recent years that what Winston Churchill called, "The best kept secret of the war", became known. We and the other Women's Services were truly "his geese who laid the golden eggs that Bletchley Park cracked". We have been on a day trip to Bletchley Park and they have a photograph of my Watch at Forest Moor, taken in 1944, - I now know I am a museum piece!

By Cynthia Humble

The Listening Stations Kedleston Hall, Beaumanor, Chicksands and Shenley were manned by ATS Intercept Operators, and I was one of those Operators. We certainly became familiar with the German operators' styles, which helped us to recognize the transmitting stations. We had to know the call signs and frequencies of whichever stations we were listening for. It was often a difficult job to pick out the transmissions as the airwaves were exceedingly busy as you may imagine, with countless messages being transmitted 24 hours per day, plus the dreaded QRM which was jamming and interference and also the atmospherics.

All the messages were in code of course, so we rarely got to know exactly what information we had intercepted. However, we do know that a friend of mine who was on my watch intercepted vital messages which led to secret information regarding the whereabouts of V2 Rocket Launchers, also of the German Missile Research and Development site. My friend received an official letter of acknowledgement signed by Winston Churchill. Stirring times indeed!

By Winifred Handley

Daily Express, 3 May 1945

DAD'S ARMY AT ERICSSON'S
By Peter d'Auvergne

Most of us have had a good laugh at the antics of Captain Mainwaring and his men in the TV series Dad's Army. The Home Guard was meat and drink for radio and music hall comedians right from the outset, but most of the members took it all in good part and many like myself thoroughly enjoyed the TV series. Mainly I suppose because so much of it is true to life.

Although it is easy to sit back and see the funny side all these years later it should never be forgotten that the Home Guard played a very important part in the defence of this country for almost five years and were instrumental in releasing many of our soldiers for service overseas. Home Guardsmen took over many guard duties from the army and even manned anti-aircraft guns during air raids and doodle-bug (flying bomb) raids in London.

In July 1940 we stood alone against the might of Germany. Every other European nation with the exception of a few neutrals had capitulated to Hitler's hordes. The Americans still sat firmly on the fence. Only the shock of Pearl Harbour brought them down to reality.

Winston Churchill made his famous speech reference fighting the Germans on the beaches and in the streets, 'We shall never surrender' were his immortal words and he appealed to all able-bodied men not already in the forces or Civil Defence to volunteer to repel the forthcoming invasion. The name of the volunteer force was the LDV (Local Defence Volunteers) and millions rallied to the call, many in their teens and also in their seventies. A lot of the older men had served in the trenches in the 1914-18 war, and many of them still bore the mental and physical scars.

I was in a reserved occupation at the time. Not allowed to volunteer for the forces and yet ironically had it not been for the outbreak of the war I would have been doing six months service as a militia man.

Aerial view of Ericsson's in 1939

I was glad of the chance to take what I considered to be a more active part in the defence of the realm and together with many others reported to the Police Station to register for service. I was instructed to report to Ericsson's cricket field on the following Sunday morning where I was greeted, together with a number of my fellow workmates, by exRSM Loat, who during the day served as the work's commissionaire. He was a real army veteran, about 6' 3" in height with a voice like the proverbial foghorn. He spent most of the morning explaining how to load and fire a rifle and taught us the rudiments of rifle drill.

During the following week I was instructed to report for guard duty a few evenings later. I reported to the company armoury on the firm's premises and was supplied with an army uniform, army boots, a Sherwood Forester's cap badge and a steel helmet. We were then marched off by our guard commander, Sgt. Ted Jones, to a hut in a field at the rear of the factory near the railway lines.

I said we were issued with army uniforms. I suppose we were more fortunate than a lot of the other volunteers who were supplied with denim trousers and battle dress blouses. Uniforms became general issue some time later. I suppose we were privileged because we were guarding a site of military importance.

We originally wore armbands bearing the letters 'LDV' on our arm, but this was soon replaced by 'Home Guard' badges. In effect we looked and behaved like real soldiers except for the fact that we still carried our civilian issue respirators in little square boxes, and wore black gaiters. Many of the veterans had campaign medals but few seemed to wear them.

Back to Sgt. Ted Jones and his guard patrol; as I remember there were ten of us and we took turns to patrol the factory environs armed with loaded rifles. In our patrol in addition to Sgt. Jones there was L/Cpl Ted Foster who had served in Northern Ireland, Tom Pearce an exRoyal Marine, Percy Green exSouth Notts. Hussars, Cis Coleman, George Robinson (his drinking partner) John Ivor Jones from the Welsh valleys, Walter Greenslade and myself. All but the latter three were exempt from military service due to both age and occupation. We generally had regular patrol partners but I was the odd man out and seemed to have someone different as a partner (not one of the regular patrol) every guard duty.

We were part of the Beeston Battalion of the Home Guard who met in the Lads' Club premises and I understand were present there in considerable numbers every night.

Those of us on guard patrol at Ericsson's saw little of them although one of their senior officers occasionally made a spot check on us when we mounted guard or during the night.

Other members of the Ericsson's company were Lt. Maxwell-Smith our OC and Lt. Albert Street his second in command. I don't know how the officers and NCOs were originally chosen but it seemed to be based on previous military service or position of responsibility within the company.

There was certainly no lack of enthusiasm, military experience or competition for advancement. During my service of approximately ten months before I was released for military service, I experienced quite a number of amusing and exciting incidents, which indicates how easy it must have been for exHome Guardsmen with four years experience to write the script of Dad's Army. The writer of the television programme was the boy who wore a scarf which is about where I fitted in. I soon got used to the regular routine of guard duty but received virtually no further instruction on the use of firearms, or drill, mainly because like many of my fellows I was working a six or seven day week.

Conditions in the hut were cosy but distinctly unhealthy. There was electric light but the heat came from the traditional coke-burning pot-bellied stove and as the windows were of necessity 'blacked out' there was no ventilation. There was no rule against smoking in the hut and by about ten o'clock the fug was akin to a gas attack. We were supplied with tea and sandwiches for supper from the work's canteen and despite rationing, a hearty breakfast when we stood down at around 6.45am.

Although the works' cloak rooms with sinks and hot water were only about fifty yards away it was the usual custom for all of us to wash in the same bucket of water. Even on active service our rules of hygiene hardly ever sank that low. When the guard were assembled in the hut it was general practice for Ted Foster, Cis Coleman and George Robinson to ask permission of Sgt. Jones to slip away for an hour. None of the others objected and I presume they went off to the Boat Inn or the Vic. They reappeared with their breath smelling accordingly. There was no great shortage of beer at that time.

Lt. Maxwell-Smith, who had no previous experience as a military man, came round to inspect the guard one evening about 10.30. Fortunately Ted Foster and his mates had returned from the pub and were chatting around the table. The remainder of us including myself, with the exception of the two on patrol were dozing on the two tier bunks provided.

Lt Maxwell-Smith had only been in the hut a few minutes when the phone rang. The security man announced that someone was trying to climb the fence into the factory grounds. The lieutenant said, "*We must take action immediately*". Excitable Cis Coleman like the little "*Don't panic*" L/Cpl. in Dad's Army responded immediately, "*I'll come with you Mr Smith*", he shouted and grabbed a loaded rifle, pulled the trigger, and a bullet went straight through the roof. In the enclosed space it made a terrific bang and the angle of the rifle was directed straight at the bunk where I lay. "*My God! You've killed him*", shouted Ted Foster. "*Yes you've shot me right through the foot*", I said. There were sighs of relief all around and I can't remember whether any further action was taken regarding the suspected intruder. All I know is that I came nearer to death that night than any time during my five and a half years active service.

We had a considerable store of rifles and ammunition and rifles were kept in immaculate condition by a little man named John Brown. John seemed to be a full-time Home Guard, as on those evenings when he wasn't in the armoury cleaning rifles, he was deputising for someone unable to turn up for guard duty. Thus he was hardly ever out of uniform and was the recipient of numerous free lunches, suppers and breakfasts. This appeared to suit him as despite the fact that he had a large family he had a rather unhappy domestic life.

On several occasions he was my partner on guard which was quite an experience to say the least. He was a First World War veteran, rather deaf and extremely trigger happy. Thus he struck fear into the hearts of the Security Staff, particularly a fat man nicknamed Sydney Howard (he was the double of a comedian of that name). On one occasion as John and I were patrolling the factory grounds Sydney emerged from behind one of the factory blocks. John shouted like lightening, "*Halt or I fire*" and pointed his rifle. This terrified Sydney as he had no doubt that on the slightest provocation John would fire. "*It's me! It's me!*" he shouted, "*you silly old fool*", and John reluctantly lowered his rifle.

One of our members was unfortunately killed in an accident at the level crossing. His widow gave permission for his fellow Home Guardsmen to act as bearers and provide a guard of honour. This gave Mr Loat the opportunity to show his expertise as a Sgt. Major. On the evenings prior to the funeral he drilled us up and down one of the main corridors in the factory. In the end he complimented us and we gave quite an impressive show to bid our comrade farewell.

As Christmas drew near we became aware that we should be on guard on Christmas Eve and Christmas Day, which caused us all concern and dismay. However, it was decided that we were to carry out our usual duties on Christmas Eve and throughout the night but would be released at 7.30am and replaced by a skeleton guard of volunteers during Christmas Day. Christmas Eve passed quite pleasantly. Cis and his mates paid their usual visit to the pub and the Company did us proud by providing turkey sandwiches for supper. As I remember there was no enemy action or military activity during that Christmas.

In the late spring, Nottingham was blitzed and we carried out our patrols to the sounds of heavy anti-aircraft fire and the loud explosions of falling bombs. No bombs fell on the factory but shrapnel hailed down around us throughout the night.

The next day was the first day of my annual week's holiday and I was given permission to stand down at midnight. I spent the afternoon playing cricket for Beeston Town against the City Mental Hospital. I batted for a long time for quite a high score and throughout my innings delayed action bombs kept exploding in the city, much to the delight of the hospital inmates.

I only did two more guards prior to departing to join the real army, but I must say that I thoroughly enjoyed the comradeship in Dad's Army and I feel that the country owed them a great deal. God bless 'em all!

Beeston Square in 1940

The Council Offices are in the centre and on the left is the National Provincial Bank at the corner of Station Road, now Bird's bakery shop.

MEMORIES OF WORLD WAR TWO
By AJ Horton

Although I was only a little boy during the war most of my recollections are very clear. My overriding memory is of the searchlights and their criss-cross patterns creeping across the sky with an incandescent and eerie glow. I remember hearing distant gunfire and seeing the flashes of bursting shells high in the sky. This was of course always preceded by the dreadful wail of the air raid siren. It seemed specifically designed to instill a sense of urgency and fear. Immediately the siren sounded mum and dad would take us down the garden to the air raid shelter that dad had built for us. At this point I would occasionally run off towards the sound of the gun fire. For a little boy it was a very exciting time. No doubt my parents had a very different opinion! I was fascinated by the searchlights and the sound of the aircraft overhead, probably heavy bombers.

In our box room I found a box of gas masks, a fascinating find for a little boy! I proceeded to work out how to wear them and then I would scare members of the family to death by suddenly appearing before them in a gas mask.

I remember going out in the car with my father one day and in the countryside we saw Italian prisoners of war helping with the harvest. As mice and rats ran out of the stubble the Italians killed them with sticks.

My last strong memory of the war is of barrage balloons. Those huge silken-covered monsters shimmering in the sun and dotted about the sky sometimes in small clusters depending on what they were protecting. They seemed to hang as if by magic suspended on an invisible thread when in fact they were anchored by cables, and they made quite an impression on me. It's amazing to think how effective they were in Britain's defence system. They were a successful deterrent against surprise low-level attacks by enemy aircraft.

After the war my strongest memory is of the rationing and ration books, walking along Beeston High Road and gazing into the empty food shops. Especially Mr. Whiteman's sweet shop situated next to Pounder's shoe shop, it is now a camping equipment shop. He would stand sombrely in the doorway while I would stand and gaze, equally sombrely, at the empty shelves in the window and ask him when he would have some sweets. Disappointingly, he could never say.

BARRAGE BALLOONS

In 1938 when the prospect of war loomed it was decided that industrial areas, harbours, ports and other vulnerable sites would be protected from low-flying dive-bombers with a barrage of large balloons anchored by steel cables. The balloons could be up to 500 feet above ground level thus forcing enemy aircraft to fly high which made them less accurate and brought them within range of anti-aircraft guns. They were crewed mainly by the Women's Auxiliary Air Force who had the difficult and dangerous task of putting them up. The largest ones measured 62 feet long and were 25 feet in diameter. They could of course be easily shot down and many were struck by lightning though this problem was eventually overcome.

In 1944 many German V1 flying bombs snagged on the cables of the balloons set up to protect London. Smaller balloons were suspended over the landing craft on the Normandy beaches on D-Day to protect Allied troops from the low-flying German aircraft attacking men and ships.

A PRISONER OF WAR REMEMBERS
By William Mackrell

Introduction

William Mackrell was born in the village of Bridge of Allan, Stirlingshire in 1917. He began working life as a milkman, making his deliveries with a horse and dray. When war broke out he volunteered for service even though he had just trained as an engine driver. He was posted to Aldershot and became a driver with the Royal Army Service Corps. He was taken prisoner at Dunkirk and held by the Germans for five years in many different camps in Germany and Poland.

After the war when he was well enough to resume civilian life, Mr Mackrell worked as a porter at Beeston Station. He then worked from Central Ordnance Depot, Chilwell distributing Army surplus supplies, tanks etc., to various parts of the country. He married and settled at Broxtowe and later became a driver with the Hoveringham Gravel Company. During this time he also served with the Army Reserve for ten years. A stroke forced his retirement at the age of sixty-two. He returned to Bridge of Allan and died there in July 1995. Understandably the months of being force-marched across Europe took their toll and for the rest of his life he suffered terrible problems with his feet.

Here is the story of his Army career and horrendous years as a prisoner of war at the hands of the Germans. (Illustrations from the collection of William Mackrell).

Mr and Mrs William Mackrell on their wedding day, 8 December 1945

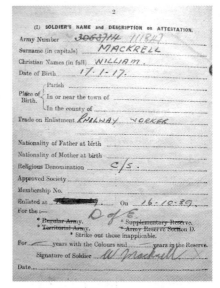

Details from pay book

I joined the army on the 14th October 1939 and became No.3053714, Driver RASC and was drafted to Buller Barracks in Aldershot. The paperwork had to be done first and then I was kitted out and on my way to France. We landed at Cherbourg and caught the train to a place called Poniche on the west coast near the Spanish border where we had our inoculations and were billeted under canvas. The weather was very warm and I became sun-tanned, it was like a ten-day holiday. Then we left for Dieppe where we joined our Company. There were about twenty-five men in our Company and only three of us were Scottish. We were there till May 1940 and the first job I had was being called out at 1.00 a.m. to get an ambulance to the docks to pick up a body that had been fished out of the water. I had an Orderly with me and he did all the talking with the French Police. We managed to get the man's pay book but he had no money on him. We took him to the morgue and that was my first casualty in wartime. We had a number of these jobs because we were billeted there much longer than expected.

Next we had a run to Marseilles to fetch a load of four-gallon cans of petrol. It took us a week after which we moved to a place called Le Treporte where I was on ambulances for long stretches or lorries for just a week at a time.

After a month we moved to Le Havre and I was sent to a place called Tervue which was a Medical Corps under canvas. It was nearly Christmas and snowing heavily. I pulled up and went inside a big marquee and looked round for the medic or an Orderly. I found a Sergeant and told him I was the driver of the ambulance and was here for two weeks and I wanted some dinner as I'd had nothing to eat that day. He took me to the Mess and gave me dinner and a tin of cigarettes. I was posted to this hospital over Christmas and New Year but had to sleep on a stretcher in the back of the ambulance until one of the Sergeants gave me a mattress on the floor near the fire as I was on call at night as well.

When I reported back to base at Le Havre I was told to take sick men from the hospital to the ship in Cherbourg Harbour. We fetched men from all the hospitals in the north and east of France. We had no maps, just a reference number and had to look at the office map and then memorise it.

When spring came I knew there was something on the go, I could feel it in the air. I had my leave for ten days and it took two days to get home and two days to get back and three days to find my unit because it had moved to a place called Doullens where the Medical Officer asked volunteers to give a pint of blood each as the blood wagon had been blown up, it was put in my pay book and initialled by the MO.

Our next job was at a place called Dourne to pick up a batch of wounded soldiers and take them to the boat at Boulogne. But we did not arrive as we were bombed and machine gunned for two days and were getting a bit edgy. We could see the dust in front of the wagon and made a beeline from the cab into the ditch. In this way we made it to a crossroads where we saw a scout car and three big tanks firing guns. We were caught in the crossfire from the tanks and a French machine gun crew behind us. Three vehicles were lost in that lot. Mine was the first to be shot at but it was the engine that was hit, but not disabled. The second caught fire and the third was also hit in the engine. For about two hours we struggled to turn the vehicles round, then we set off back to base with, remarkably, only one casualty. It was the Sergeant from the Medical Corps, who had a bullet in his shoulder. He was responsible for getting all the men and casualties back to the boat but in the event all were taken prisoner.

Parked under cover of the trees, we made tea and three ambulances pulled up and asked us for the road to Dieppe. We told them and said we had a Sergeant with a shoulder wound and could they take him. They said they could, so I wished him luck and we shook hands.

Things were getting desperate so we decided to get back to base as quickly as possible. It was hell on the roads. Refugees were lying by the side of the road, either dead or wounded. There was a terrible smell of dead animals and humans. We tried to comfort the women and the children, but there was nothing we could do.

Eventually we arrived at base to find it wrecked and deserted. We sat down to discuss what could be done and wanted to know what had happened and why. It was decided to take the wagon and carry food to last a week, tins of meat, stew, tea, sugar and Nestlés milk. There was no bread, but there were some Iron Ration biscuits called Hard Tack.

All roads were blocked with refugees. It was a nightmare and we had to constantly dive into the hedge bottom to get away from the machine gun fire and bombs from the aircraft. When it was getting dark we parked the lorries, made the petrol cooker work and cooked some food, after which we tried to sleep. It was impossible with the shells firing all night. We were seven drivers with wagons and ambulances, without officers or NCOs, and nobody asked us where we were going. It was a proper mix up. I said so in stronger language to the Infantry as they were walking alongside our wagons.

After a while we picked up a passenger, a Church Army man who ran a canteen. He was exhausted, had blisters on his feet and was unable to walk any farther. His little case was full of chocolate bars. He collapsed into the seat and told us that we were surrounded and that we must head for the coast as there was nowhere else to go if we turned on to a different road. We caught up with the refugees and the dead cattle and horses and there was always the smell of death. I was getting used to it by now. We entered a village where the roads were all blocked and everything was at a standstill, everybody was looking up for aeroplanes.

In front of me was a car and in front of that a wagon of French soldiers. The driver of the car seemed to be struggling with his wife. He got out of the car holding a revolver, he fired into the wagon and four soldiers fell onto the road. At this the Church Army chap fainted. The French soldiers were loaded back onto the wagon. The other soldiers got hold of the man in the car but I do not know what they did to him as I saw a gap in the traffic and pulled out of the main convoy. We carried on our weary way with, seemingly, something exciting happening every moment.

We drove on at about five miles an hour with my Church Army friend jumping about in the cab, he was so frightened of the Jerry planes, I did not like them myself and we had to take cover in the ditch a few times. After a few more miles we stopped again to make some tea but did not have any sugar so I went along to see if I could get some from the back of the convoy, which I did. I swapped some tins of stew for tea and sugar then fetched the little cooker from the back of my wagon and made tea in a big can. It was good. I brought my mates together and we all drank the tea, the Church Army man could not keep his eyes off the sky.

Off we went again and the next time we stopped my Church Army man decided to go it alone on foot across the fields. We said farewell to him and he gave us a carton of chocolate, we shook hands and that was the last I saw of him. We continued our journey for about three hours until it was getting dark and we were near the coast. We decided to get some sleep in the wagon because the bombers would not fly at night, but at four o'clock in the morning they started up again.

It was very misty when we awoke and we knew it was going to be a hot day. We left the lorries by the roadside and walked towards the beach, I was amazed at what I saw. The Jerry bombers were starting again and all hell was let loose. It went on for half an hour. When we were walking back along the road we met an Officer who was Captain of the Medical Corps. He asked us if we were Transport and we told him we were drivers. He asked us to take six wagons to a little casualty clearing station and load them with stretchers. With the Germans firing at us continually we returned the wagons to a road near the beach and the medics were to carry the wounded onto a boat. Some looked very bad and some had gangrene in their wounds, the smell was terrible. It took five trips, two wagons were on fire and the others were riddled with bullets. I never saw the captain again, I do not know if he was killed or drowned.

When we had taken all the wounded to the beach I knew that we wouldn't be able to get on a boat ourselves. The enemy was about a mile away, we discussed tactics and agreed to set fire to the wagons and take the bolts out of the rifles as we had no ammo left. All we could do now was to pack it in.

A Jerry flung a grenade among us and I got a piece in my leg and some of the others had fragments in their arms, I think it was an Anti-Personnel Grenade. That was why we gave ourselves up. I bandaged my leg with a shell dressing that I had in my pocket. The Germans told us to stand up and put our hands above our heads. It was very degrading; they took our rings and watches, money and lighters, the lot. We were herded along to join men from other

Regiments.

After about half an hour we were marched along a road towards the Belgian border. We marched through many villages and people would put buckets of water or sometimes wine out for us but the Jerry (German) guards kicked them over. There were machine guns on the back of the lorry ahead of us and two on a lorry along side us, trained on us all the time. We had no food for three days and then two new lorries of guards took over who were not so strict, they let us have water to drink and some food from the civilians. We had potatoes boiled in their skins for which we were extremely grateful.

I had my leg bandaged by a Belgian Red Cross Nurse who spoke good English and asked for my name and address so that my next of kin could be informed. We resumed our journey and after about two hours were told to sit down in a field where there were two functioning field kitchens. The Jerry guards had first helping then they watered ours down, but we were glad of it. We slept that night in the field, I had a blanket I picked up somewhere on my travels, it kept me warm that night and a lot more nights to come.

The next day I saw the Campbells walking in the opposite direction, I do not know where they were going. There were about forty men and eight guards. I shouted to them and they answered me back, but I didn't see them again until the war was over.

We carried on walking through Belgium and Holland, worn out and starving, getting weaker day by day and infested with lice. There was no food, we could not get a wash and my feet were in very bad condition. At the end of each day we were given soup but no bread after which I just lay down and went to sleep. I shared the blanket with my mate Bill Hanley from Nottingham who was a bus driver in peacetime. When it rained we were wet through, when the sun shone we dried out again. It was the only time we had a wash, when it rained. Sometimes we had a couple of hard-boiled eggs from the civilians although food was really scarce by now and the guards were hitting the civilians and us with their rifle butts. I think I had walked about 250 or 300 miles, my feet knew it and my legs were very tired.

It took about a month to walk to the Dutch/German border and we all knew what was in store for us. One day we picked up a loaf of bread that was filthy, and covered in green mould, hard as a brick, but we still ate it all, it was to last us for three days.

The notification of William Mackrell's imprisonment, received by his family

We eventually arrived at a river or canal and I heard an accordion and saw a man in a little boat playing a song called *Au Revoir*. There were barges for about one hundred yards and we were told to go down into the hold of one that was black with coal dust, we were packed like sardines, they battened down the hatches and we were off. Three barges behind a tug, we zigzagged from bank to bank as we were being bombed by the RAF. I think they took us for ammunition barges. We had to stand for three days and two nights because of the state of the steel floor. It was incredibly filthy and we could not sit down for the urine and the excrement, the smell was terrible.

At last the barges stopped and the hatches were opened. I could not see a thing for about five minutes. When I looked down at the bottom of the barge I found the squalor disgusting but there was more to come before the war was over.

I think we landed at Dortmund or Essen. We were in very poor condition; we had lice and were starving. We were marched off in three ranks but we couldn't understand what the guards were saying so they laid into us with rifle butts and the women spat on us and threw stones. It was a two-mile march to our camp which was a factory or a store with a concrete floor and straw to sleep on. We were given some soup and green mouldy bread, it was repulsive but it helped to satisfy our hunger.

The new guards were absolute swine. Suddenly a German Officer came over to me, he was shouting and grabbed me by my jacket, he pulled out a revolver and put it to my head. I thought I'd had it. He hit me at the back of the neck and I fell down but I soon got up again, he put the gun back in the holster.

We were the scruffiest, most ragged bunch I ever saw. Next morning we were given ersatz coffee, no sugar and milk. At least it was wet and warm but we had nothing to eat. We fell into three ranks and were made to march three miles to a train that took us to a Prisoner of War camp at Marienburg. Here there was a machine gun every hundred yards and three rows of barbed wire with trip wire in front of that.

We then set off again by train to another camp. There were forty men packed in each cattle truck. After five hours we pulled into a siding, the guards pulled the doors open and we fell out on to the platform. We were given a drink of water but nothing to eat. An hour later we were bundled into our trucks again, I had no idea of the time and I was so tired I kept falling asleep on my feet. Eventually the train slowed down and stopped. We were there, thank God for that.

We made it slowly to the camp and through the gates. There was food, I was amazed! I soon got my dixie, (cooking pot) but we were allowed only one ladle of soup and half of a small black loaf. I thought it was my birthday! It must have been about nine o'clock in the evening and we had been standing since six that morning. We had a roll call, of the sort that only happens in a POW camp. It took about two hours to count two hundred men, then we had to find a bed. There were two tier bunks of board with a little straw to sleep on and I soon went to sleep but all I dreamed of was food. It is a terrible thing, starvation.

At six o'clock we got up and had some ersatz coffee. It was made of roast barley and roast acorns, ground down and boiled. We had a roll call and it took them one and a half hours to sort us out. We didn't help them. First of all we took our clothes to be deloused, and then we had a cold bath, our heads shaved and our photo taken. They put numbers on the photos, mine was 19101.

Two guards got hold of me and marched me to a building, up the stairs and into a room where a German Officer sat at a table. I knew by the skull and cross bones on his cap that he was Gestapo. Surprisingly he spoke perfect English. He asked me a few questions and I told him my rank, my number and my regiment. That was all I was going to tell him. He asked me what my Grandma's maiden name was but I did not know. He was getting a bit hot under the collar and asked me what my nationality was, when I said that I was a Scot I got a bit of a punching but I was getting used to it. So now I was a registered prisoner of war.

Although the water was cold and there was no soap I decided to wash some of my clothes. They hadn't been washed for three months. I still had my old trousers and jacket but I had no socks, only some foot cloths I wrapped round my feet to wear with my old boots. Then it was roll call again! Another two hours! We kept moving from the end of the line to the beginning, that meant we had to be counted again. The Jerries said they would shoot the lot of us if we did it again.

The next morning we had our ersatz coffee and then walked two miles to unload some barges. It was

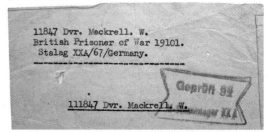

William Mackrell's details at a further Prisoner of War camp

110

7.30a.m., I had my dixie slung on my belt and found there was a boiler of soup so I had a dixie full and a hunk of black bread. I did that job for about a week. I always tried to get work because it meant more food and I was able to sleep better at night.

Eventually we were moved to another camp. We walked two miles to the station where we were herded into trucks. The journey lasted all day and all night and when we stopped it was about five in the morning. We had a roll call that took an hour and were then marched nearly four miles to the camp. We were sleepy as we walked so the guards gave us a few rifle butts in the ribs to wake us up. The camp was badly run down but it was dry and we had some straw to lie on. We were only there for about a week. By now it was nearly autumn and I knew that we were about to have another move. This time we were taken to Poland.

The journey took two days by train, packed in cattle trucks. No luxury travel for us but we were getting used to it. We only had half a loaf and a drink of water before we arrived in Poland. My first impression of the people and the transport was that they were about fifty years behind our times. This place was called Lublin and we had to walk two or three miles to the camp which was an old wooden building that had housed pigeons. It was a Polish Army Barracks and we found some pigeon baskets in the loft, we brought them down and broke them up to put in the stove to keep us warm. When the guards saw the smoke coming out of the chimney, that was it! We had rifle butts in our backs and three hours punishment outside on the parade ground in the freezing cold. We had no food and it was too cold to go to sleep.

Next morning we were given some ersatz coffee and a slice of black bread. I was given the job of peeling potatoes for the guards, which I didn't want to do, but it was warm and beggars can't be choosers. The Jerries searched us to make sure we didn't have potatoes in our pockets. We were given a bowl of soup at night and that helped us to sleep.

We were in Lublin for two weeks after which we went to a camp called Thorn. It started off quite small but it became larger as time went on and it became the headquarters of Prisoner of War camps. I didn't see much of the camp as I was out on working parties which meant I was given more food. My first job was clearing snow from the runway of the aerodrome. I had two bowls of soup, a big piece of black bread and two roast potatoes for that. My feet and legs were wet but my belly was full so I was satisfied.

It was December, we had a foot of snow and it was my first winter in captivity. One day as we marched along the street a woman gave me a small loaf. It was a risk as the guards were walking back and forth and as she disappeared I thanked her. She would have been shot if caught. I went on the same job the next day, we had a little bread and a drink of coffee before we started work and after we finished for the day we had some soup and bread.

That job lasted for a week and it ended because two RAF pilots tried to steal a plane but they could not get it started because of the cold weather. This caused the Germans to vent their wrath on us. I don't know what happened to the airmen but I do know we were on parade for over two hours in the freezing cold. Because we were British and therefore, to the Germans, connected with the attempted escape we were confined to camp for a month. There were no working parties and no extra food and by way of punishment I was taken to Fort 13 for a month where I had to exist on just bread and water. I lost some weight again and felt I was getting weaker. We were all starving. Another chap and I managed to get some potato peelings from the guard's compound but if we had been caught we would have had another beating. We were also rationed for fuel; we used it for heating and boiling our potato peelings. Everyone tried to get warm around the stove but we couldn't light it until 6 p.m.

Again I was moved to another camp and this time it was out in the wilds. Fifteen of us walked about three miles from the station with four guards. I was given the job of pile-driving with a steam hammer and we had to shovel concrete behind the piles. That is where I got my jackboots with wooden soles. They were warm and I was given them by the foreman who was a German civilian. He must have liked me. The food was good too, soup, bread and roast potatoes. That job lasted for a month and then the weather closed in. There was ice on the river and we had a lot of snow so we had to pack up and go back to the big camp. Back to the starvation diet again.

We returned to Thorn and received some clothing from the Red Cross. I had a second hand battle dress, a vest and pants but no socks. I still had my jackboots with wooden soles to keep my feet warm. We had not yet received any Red Cross food parcels.

They gave us the job of unloading sugar, flour and sometimes coal from barges. Coal was very scarce and it was a crime to bring coal into the camp. We were searched before we entered the gates. The Polish people risked their lives by giving us bread and a little tobacco, they could have been shot. They took a lot of chances and I greatly admired them for their kindness and bravery.

When all the barges were unloaded we were out of work and so it was down to bare rations again, one loaf of bread between seven men and a bowl of soup each per day. A loaf was eight inches by four inches, not much to eat. We were burning all the wood we could get, even some of our bed boards, so that we could keep warm. It was very cold and I only had one blanket.

Then I was put on a civil contractor's job, there were thirty of us with four guards. We travelled in a carriage with wooden seats but I was unable to guess our location as all the signposts had been taken down. Two huts surrounded with lots of barbed wire were allotted to us and each had a large stove with plenty of coal so we were warm all night. We were also given an extra blanket. We walked a mile to work each morning carrying a pick

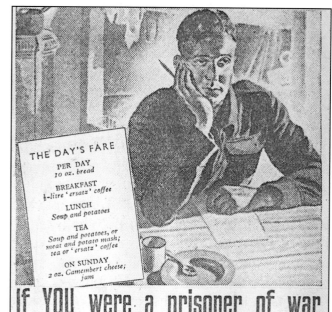

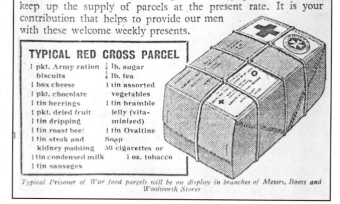

Empire News, 25 May 1941

and shovel. The work was hard, but I did not mind as we were given plenty of food and we were warm at night.

After a few weeks on this job we worked in an old graveyard that I think was about a hundred years old. The Gestapo, in plain clothes and carrying revolvers, arrived. I thought they were going to shoot us but they just sat and watched us without saying a word. After a while they sifted through the bones looking for jewellery and other valuables. We had a rest while they did this, but they did not find much, only a few rings. When they left we breathed a little easier.

Our next job was in a little old derelict village where we had to break up stones and lay them on the roadway. All by hand, there were no machines. We were very sunburnt because the temperature was ninety degrees, but it was cold at night. There was no work on Sundays, so we did our washing and had a bath. The water was cold from a hand pump and there was no soap. I was there for eight months until the weather closed in and we had to stop.

We were on our way again, back to Thorn camp where we had a surprise waiting. The food parcels had arrived for us through the Red Cross. We had one parcel between four men for which we were very thankful as we did not get them very often. It was nearly four years before I had a parcel to myself. When I walked to the gate to see if there was work, I had to carry all my tins with me in a haversack. If I didn't the men would have stolen them. You could not trust your mates. Hunger made men into animals.

Stalag 20A Thorn was about two miles square and consisted of many smaller camps for the Russians, the French and the British. Each camp was partitioned in lanes with barbed wire each side. The guards patrolled in the lanes. We stood near the gate looking for work; we were always looking for work.

One morning we were marched two miles to a big house. There were six men and one guard and we arrived at eight o'clock. It was a German Officers' Mess Club and we were taken into the kitchen where there was a big wooden table. We sat down and were given a cup of coffee, two slices of bread and some cheese after which we were given the job of chopping wood, each tree had to be cut into twelve inch lengths to be used in the oven for baking bread. It was a seven days a week job but it got me fed in the winter.

A piece of German wartime propaganda
The caption reads
"BEFORE MAKING HIS HISTORIC SPEECH FROM BUCKINGHAM PALACE, THE FUEHRER REVIEWS HIS VICTORIOUS TROOPS."

All I wanted was some decent food for myself. I missed my freedom, there was a gun at my back all the time and everywhere you looked there was barbed wire. I was getting what we called barbed wire fever. Now if I see a barbed wire fence I think of my days as a POW.

I think it was New Year 1943, just an ordinary day at work, when we were given a bottle of beer by the cook. He was a nice chap and he spoke English because he had been a cook in a hotel in London before the war. Although he was a nice man he was also a German and our enemy. That thought always stuck in my mind. We were there for another three months before we had to go back to the big camp in exchange for Italian civilian workers.

We managed to get odd jobs, such as unloading barges onto lorries but we had to steal food. Some of the guards searched us and others did not. One of the bargees kept two or three hens on his barge, he gave me three eggs which I took to the camp, boiled them and ate them with a piece of dried bread, it was delicious. When there was no work there was no food. Sometimes there was work but there was no food at the end of the day. We had nothing from our captors. What we managed to steal from the Germans we kept to ourselves.

I was taken back to Stalag 20A again and was getting all the news about the war because we had a secret radio in the camp. There were a lot of spies about, although they wore British Army battle dress they were Germans. We could tell, they could speak English but they could not pronounce a 'w'. The news over the grapevine was good. It bucked us up a bit and I knew we were going to win the war. The guards were changed to older men and they were an improvement. The young ones were being taken to the Russian Front; the Germans were getting very hard up for manpower. They put all the Irishmen into one part of the camp and asked if they would fight against the Russians; only against the Russians and not against Great Britain.

It was late summer 1943. I was thinking of escape because I wanted to be free. But how? I had no papers; I had no way of speaking the language. I could speak a little German but could not get into conversation with people. If you were an Officer you could get the papers you wanted. They were all counterfeit of course. But you had to be in the Officers' camp to get into the Escape Committee. They received coded letters from MI5. I was not one of them, so I had to carry on with my captivity. How long, I did not know.

I had a job for a few weeks at the barges down on the river, loading flour and sugar, but it meant I could have a little food. When we returned to the camp we always picked up something to eat. Escape seemed out of the question, so I carried on as usual. My thoughts were confused and I was getting a bit low. Each night I hoped the next day would be a better day.

But the next day found me hanging about round the gate looking for work as usual. When I did get a job it was heavy work. A German civvy picked me up; he looked me over and said "You'll do". We were transported by train to a place down at the south of Poland, near the Silesian border. When we alighted there was a three-mile walk to a civilian camp. Some inmates were Poles and some were Germans and we were put into a little lumberjack camp with barbed wire and guard boxes and given a bowl of stew, which I was ready for. Our job was to saw down trees and strip the branches. I was there for six weeks and it was hard work but we had plenty to eat.

After the six weeks we were taken back to Thorn, but I did not know why. We couldn't ask questions, ours not to query. So I was back at Camp Thorn again. I didn't like it at all and I was trying to get away from it. After about a week a board was put up on the wall of the guard's billet near the gate, which hadn't been done before. I looked at it every morning, and one day my name was on it, along with nineteen other men. We were leaving at ten o'clock to work at a place called Ober Gruppe. I will never forget that name. Six guards were with us and we were marched off to the station.

The guards were a bit older than usual, one being about fifty years old and they were not what you would call Nazi guards. They were friendlier and told us where we were going. It was to north-east Poland near the Russian border. I talked to these guards and they seemed to be all right, but at the back of my mind I could not forget that they were Germans and they were the enemy.

Our train pulled into Thorn station and it was the first time in three and a half years that I was taken by passenger train, it had always been by cattle trucks. The journey lasted for about three hours until we got off at a place called Groudets which was a little station in the country.

The village was on the River Vistula which ran into the Baltic Sea. We gathered ourselves together and marched off down the small road. It was about two miles to the village and we saw people lined up at the side of the road. They looked at us with a slight smile on their faces and we knew that they had never seen a British POW soldier before. They seemed to like us and we felt proud.

The camp was situated in an old school house where there was more barbed wire, but only one strand instead of two. I think they must have run short of barbed wire. In the middle of the floor was a large stove and I was to be the warmest I had been for three and a half years.

The next morning we marched to the farms that we had been allocated to, four men to each farm. A guard was talking to the man in charge of one of the farms, he was the burgomaster and he was told that I was the tractor driver. They both spoke in German but I could make out what they were saying. The boss was a tall man, about 6 ft 5 inches and as straight as a poker. He was an East Prussian and wore jackboots and carried a little riding whip with which he was always tapping his boots. I did not like him at first, but he gradually calmed down and became more amiable. He was a swine to the Poles who worked for him, but they could not do anything about it. We did a few jobs and had our dinner and the guard took us back to the camp at about seven o'clock.

It was autumn-time so our working hours were getting less as the nights drew in. The land was flat with the River Vistula running along one side. Big boats were back and forth on the river until it froze. We had to saw the ice from the river and carry it to the freeze-house at the farm where all the meat was kept. I did little jobs about the farm while I was waiting for a tractor to come from Germany.

When at last the tractor arrived the instructor told me what had to be done and that afternoon I worked with him, up and down the field, to learn how to plough and I soon got the hang of things. The residents had never seen a machine like this one before and they stood with their mouths open to see a British POW driving it. Life was getting a little better now, but it did not last long. I soon started to plough on my own with no guards watching over me and I was on the go from sunrise till dusk. All the fields I ploughed were grassland and then planted with wheat. At the end of each day I left the tractor in the yard, had my dinner and then a guard would walk with me back to the camp. It was a seven-day week.

I finished all the fields on our farm then had to move to another that was owned by a Polish priest. He was pleased to see me and made quite a fuss. He was a good man. He had a radio in the cellar and told me never to repeat anything I heard about the war news on the BBC. I had breakfast with him although it was the second breakfast I had that day. He then gave me a bottle of wine from his cellar and a packet of cigarettes. I stayed there for a week and he always gave me bread and cheese to take back to the camp for my supper.

After this I went to seven more farms. The threshing machine was worked by the tractor on a belt and there was plenty to do, but I did not worry about the work as I was getting plenty of food. The war news was good and I was sure we were going to win. I did not see many guards. Sometimes I walked on my own at night and I often thought about escaping but there was no point; where could I go? I thought I would stick it out as we seemed to be on the winning side.

One night when I returned to the farmhouse I saw bare-footed women standing by the stables. They looked at me as I was walking back from the tractor and then shot off through the stable door and disappeared. I went in for my dinner and then walked down to the camp and when I arrived I asked one of the others who these women were and was told they were Russian women POWs and were to look after the stables. I did not know about this as I had been away ploughing for six weeks.

We finished ploughing for the winter, and then the tractor had to be sheeted down. The next job was cutting the willows down by the side of the dykes and the little streams. We also had to round up the cattle. This was the first time I had ridden a horse and I did not know the words in German for go or stop. A few days later one of the Poles and I had to get a year-old horse to the blacksmiths to be shod. It had never had shoes on before and put up great resistance that resulted in me becoming black and blue all over. It took all day to get him to the blacksmiths and then we had to chop down a tree and cut it into one foot lengths for the bakery.

It was winter now and very cold and we had a horse pulling a sort of sledge that smoothed the entire roadway so that when it froze the road was like tarmac. It stayed like this all winter. We had to cut ice in blocks from the river and I think if one of us had fallen in we would not have come out again. The Red Cross sent us some new clothes so we were warm for the winter.

We were getting into 1944 and it seemed a long time since I saw home. The news was good. The Russian Front was advancing to the Polish/German border. We carried on with our jobs on the farm from seven o'clock to five o'clock each day and just kept our fingers crossed. It was very cold so it was time to get out my jackboots with the wooden soles, they kept my feet warm, but alas the soles were getting a bit thin. I hoped they would last for the winter. The guards took us to work in the morning and back at night, because it was dark. Yet when it was daylight we walked on our own. It did not make sense to me.

I had to take a couple of horses to the blacksmiths and I had to kill a pig. The Pole I was working with swung the sledge hammer and missed the pig, so I took the hammer and he cut its throat. We pumped its leg and the blood went into a bucket. The Pole cut a piece of fat from the pig and ate it. Then we carried it down to the ice house to hang for a few days, and then he cut it up and hung all the parts on different hooks.

The next day we chopped some more wood for the fires as there was no coal left. We had to take it in turns to stoke the fire in the middle of the night because it was freezing. We always had something to do. It passed the time and we were getting fed.

When spring approached we had plenty of work to do. Then we felt the heat of the sun and it was summer, then harvest time and time to get out the binder. It was pulled by four horses and I rode the first horse and became saddle-sore. I was a real cowboy before the end of the summer.

Infantry crossing an improvised bridge at night to take Goch, near the Dutch border, 18-19 February 1945

Talking to one of the Poles I was told that our troops had landed in France in June and it was now the beginning of September and we were very pleased about the news. After we had done all the threshing it was time for the ploughing to begin again. The first farm to be ploughed was that of the Polish priest who told us that our troops were advancing across France and the Russians were nearing the Polish/German border. When I got back to the camp I told all my mates and they were full of joy. The guards must have known what was going on.

I finished off the ploughing and said good-bye to the old priest and he gave me a little bottle of schnapps. That was the last I saw of him. The weather was closing in and the frost made the ground too hard to plough so we put the tractor away for the winter. Little did we know what was in store for us.

In January there was about nine inches of snow. When we came out of the camp one day we saw some German Infantry standing along the road, this was very strange. I could hear gunfire. We walked along to the farm and could see the farmer and his wife packing their belongings into a wagon pulled by a couple of horses. They climbed aboard with their two children. It appeared we were between two firing lines and they were being evacuated to Germany. At dinner the guards told us we were to pack up and get ready to leave in the morning. Then we had another order to leave immediately. It was four o'clock in the afternoon on the 23rd of January 1945. We packed all the food we could into our rucksacks, but we could only take one blanket. I had Red Cross tins and I rolled my blanket up and slung it over my shoulder and tied both ends with a piece of string.

There were twenty of us and six guards. We marched to the station and took off our gear and sat down for a while. By now it was dark and suddenly there was a terrific explosion. I did not know if the Germans had blown the bridge or were breaking the ice on the river. There were many horses and wagons going across the ice on the river, the ice cracked and they all sank. It was a terrible way to die.

We picked up our packs and were ordered on our way. It was dark and snowing and we walked for about two hours. The guards were scratching their heads and looking at the maps. They were lost and we could not see the roads or fields. We came across an old barn, so we all piled in and lit a fire and melted some snow in the billycan to make tea. We had a little bread left over so we shared it with the guards and gave them some tea. We could not leave them out as they were old men. They were not Nazis. We ate our food and found some straw at the other end of the barn and bedded down for the night. It was nearly midnight and I was asleep in two minutes.

When I awoke in the morning there was a big rat sitting on my chest. There were dozens of them running about. The guards told us we had to march about fifty miles to a railhead for a train. It took us three days to march the fifty miles, but there was no station, just a line. Another thirty men and five guards joined us from another camp. They had been on the road for six days and did not look very good; they said the food had been poor at their camp.

We pushed on but to where I did not know. The guards did not know either and we did not see any civilians about, they must have been evacuated. We were looking for a barn so that we could get out of the snow and cold when I heard a wagon coming along the road. Inside were more guards. We found somewhere to spend the night and get out of the wind and have something to eat. It was not much as we were rationed. We had one meal each day, then it got to be one meal every two days and when our food ran out we had to steal it where we could.

After we had been on the road for two weeks we were getting very hungry. The Germans did not give us anything to eat at all. We came to a little village, but there was nobody there. I saw an empty shop and looked about for a while and found a bag of sugar, which I shared. We carried on our way and managed to get a few potatoes here and there and ate them raw and a cabbage now and again, they were a bit frosted, but we still ate them.

One night we were marshalled into a field where another group of men were already waiting. That made us up to seventy-five men and twenty guards. There was a wagon towing a field kitchen for soup and another wagon towing a field kitchen for coffee. It was the first thing the Jerries had given us for over a fortnight and that was the last we ever had from them. It was also the last time the guards were changed.

I was getting so tired every day. Sometimes we were able to get into a barn at night and sometimes we had to sleep in a field. One day we came to a little hamlet where there was a stone building in which were three boilers. Outside was an old hand pump for water so we started a fire and half-filled one of the boilers with potatoes we had found. It was a feast. We stayed there for three days and one of the men, who was a butcher, killed a cow and boiled it up, but it gave us all diarrhoea and stomach pains, so we had to throw it away. The twenty men from our camp always kept together and shared everything. If anyone fell behind we would take his arm and help him along. It was nearly the end of February, and a lorry brought food for the guards every day.

There were about two hundred of us now, scattered along the road for about a mile and we hadn't a clue where we were. We did not know if we had crossed the border into Germany or not. We were always hearing gunfire behind us and knew it was the Russians. We did not know whether to hang back and let the Russians take us or carry on to Germany to find our own troops. We kept going hoping to get somewhere in the end. I hoped it would be home. Things were getting rough, we were ill and my memory was hazy. Some of the men had to be carried and some died on the road.

We were in very bad shape but knew we were in Germany now as our own planes were machine gunning us, so we decided to escape from the rest of the convoy. We sat down by the trees until all the men had gone and when it became dark we started to walk through the woods where we found a little croft but could not ask for food as the man was probably German and would have a shotgun, so we had to wait until he was in bed. Then we searched for food and found some eggs and potatoes and a chicken. It was a struggle to get the chicken as the hens were making a terrible noise. I could hear a dog barking so we left quickly. About a mile away we started a fire although it was risky. There was plenty of water as the

Allied tanks smashing a powerful German steel and concrete fort during the last great battle west of the Rhine, 5 March 1945

*Crossing of the Rhine at Wesel,
23 March 1945*

snow had melted and formed many streams in the area. The food was quickly cooked and eaten and then voices were heard so we had to move quickly. Water was poured from our potatoes and eggs into the fire and we grabbed the chicken and ran. After a while all was quiet so we sat down to eat the chicken. It was not properly cooked, but we still ate it. The next day we were all doubled up with pain in our stomachs and had to rest all day. Then we struggled on but had to keep stopping to rest.

That evening the setting sun made us realise we were heading in the right direction. The next day we came across a railway station that had been bombed and the lines were twisted. There was a crowd of Italian civilians and we avoided them because Italians couldn't be trusted. That night we slept in the woods, I still had my old blanket to keep me warm. I didn't know what the date was, but knew it was getting near the end of March as the sun was getting warmer.

Feeling braver we took to the main roads. Nobody took any notice of us, they thought we were tramps. We arrived at a civilian camp surrounded by lots of barbed wire. It seemed to me that in Germany they were short of a lot of things, but not barbed wire. There was a mobile soup kitchen, so we got in the queue and were given some soup. One of the men beckoned me over and said he had been watching us. He was a Belgian prisoner of war and knew that we were British prisoners of war. He told us to look to the west at night to see the flashes of guns that would keep us in the right direction. We followed his instructions and walked right into a bombardment from our own guns. We managed to get into the air raid shelter and if they had known that we were British, the Germans would have cut our throats, so we had to get out before daylight. Luck was on our side and when "the all clear" went we left hurriedly.

We could have been hit by a sniper as the bullets were flying all over the place. When the firing stopped we walked a little and then slowed to a crawl, we were all in, but the feeling that we had nearly reached freedom kept us going. Our hearts were banging on our ribs but felt we had to keep going till we dropped. And that is what we did.

Lying on the pavement exhausted we saw a British tank. I thought we were seeing things. But it was real. Behind the tank came the Infantry, we were in no man's land, but not for long. The soldiers came across to us with their rifles cocked and we thought there was going to be trouble. We spoke to them and showed our identity disc and our POW disc so that they knew we were British. Then a jeep with a radio arrived. One of the men radioed for some transport to take us four POWs to hospital for treatment. We sat there for about half an hour and the soldiers came to protect us and tell us the news about D-Day.

The ambulance came and the driver told us to keep our heads down as there was a lot of firing. About two miles out of town we came to a large building beside which was a marquee and that was where we had our treatment. An Orderly gave us four big mugs of tea and slices of bread and butter. It was like cake and wine to us. Then they had to cut my boots off. He said my feet were like pieces of liver. They bandaged my feet and sprayed my hair and body with DDT powder to kill the lice. Then my memory went blank and I don't know whether I went to the Brussels hospital by plane or road. My mates had all gone. I suppose they were sent to other hospitals.

The nurse took all my clothes off and I went into the bath. My body ached with the louse scars and my feet were in a lot of pain. The bed had white sheets and a pair of pyjamas was laid out for me. I couldn't believe it was real; it was like being in heaven. On my casualty card it said I had gastro enteritis, malnutrition, louse scars and bad feet. After a chocolate drink I went to sleep for about twenty-four hours and when I woke up it felt as if I was in a trance, I couldn't think properly. I suppose it was the change of circumstances but I was feeling a little better and was being fed and cared for.

On the fifth day I got out of bed, very shaky but I made it and knew that I was going to be all right. I asked if I could go, but the nurse said not until the next day when the doctor would be round to see me. I hobbled around my ward and when I got back to my bed I was exhausted and nearly fell into the chair. I was very grateful for all the nurses did for me.

The next day when the doctor came he told me I could go to England; I was taken to the airport, got off the lorry and walked up the tarmac in my carpet slippers. Then it suddenly dawned on me that I was free. I stopped, put both my arms in the air and shouted, "This is my finest hour." Tears ran down my cheeks and I cried like a baby. When I looked at the other chaps, they were in tears too.

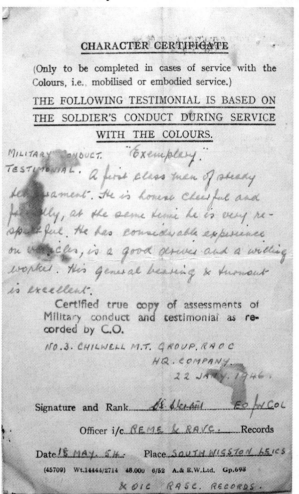

It took us all that day to get a flight home. The navigator asked me where I was taken prisoner and when I told him Dunkirk, he said we were going that way and the pilot dived down to Dunkirk and flew along the beach. I looked back along the plane at the lads and there was no one with dry eyes. It was an emotional ten minutes when we crossed the channel. When it was getting dark I noticed the towns were all lit up. I supposed the war was nearly over now. We got ready for landing, then we were on the runway, the door was opened and we were on British soil at Lynewood.

We were the first prisoners to come in. Red Cross and RAF nurses escorted us to a big marquee. Inside were tables and chairs and from here we were drafted to different hospitals. But first we had a meal of fish and chips, the first for six years. We were given a bar of soap and a towel by the RAF. I had no razor, only had what I stood up in and I still wore my carpet slippers.

First thing in the morning I was taken by lorry from Lynewood to the railway station. We walked up the platform where there were about twenty-five or thirty patients and I asked one of the Orderlies where we were going. He told me we were bound for Newport in Wales and that we would have a Red Cross coach on the train. Eventually we arrived at Newport and lorries took us to the Auxiliary Military Hospital where I had treatment for my malnutrition. After two days I was given a pair of shoes that I tried to put on but could not because of my injuries. I persevered each day and eventually was able to wear them.

One day at about five o'clock the nurse said that I could take a mate with me and walk a little. It was to see how we would react to the outside world. We walked up the street and looked in the shops and realised we had no money, so we walked back to hospital. I was tired out and ready for a sit down and a cup of tea. There was a dining hall where we could play darts and dominoes and there were magazines to read. The next day I had some thin porridge and three slices of toast with marmalade and two cups of tea and then we had our walk round the town and back. The day after, I had a check-up with the doctor who said that I was fit to travel so I packed my kit bag and obtained all my travel warrants and some money. Six of us were to go home.

It was a sentimental journey, six years was a long time. We changed trains at Crewe, shook hands and said good-bye and boarded trains going in all different directions and never saw each other again. I was used to it. You had a mate for a few months then he was taken away to another camp. I boarded my train for Stirling and home. I put my kit bag on the rack and sat down to read the paper for an hour.

I fell asleep and when I awoke there was a WAAF officer and an RAF officer on the opposite seat.

William Mackrell, on the right, with his army lorry at the Army Surplus Base at Castle Donington in 1947

They asked me if I had had a long journey and I told them that I had and that I had been force-marched from the Russian border to the Dutch border. They were very interested in what I had to say and they bought me tea and sandwiches at one of the stations. I answered their questions and told them my story. We arrived at Stirling at about 5.30am and I said good-bye to them.

I walked through the gates, put my kitbag down and looked around. I saw a policeman and told him I had been a prisoner of war for five years and things were very strange. He picked up my kitbag and took me to the bus station, carried it onto the bus and paid my fare. I got off at the Bridge of Allan and walked down Cawder Road. There appeared to be a celebration as the buildings were decorated with streamers and bunting. I didn't realise it was for me! Then I saw my mother open the door and I shed a few tears. All the neighbours opened their doors and shouted "Welcome home Willie". I was home at last!

The newspaper reporters came to see me, but they only printed what they wanted to. I told a few truths and nobody believed me. After a week of celebrating I was back to normal and really appreciated all my mother did for me. After six weeks furlough I had to report to Haywards Heath barracks for one month of retraining. I transferred to the Army Reserve in May 1946 for ten years until March 1956. I married and then was demobbed and went to live at Broxtowe. My first civilian job after the war was as a porter at Beeston Station and then I went to the Central Ordnance Depot at Chilwell with my friend Jim Wright. He had been a prisoner of war for three years. (He died about 20 years after the end of the war). Life seemed very strange in civvy street ………

106713   Army Form X 202/B.

CERTIFICATE OF TRANSFER to the ARMY RESERVE

Army No. T/3053714   Rank ..D.RIVER

Surname (Block letters) MACKRELL

Christian Name(s) WILLIAM

Regt. or Corps .... **R.A.S.C.**

The transfer of the above-named to the appropriate Class of the Army

Reserve (see note below) is confirmed with effect from 24.5.46 .

*The date to be inserted here will be that following the day on which Release Leave terminates, including any additional leave to which the soldier may be entitled by virtue of service overseas.

Note.—The appropriate Class of the Army Reserve is as follows :—

(i) Royal Army Reserve—in the case of a regular soldier with reserve service to complete.

(ii) Army Reserve, Class Z (T)—in the case of a man of the Territorial Army, including those called up for service under the National Service Acts :

(iii) Army Reserve, Class Z—in the case of all other soldiers not included in (i) or (ii) above.

Record Office Stamp.
R.A.S.C. RECORDS
5 FEB 1946
ORE PLACE
HASTINGS

Officer i/c **R.A.S.C.** Records.

Date ....

Warning.—

Any alteration of the particulars given in this certificate may render the holder liable to prosecution under the Seamen's and Soldiers' False Characters Act, 1906.

If this certificate is lost or mislaid, no duplicate can be obtained.

Wt. 37285/90 1,000M 12/45 KJL/1516/16 Gp.38/3

D-DAY

D-day, 6th June 1944, was the day the Allied forces under the command of American General Eisenhower launched 'Operation Overlord'. 11,000 aircraft and 5,000 ships were dispatched across the Channel. 130,000 troops were landed along a 50 mile stretch of the Normandy coastline in the greatest amphibious invasion of all time onto five beach-heads, code named Utah, Omaha, Gold, Juno and Sword.

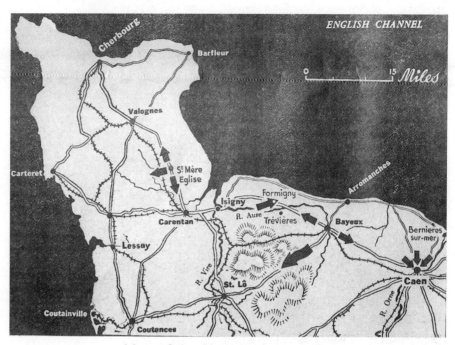

Map of the Normandy coastline

They began the liberation of German-occupied Europe. Unsuitable weather had forced the postponement of the Normandy campaign which had been planned for 5th June. Paris was liberated on 25th August after heavy fighting and Brussels on 2nd September. On 12th September troops crossed the German border.

Once Normandy was chosen as the area for the Allied landings most of southern England became an assembly point for the troops and equipment. Artificial harbours were quickly built to facilitate the unloading of vehicles and heavy armaments. They were assembled in utmost secrecy off the south coast and towed across the Channel. One of these docks was built at Arromanches and was as large as Dover harbour. It remained in use long after the conventional ports were captured from the Germans.

Most of the concrete caissons needed for the construction were made at docks in the Port of London and were named Mulberry Harbours after Mulberry Quay in the Surrey Docks, the site of manufacture.

When the Allied armies arrived in France they needed vast amounts of fuel and so in order to avoid the possibility of supply ships being mined or attacked by u-boats and aircraft, a pipeline was constructed and laid under the English Channel. It enabled fuel to be pumped directly to France and was called the Pipeline Under The Ocean, and known as PLUTO.

Mulberry Docks & Strawberry Sundaes

In the colossal chain of allied effort, forged through five years of blood and sweat, "Mulberries" — D Day's Floating Docks — were the last vital link. In that close-kept secret, Electricity was once more "the power behind the plan".

Among the sweets of victory will be the much-missed luxuries and aids to living that Electricity can bring — frozen delights for your table, effortless cooking and cleaning, all the comfort and cheerfulness of an all-electric home.

Till then, switch off whenever and whatever you can.

Electricity

Sunday Express, 6 May 1945

121

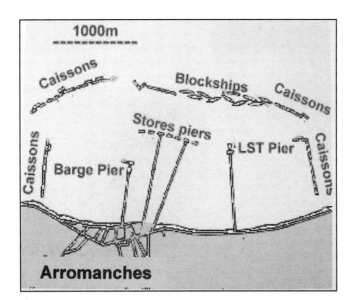

Plan of the Mulberry Dock at Arromanches in 1944

Remains of the Mulberry harbour, on the right, at Arromanches, as seen in 2000

Aerial activity over the Normandy coast

When the Allied troops landed on the Normandy beaches in June 1944 they were carrying self-heating cans of Heinz soup. A match or even a cigarette was all that was needed to light the smokeless and flameless elements and the contents of the can were hot enough to eat in only a few minutes. Collaboration with ICI had taken many years to perfect the self-heating can which was finally achieved in 1941.

D-DAY REMEMBERED

To most of the residents of Beeston the first indication of impending D-Day must surely have been the noticeable increase in the amount of air activity. Being not too far from several large bomber stations in the Vale of Belvoir, Beeston was regularly overflown by planes en route to targets on the continent, so the drone of aircraft during the night hours had become an established feature of wartime life. But during May and the first days of June 1944 a marked increase in the level of this activity became apparent, and on the night of 5/6th June the continuous rumble of planes passing overhead made it obvious that something special was happening. We were not, therefore, altogether surprised when news of the landings was announced the next morning.

My most vivid memory is of the night training flights carried out by the US airborne forces, some of which I believe were based at Newton and Wymeswold; this took the form of large formations of glider-towing Dakota aircraft passing over at low altitudes during the hours of darkness. Practically unknown in wartime, all the aircraft had their navigation lights illuminated, no doubt to assist in holding their positions, thus creating a marvellous spectacle as they swept overhead with a thunderous roar, low enough to be silhouetted against the night sky and like a moving carpet of white, green and red stars!

By Peter Shipley

I was one of the lucky ones, I was on the Channel guns at Dover. Two days after D-Day I was moved to an Electrical Artificers course at Gosport where I saw a continuous stream of ambulances coming back from France with, presumably, many wounded soldiers.

There was an equally continuous flow of soldiers in the opposite direction embarking for France.

By Eric Hopkins

Allied landing on D-Day

Photographs taken during and after the D-Day Landings

124

SOME RECOLLECTIONS OF CHILWELL DEPOT (OR MY PART IN D-DAY)
By Bill Shaw

I first came to Chilwell as a small child when my dad was posted to the Central Ordnance Depot during World War Two. We lived in a rented house just off Depot Corner - the junction of Chetwynd Road, Attenborough Lane and High Road.

In those days there were two distinct Chilwells. Chilwell the village, which still had farms with crops growing and cattle grazing. Houses where people had lived for generations in some cases. And then there was the Chilwell behind the wire fence, the Depot, with its guarded gates through which thousands of people swarmed while we were having breakfast and out again at tea time. My dad was one of them but would never tell me what happened inside those gates. "It's secret" he would say with a finger to his lips and a twinkle in his eye.

Well, secret or not, it was obvious even to us kids, going to and from Meadow Lane school and afterwards roaming the fields and woods and peering through the wire, that things were getting busier during those early months of 1944.

The depot was bursting at the seams with military equipment stacked on every available square foot and many more soldiers, some with strange accents, strolling to and from the Cadland and Charlton Arms. And even more often, columns of them marching along the roads with that unforgettable crunch-crunch of hundreds of steel-tipped army boots marching in step (modern army boots do not make the same sound!)

For us kids, a highlight of the week was Thursday night as I remember, when Thursday being pay-day, soldiers would crowd into the local pubs and we would watch from the safety of the top of the stone wall alongside the Charlton Arms car park, the fist-fights that often broke out, followed by the dramatic arrival of the 'Red Caps' who broke up the fights with even more violence.

Marshalling area, Central Ordnance Depot, Chilwell in the weeks before D-Day

The Chilwell Depot did burst its seams. The nearby fields filled up with tented camps and Nissen huts, other fields with lines of military vehicles and mysterious mountains of crates covered with camouflage tarpaulins and guarded by serious looking soldiers wearing helmets and carrying rifles with bayonets who growled 'b***** off!' when we went too close.

In May 1944 it all started to pour out! Everyone knew, of course, that the Invasion of France was coming sooner or later, but for day after day amazed locals including myself and my school chums watched as thousands of army vehicles roared through Depot Corner in what seemed endless convoys nose to tail, all "heading south" the grown-ups said knowingly.

All the vehicles, of many different types, had black and white vertical stripes painted on their doors or sides - a little like modern bar codes, which presumably meant something important.

When one thinks back on it, the logistics must have been staggering! Getting all that equipment and men from Chilwell and many other depots around the country down to the coast and on to the right ship at the right time and at the right port, without our present motorways, communications, street lighting or computers, must be an incredible story. What if they all arrived at the same time? Imagine the potential for chaos!

Anyway, some days later my pals and I roamed across the now empty fields looking at the marks on the grass where all that equipment had been, and tried to outdo each other in guessing where they had gone - of course on D-Day, the 6th of June, we knew where they had gone, - or thought we did.

Central Ordnance Depot, Chilwell from the Sandhurst Block occupied by the ATS

Troops wading ashore during the D-Day Landings

VICTORY IN EUROPE

Victory in Europe was finally achieved when the Germans were defeated by the British, Americans and Russians. The Allies invaded Italy and forced the Italians to make a separate peace on 3 September 1943.

The Germans had invaded their ally Russia at various points from the Baltic to the Black Sea, in June 1941 and after early successes were gradually driven back being completely unprepared for the severe weather and arctic temperatures. They were finally driven out of Russia in August 1944.

The Allies launched a second front at Normandy in June 1944 and advanced through France, Belgium and Holland. They continued through Germany in February 1945 despite flying bombs and rockets etc., and with the American forces linked with the Russians who captured Berlin on 28 April thus forcing a German surrender, signed on 7 May. The next day was declared VE-Day.

In Beeston and Chilwell the news was greeted ecstatically. Two days of celebrations were quickly organized; church services took place and street parties arranged with food that had been squirrelled away for this festive occasion. Flags were hung from windows and bunting and streamers draped over the streets along with emblems of the Allied nations. The *Beeston Gazette & Echo* reported that Windsor Street and Mona Street, the two streets worst hit by German air raids, defiantly put on one of the best displays. Fancy dress parades were planned, bonfires lit and firework displays arranged.

FOOD FACTS SPECIAL EDITION
FOOD SUPPLIES FOR VE-DAYS

The Ministry of Food is confident that food traders, having served the public well throughout the war years, will provide a service during the V Holiday that will enable the public to obtain their essential minimum food supplies. The Ministry makes the following suggestions to food traders and housewives :—

GROCERS should remain open on VE Day for at least one hour after the Victory announcement has been made and if possible two hours. If VE Day is a Friday grocers should open on Saturday and close on Monday, but grocers selling bread and milk should act also in accordance with the following paragraphs.

DAIRYMEN are expected to deliver milk on both VE Days just as they normally do on Good Friday or a Bank Holiday.

BAKERS should make arrangements in advance to ensure that after the announcement bread will be made and delivered to private houses and retail shops in sufficient quantities to provide at least for normal requirements. Wherever possible bakers should in addition make bread as usual for sale on VE+1 Day and on this day open their shops for one hour or possibly two hours for the sale of bread only.

Although it is expected that the public will be able to obtain bread supplies during the V Holiday housewives are advised to carry in their homes slightly more bread than usual.

SHOPS DEALING IN PERISHABLE FOODS should remain open on VE Day long enough after the official announcement to ensure that perishable goods are not wasted.

RESTAURANTS AND CAFÉS are expected to be open on both VE Days.

Every food trader is asked to display in his shop a notice telling his customers at what hours his shop will be open during the V Holiday, together with any further details useful to his customers. Retailers expecting deliveries from wholesalers on VE Day should arrange for the reception of these goods.

The Ministry of Food, London, W.I.

Sunday Express, 6 May 1945

VE-Day party on School Lane, Chilwell

Victory in Europe

Only this text in English is authoritative

ACT OF MILITARY SURRENDER

1. We the undersigned, acting by authority of the German High Command, hereby surrender unconditionally to the Supreme Commander, Allied Expeditionary Force and simultaneously to the Soviet High Command all forces on land, sea, and in the air who are at this date under German control.

2. The German High Command will at once issue orders to all German military, naval and air authorities and to all forces under German control to cease active operations at 2301 hours Central European time on 8 May and to remain in the positions occupied at that time. No ship, vessel, or aircraft is to be scuttled, or any damage done to their hull, machinery or equipment.

3. The German High Command will at once issue to the appropriate commanders, and ensure the carrying out of any further orders issued by the Supreme Commander, Allied Expeditionary Force and by the Soviet High Command.

4. This act of military surrender is without prejudice to, and will be superseded by any general instrument of surrender imposed by, or on behalf of the United Nations and applicable to GERMANY and the German armed forces as a whole.

English version of the unconditional surrender document signed on 7th May 1945 in Rheims, France, by German General Oberst Jodl, Chief of Staff of the Whermacht.

5. In the event of the German High Command or any of the forces under their control failing to act in accordance with this Act of Surrender, the Supreme Commander, Allied Expeditionary Force and the Soviet High Command will take such punitive or other action as they deem appropriate.

Signed at Rheims France at 0241 on the 7th day of May, 1945.

On behalf of the German High Command.

Jodl

IN THE PRESENCE OF

On behalf of the Supreme Commander, Allied Expeditionary Force.

W. B. Smith

On behalf of the Soviet High Command.

Sousloparov

Major General, French Army ("itness)

Witnesses were Major General W Bedell Smith of the Allied Expeditionary Force and General Eisenhower's Chief of Staff; Soviet General Susloparoff and French General Francois Sevez

General Jodl signing the unconditional surrender documents

BEESTON AND STAPLEFORD
URBAN DISTRICT COUNCIL

V-DAY

CITIZENS OF BEESTON

AN OPEN-AIR
MASS SERVICE OF
THANKSGIVING

Will be held on

DOVECOTE LANE
RECREATION GROUND

On the Sunday after V-Day at 2.45 p.m.

Service to be conducted by
REV. J. P. HALET
(Vicar of Beeston)
and REV. IRAM G. WALL
(Methodist Superintendent Minister)

All local organisations are requested
to meet on Broadgate Recreation
Ground at 2 p.m. for parade to
Dovecote-lane

Further particulars:-
WALTER HAYES
1, Elm-avenue, Beeston

Beeston Gazette & Echo, 5 May 1945

BEESTON AND STAPLEFORD URBAN DISTRICT COUNCIL

SERVICE OF THANKSGIVING FOR VICTORY IN EUROPE

(SUNDAY FOLLOWING VE-DAY)

Conducted by THE VICAR OF BEESTON & Rev. IRAM G. WALL (Beeston Methodist Church)

The heading of the Service Sheet for Beeston's VE-Day Thanksgiving Service

VE-DAY IN CHILWELL, ONE SMALL PART OF IT ANYWAY
By W H Ashton

I suppose the first thought of the children on hearing the news of VE-Day (8 May 1945) was that now all the things promised for 'after the war' would be forthcoming. Although realistically we had grown out of most of the items which carried that promise.

After the initial announcement of VE-Day the most important piece of news for the kids who had colonised the waste ground, left unused by the building trade in 1939 on Woodland Grove, was that the Hillman Estate was going to have the biggest bonfire and celebrations in all Nottinghamshire. This claim by our mortal enemies (far greater enemies than the now vanquished Germans had ever been) could not be accepted and so a great drive was organised to collect all the rubbish and unwanted combustible matter - especially blackout materials - which existed in the area over which we held sway.

Whilst this search went on the few men who were available were pressed into service to cut up the logs which had long served as barricades for games of soldiers, to form the heart of the fire. Mothers meanwhile, working miracles in their usual quiet way, produced from hiding places even we had not been able to find, a feast the like of which only the elder children could remember.

Luckily the weather was kind to us, warm for May and calm, so that after the food was all eaten we could light our bonfire, which according to neutral observers totally eclipsed the Hillman Estate effort. Perhaps also the effect was enhanced by the addition of a quantity of thunder flashes which had mysteriously found their way from Chilwell Depot where they were used for battle training. There were of course no fireworks available and we had to have some extra noises!

The celebrations went on far into the night, even the children could feel the relief and thankfulness that it was over and our future was secure once again, though I do not think we had ever doubted the outcome. I called at home at about 3am and finding

VE-Day street party on Park Street, Beeston

no one there, returned to the fire and baked potatoes, that delicacy of childhood, until well after dawn.

Altogether a day well-remembered and well worth remembering by those who had fought for our country and our English way of life, and something that should not be forgotten by those who came after us in these days of European unity.

As an appendix to these memories the later VJ-Day came as something of an anti-climax. Maybe we had got used to 'peace' and the Japanese theatre of war seemed so remote to us, though not of course to anyone with relatives or friends directly involved. Really, we should NEVER forget!

Celebrations on Dovecote Lane Recreation Ground on the day after VE-Day

I REMEMBER VE-DAY 1945; OR MARTON ROAD CELEBRATES HITLER'S DOWNFALL
By Bill Shaw

I was nine years old when the war ended; we had spent the war years in Marton Road, Chilwell, just off Depot Corner.

As VE-Day on the 8th of May approached, excitement grew, we were to have a street party! I am not sure who organised it except for Mr Pilling who played a leading role, although many of the parents must have been involved. Quite a few of the dads were away in the forces.

Marton Road was a close-knit community then, the war had seen to that. Kids played in the street much more than today. Traffic-free Marton Road looked like a school playground some times. It was also a 'dead-end' terminating in an earth bank and a sloping field. There were no buses or cars, just the regular visit by the Hollingsworth grocery cart pulled by 'Tater Bobbo' - the 'bobbo' that brought the 'taters' was the gentle horse called Daisy much petted by the local children. There was a brick and concrete air raid shelter at each end of the road to provide for those without a family shelter in their garden and in the days prior to VE-Day they were stripped of bunks, doors and anything combustible for the bonfire in the middle of the road. I remember young off-duty soldiers from the Garrison leading parties of kids in wood-gathering. As the bonfire grew to fifteen feet high, some concern was expressed that the heat would set light to the houses and that would give Hitler the last laugh!

Flags and old bunting appeared on many of the houses, and on the great day tables and chairs were carried out and lined up in the road. Mums got busy and in no time at all the tables were laden with food. All the kids were rounded up, scrubbed down and made to look presentable and then we sat down at the tables outside.

After posing for photographs we were ordered to tuck in. All the traditional food was there - sandwiches, jellies, blancmanges and cakes (hamburgers and hot-dogs were unheard of). The mums scurried about, some with tea pots, others refilling plates. After tea, games and races, farther up the street organised by the dads kept the kids happy while the tables were cleared away.

At dusk the bonfire was lit, I don't remember fireworks; I suppose they were not yet available. A gramophone and amplifier started to pour out dance music and for the one night in its history Marton Road was filled with dancing couples. More food and drink was produced and the party went on long after we kids were winkled out and packed off reluctantly to bed. I do remember, as we kids ran about through the dancing couples, there were quite a few soldiers in uniform, some were dads, others from the Garrison so there was no shortage of dancing partners for the mums and grown-up daughters.

Next morning the adults cleared up the street, but the crater left by the bonfire remained for months.

When VJ-Day came it seemed a bit of an anti-climax, although Marton Road celebrated, it was as I recall a much quieter affair.

*VE-Day Street Party
Clifford Avenue,
Beeston*

VE-DAY IN INDIA
By Peter d'Auvergne

VE-Day, 8th May, was the last day of a fortnight's leave in Bombay. Half a dozen of us, at that time serving in the Royal Signals attached to 14 Air Landing Brigade, had been advised to take all the leave due to us, as more leave in the foreseeable future was very uncertain. Our division (44th Indian Airborne) was preparing to drop on one of the Japanese-occupied islands in the Pacific.

In view of what had happened at Arnhem and to the Yanks at Wake Island, the chances of survival were not particularly rosy. As a result we all drew all our available cash, took the sleeper to Bombay, hired a flat near the sea front and spent a wonderful fortnight bathing, sightseeing, attending concerts and cinemas and eating in good restaurants.

On the day the war ended in Europe we were all nearly broke and looking forward with some trepidation to our return to the unit on the following day. We knew the war in Europe was almost over, just a question of who got to Berlin first.

On the last evening we went to the cinema to see Eleanor Powell in one of the typical war time frothy musicals made especially to boost the morale of the lads overseas. We had just settled down in our seats after the interval when three or four sailors burst into the entrance nearest the screen. One of them was rolling drunk. "*'ooray*" he shouted, "*the b***** war is over*". "*Sit down and shut up*" roared the audience, composed almost entirely of members of the British Forces on leave, many in the same circumstances as ourselves.

The next day we spent buying last minute presents and having one last swim at our favourite beach called *Breach Kandy*.* Then we packed and took a taxi to the station to catch the sleeper back to our unit. There had been no VE-Day celebrations in Bombay. The civilians were still living in fear of the Japanese and those of us in the forces knew only too well, that for us, this was just the beginning of another campaign even bloodier than those in Malaya and Burma.

When I checked my possessions I realised that I had lost my pay book, and as I stood looking out of the train at the last lights of Bombay disappearing, I was wondering what would happen when I was put on a charge on my immediate return. VE-Day was not a particularly happy day in South-east Asia.

* Breach Kandy was a club in Bombay with swimming facilities and where soldiers could get meals.

VE-Day street celebrations on Farfield Avenue

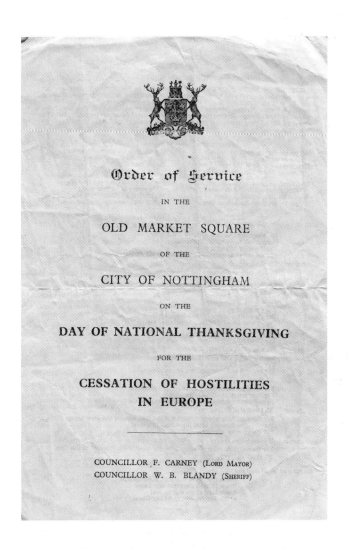

VE-Day party at the rear of the fish and chip shop, 84 Chilwell Road. Standing, Mr Jennings of the chip shop and Mrs Newbold of the baker's shop.

VE-Day Street Party on Derby Street, Beeston

VICTORY OVER JAPAN

Japan had been at war with China since mid-1937 for control of their minerals and oil. This alarmed the US and they increased financial and military aid to China. In July 1941 the west effectively halted trade with Japan who badly needed raw materials they couldn't produce themselves. As a result they planned to seize the oil and mineral-rich East Indies and Southeast Asia. War in the Pacific seemed inevitable.

On 7 December 1941 the Japanese Imperial Navy launched a surprise attack on most of the US Navy's fleet of battleships at anchor in their deep-water naval base in Pearl Harbour, Hawaii. There had been no formal declaration of war and it was completely unanticipated that Japan would attack in the west. The Japanese thought the disablement and sinking of large numbers of US naval vessels removed a possible threat to their southward expansion. America, unprepared and considerably weakened, was brought into World War Two. The Japanese then eliminated much of the US Air Force in the Philippines and put an army ashore in Malaya. Japan's allies Germany and Italy declared war on the USA on the 11 December and Japan controlled Southeast Asia and Burma within four months.

US naval victories in the Pacific in June 1942 stemmed the advance but bitter fighting continued until 1945. When Japan was on the retreat after defeat by the British in Southeast Asia and by the Americans in the Pacific, they refused Allied demands for unconditional surrender. After the USA dropped two atomic bombs on Hiroshima and Nagasaki on 6th and 9th August 1945 Japan surrendered on the 14th and World War Two had ended at last. The 15th was declared VJ-Day.

JAPAN GIVEN CHANCE TO SURRENDER

PROCLAMATION BY BRITAIN, U.S. AND CHINA

BERLIN, Thursday.

Britain, the United States and China have delivered a joint ultimatum to Japan to get out of the war on their terms now, or be inevitably and completely destroyed by "prodigious forces now poised to strike the final blows."

A proclamation, signed by Mr. Churchill and President Truman while they were in Potsdam, and approved by Marshal Chiang Kai-shek by radio, sets out terms which amount to unconditional surrender.

Daily Telegraph, 27 July 1945

The weather here was dull and showery but this did not dampen the enthusiasm of Beeston and Chilwell people. It was announced at midnight that the war had ended and *The Beeston Gazette & Echo* noted that within a few minutes bonfires were lit on street corners, fireworks let off and pyjama-clad people danced on the High Road! That day and the following day saw mass celebrations around the area. Less than three months after the Victory in Europe festivities decorations appeared everywhere again, flags and bunting were hung from windows and across the streets with streamers and emblems of the Allied nations. Public service vehicles, even ambulances, were decorated. Churches and Chapels held services of thanksgiving and remembrance. Many streets arranged alfresco tea parties again.

In Meadow Lane, Chilwell a tea party was held for over 60 people in two marquees borrowed from the Chilwell and Attenborough Sea Cadets. The residents consumed ice cream, trifle, meat, salad, fruit, cakes and 'other delicacies that had been missing from the table for such a long time'.

Stoney Street in Beeston also celebrated with a tea party. A small committee had been formed to arrange the VE-Day festivities and they were pressed into service again. They organized the party along with a firework display and a fancy dress parade.

More than 2,000 children took part in a sports display on Dovecote Lane Recreation Ground after which 6,000 people enjoying open-air dancing. Floodlights on the bandstand were lowered at ten o'clock, dancing ceased and a huge firework display began.

Victory over Japan

The Japanese surrendered on 14th August 1945 after atomic bombs were dropped on Hiroshima and Nagasaki. The official unconditional surrender documents were signed aboard the battleship USS Missouri at anchor in Tokyo Bay on 2nd September.

Translation of Emperor Hirohito's Receipt of the Surrender Documents

PROCLAMATION

Accepting the terms set forth in the Declaration issued by the heads of the Governments of the United States, Great Britain, and China on July 26th, 1945 at Potsdam and subsequently adhered to by the Union of Soviet Socialist Republics, We have commanded the Japanese Imperial Government and the Japanese Imperial General Headquarters to sign on Our behalf the Instrument of Surrender presented by the Supreme Commander for the Allied Powers and to issue General Orders to the Military and Naval Forces in accordance with the direction of the Supreme Commander for the Allied Powers. We command all Our people forthwith to cease hostilities, to lay down their arms and faithfully to carry out all the provisions of Instrument of Surrender and the General Orders issued by the Japanese Imperial General Headquarters hereunder.

This second day of the ninth month of the twentieth year of Showa

**Seal of
the
Empire**   Signed: HIROHITO

Countersigned: Naruhiko-o, Prime Minister; Mamoru Shigemitsu, Minister of Foreign Affairs; Iwao Yamazaki, Minister of Home Affairs; Juichi Tsushima, Minister of Finance; Sadamu Shimomura, Minister of War; Mitsumasa Yonai, Minister of Navy; Chuzo Iwata, Minister of Justice; Tamon Maeda, Minister of Education; Kenzo Matsumura, Minister of Welfare; Kotaro Sengoku, Minister of Agriculture and Forestry; Chikuhei Nakajima, Minister of Commerce and Industry; Naoto Kobiyama, Minister of Transportation; Fumimaro Konoe, Minister without Portfolio; Taketora Ogata, Minister without Portfolio and Binshiro Obata, Minister without Portfolio.

VJ-DAY
By Peter d'Auvergne

The day before VJ-Day we had just returned from a three or four day jungle exercise. Probably our last prior to our drop on some Japanese-occupied Pacific island.

We were all very tired, hot, dirty and footsore. All eager for a shower, a good meal and a good night's rest. There were six of us in my tent and as we were unpacking our gear one of the lads switched on the radio, probably hoping to hear one of the popular wartime shows starring Rob Wilton, Tommy Handley or Arthur Askey. Almost immediately we heard the announcer say that a meeting to discuss peace terms was taking place between General McArthur (the American C. in C. South Pacific) and the Japanese High Command. No mention of 'the bomb', just a suggestion that a horrendous event had taken place.

By ten o'clock that evening we knew that at last the war had really ended, and that we could have the next day (VJ-Day, 15 August) off to celebrate. The Indians were to stay on duty and have the following day off.

Sports were quickly organized. The Black Watch ran a Donkey Derby and then nearly caused another war by trying to start a rodeo with some of the cows and bullocks they found wandering around the camp. (The cow is a sacred animal in India). However the officers quickly intervened and put a stop to it before too many of the Indian troops realised what was happening.

The impact of the end of hostilities did not really seem to affect us until darkness fell, then soldiers of all ranks and from various units, started walking into our tents brandishing bottles of whisky. Where it all came from I'll never know. I hadn't seen a full bottle of Scotch opened for years.

By about nine o'clock everyone was in a party mood. Some of us were very jolly. A few had imbibed a little too well and were fast asleep on their charpoys completely unaware of the celebrations going on around them.

Around ten o'clock my officer came into the tent, made a beeline for me and said, "Sorry Peter, but I'm afraid you'll have to go and take over in the Signal Office, there's a load of Top Priority Messages coming in and the Indians can't cope".

So off I went and spent the next four hours receiving and supervising delivery of an endless stream of messages listing hundreds of names of men in the brigade delegated to parachute into Hong Kong, Singapore and numerous other Japanese-held territories to effect the release and evacuation of our POWs, most of whom had been held for over three years. This went on until about two o'clock the following morning. Then I was able to hand over to the Senior Indian NCO and return to my tent about a hundred yards from the Signal Office.

The camp was in complete darkness. All the revellers were fast asleep and I was soon into my charpoy and oblivious to war and peace like the rest of them.

That was the official VJ-Day, but my real VJ and VE-Day came about three months later when I sailed down the Mersey on a cold, foggy Friday afternoon about three weeks before Christmas. Bands were playing and waving crowds thronged the dockside and 'wonders will never cease', I was able to spot my wife among them. The first time I'd seen her for almost four years.

THANKSGIVING WEEK
By Gwen Price

In May VE-Day was celebrated and VJ-Day in August. Here in Beeston we had a *Thanksgiving Week* later in the year.

My husband was still overseas in the Far East, (eventually returning home in May 1947), but he kept the hundreds of letters I wrote to him. In a letter dated November 3rd 1945 this is what I had written:

It was a marvellous sight, hundreds and hundreds of flaming torches made the High Road a mass of moving light. Everybody marched up Wollaton Road to the Wakes field singing 'Land of Hope and Glory'. A huge bonfire was lit.

An electric organ played for community singing, and baked potatoes were on sale.

All that week there were dances, whist drives, processions and at the Astoria Cinema, now an office block near the corner of Derby Road and Woodside Road, if you bought a 15 shillings (75p) National Savings Certificate at the pay box you received a free ticket for the best seats.

Before Bonfire Night that year, the rush for fireworks was so great that two policemen were on duty controlling queues at the toyshop on the High Road. Truly a week of celebrations!

PEACE HAS ONLY BEGUN

Peace has begun – begun to dismantle
bomb shelters and road blocks,
mined beaches and wire.
The road signs are back
on the roads of our Island,
the roads that wind safely
to Mother and Dad.
The boys are preparing
for joyous reunions,
for work and careers;
the girls for new homes.
The black years are over
the grim task is done,
the long war is over, and peace has begun.
Now on to the future!
New tasks, new plans, new problems,
new sowing, new harvest –
the harvest of peace.
For this new beginning,
this mighty New Hope,
this Glorious Opportunity
Let us give thanks.

THANKSGIVING WEEKS

Local THANKSGIVING SAVINGS WEEKS are being held throughout the Country. Look out for the date of your own Savings Week and back it for all you're worth.

*Beeston Gazette & Echo
22 September 1945*

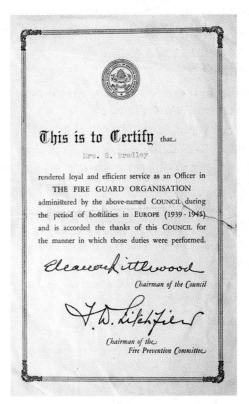

*Certificate of Thanks to Mrs S Bradley
of Beeston for Services as Fire Guard
in World War Two*

BEESTON
THANKSGIVING WEEK PROGRAMME

SATURDAY, OCTOBER 27, 1945

GRAND OPENING PARADE

ASSEMBLE 1.30p.m. Move off 2.15p.m. from Dovecote-lane Recreation Ground, Queens-road, Humber-road, High-road, taking the salute in Post Office-square, and dispersing in Foster-avenue, Chilwell-road and Devonshire-avenue.

Procession headed by the Sherwood Foresters' Military Band, and including the R.A.O.C. Pipe Band and Boys' Brigade Band, will comprise the following units:- Military Personnel, A.T.S., R.A.F., W.A.A.F, Air Training Corps, Army Cadet Corps, Beeston Boys' Brigade, Civil Defence, and other local organisations.

Parade Marshals:- Major P. R. Mennell and Warrant Officer E. A. Woodward.

CIVIC OPENING
At the BEESTON TOWN HALL, by
Lt-Col. A. H. MITCHELL, M.B.E. M.C.

See Two Grand Exhibitions

ART GALLERY in the CHURCH FELLOWSHIP YOUTH CLUB ROOMS, STATION ROAD, BEESTON, showing collection of pictures of Dunkirk, D-Day Landings, the Mulberry Harbour and other features up to the final victory. Open at 3.0p.m. Admission Free.

Also EXHIBITION and COMPETITION in the BEESTON LADS' CLUB, STATION ROAD. Official Opening at 7p.m. by Councillor Mrs. Littlewood, M.B.E., J.P. Exhibits include Toys and Models; Special Stand by Ericsson Telephones Ltd.; Model Farms in Peace and War; Kitchen Equipment for new Permanent Houses; Poster Display by Beeston Fields Senior Boys; Modern Lathes for Toy making by Myfords; R.A.F. Dinghy, Parachute, etc.; Show on Monday, Tuesday and Wednesday.

Don't Forget to Buy Your Thanksgiving Flag

ADDITIONAL SELLING CENTRES:- Messrs. Boots, The Square; Messrs. Woolworths, High-road; Gas Show Rooms, The Square; Astoria Cinema, Lenton Abbey; and specially decorated Barton Bus.

TARGET CHANGING

The figures will be altered daily on the Main Indicator in Post Office-square, Beeston, as follows:- Monday, Lady Belper; Tuesday, Mr. A. R. Baldwin (President, Rotary Club of Beeston); Wednesday, Mrs. Littlewood, M.B.E. (Chairman, Beeston and Stapleford Council); Thursday, Two Schoolchildren from Toton; Friday, Corpl. H Nicholls, V.C.; Saturday, Alderman L. W. A. White; Monday, Councillor A. Redwood (Vice-Chairman, Beeston and Stapleford Council.

SUNDAY, OCTOBER 28

GRAND VARIETY CONCERT
In the MAJESTIC CINEMA, QUEENS-ROAD, at 2.30p.m. All Star Artistes include John Kirkland (violin), Frank Britton (piano). See special announcements.

MONDAY, OCTOBER 29

LADIES' INVESTMENT LUNCHEON
HANDS' CAFE, CHILWELL-ROAD at 1.0p.m. Guest of Honour, Lady Belper, J.P., C.C.

TUESDAY, OCTOBER 30

ROTARY CLUB OF BEESTON
INVESTMENT LUNCHEON, at 1.0p.m. Speaker: Mr. H Dakin, M.B.E., Regional Commissioner for National Savings.

GRAND VICTORY BALL
At BEESTON LADS' CLUB, from 8-30 to midnight R.A.O.C. Blue Rockets Dance Band. Tickets 2s. 6d.

WEDNESDAY, OCTOBER 31

BEESTON STREET GROUPS
WHIST DRIVE at 7.0pm
At OLD BOYS' CLUB, MIDDLE STREET.
Good prizes. Admission 1s.

THURSDAY, NOVEMBER 1

CHILDREN'S FANCY DRESS PARADE
NETHER-STREET SCHOOLS, at 2.30p.m. Parade at 3.30, Nether-street, The City, Humber-road, High-road and The Square, where target figures will be changed at 4 p.m.

TORCHLIGHT PROCESSION
Grand Evening Spectacle
Arranged by Beeston Youth Committee. Assemble 7.30p.m. at Dovecote-lane Recreation Ground, and move off via Queens-road, Humber-road, High-road and Wollaton-road to the Wakes Ground. Bonfire, Fireworks, Music by Charles and his Organ, and Community Singing.

FRIDAY, NOVEMBER 2

CHILWELL STREET GROUPS AND W.V.S.
WHIST DRIVE at 7.0pm
At CHILWELL MEMORIAL HALL. Good Prizes. Admission 1s. 6d.

Beeston Gazette & Echo, 20 October 1945

Ex Prisoners of War and wounded ex Servicemen outside the Manchester Unity (now The Cow public house), on Middle Street, 1945.

BEESTON VICTORY CELEBRATIONS
SATURDAY, JUNE 8

All to take place on

Dovecote Lane Recreation Ground

10 a.m.—150 MINUTES CHILDREN'S AND YOUTHS' SPORTS
No Entrance Fee. Scores of Prizes, Come Lads and Lassies, and join in.

2 p.m.—MAMMOTH FANCY DRESS CONTEST
Class A.—Up to 10 years.   Class C.—13 to 18 years.
Class B.—10 to 13 years.   Class D.—18 and over.
NO ENTRANCE FEE.   PRIZES.
Entries on the Ground at Information Marquee.
Enter all the Family. Dress up and enjoy yourselves.

4 p.m.—OPEN-AIR FREE TEA for all Beeston Schoolchildren
Bring your own cup or mug.
Tickets obtainable from your school or on the ground.

6.30 p.m.—LOCAL TALENT CONTEST FINALS
Come and hear and support Local Discoveries

7.45 p.m.—CHILDREN'S OPEN-AIR DANCING
To Charles who will play all your favourites on his Organ.

8.30 to 11.45 p.m.—OPEN-AIR FLOODLIGHT DANCING AND CABARET
CHARLES AND HIS ORGAN, WALLY OLDHAM AND HIS UKELELE
JOHNNIE GREEN, B.B.C. COMEDIAN, KATHLEEN PEARCE, SINGER
MARJORIE HURT AND HER ACCORDION
Punch and Judy, Miniature Railway, Children's Swings and
Roundabouts. Lemonade. Ices. Music and Fun all day.
SEE SPECIAL FLOOD-LIGHTING at 10.30 p.m.

11.45 p.m.—GRAND FINAL VICTORY GOOD-NIGHT

THURSDAY, JUNE 6, 4.30 p.m.—BEESTON OLD AGE

PENSIONERS' MAMMOTH PARTY

In Chilwell-road Methodist Church, Lads' Club, and Station-road Schools.
Tickets should be obtained by Monday next from:—Mr. Gray, Newsagent, Chilwell Road;
Mr. H. A. Price, Newsagent, High Road; Mr. W. H. Smith, Newsagent, opposite Palace Cinema,
High Road; Mr. A. Chambers, Newsagent. Wollaton Road; Mr. Underwood, Butcher,
117, Central Avenue; Mr. Wakefield (hon. secretary of Old Age Pensioners' Association),
23, Leslie Avenue; Councillor S. Butler, Beech Avenue. If you are over 65 there is a ticket for you.

SUNDAY, JUNE 9, at 8 p.m.—OPEN-AIR SERVICE OF THANKSGIVING

Supported by all Denominations and Choirs. Charles at the Organ.
Special Souvenir Order of Service Sheet. Come and give thanks that we are able to have a Victory Day.

Further assistance required to promote this huge programme.
Give your name to Mr. Walter Hayes (hon. secretary). Victory
Celebrations, Town Hall, Beeston.

*Beeston Gazette & Echo,
1 June 1946*

8th June, 1946

To-day, as we celebrate victory, I send this personal message to you and all other boys and girls at school. For you have shared in the hardships and dangers of a total war and you have shared no less in the triumph of the Allied Nations.

I know you will always feel proud to belong to a country which was capable of such supreme effort; proud, too, of parents and elder brothers and sisters who by their courage, endurance and enterprise brought victory. May these qualities be yours as you grow up and join in the common effort to establish among the nations of the world unity and peace.

George R.I.

1946 & 1947 THE FLOODS

Severe weather in the winters of 1945/46 and 1946/47 resulted in widespread flooding, an invader of a different sort. Many homes were badly affected. The war was over but everything was in short supply, rationing had been increased and people had to tighten their belts still further. The winter of 1946/47 was particularly harsh. This was the culmination of nine troubled years in the history of the Beeston area.

BEESTON RYLANDS UNDER WATER

39 Sheep Carried To Safety After
24 Hours' Unceasing Labours

BOATS CARRIED RESIDENTS HOME

IT is 14 years since any serious flooding took place at Beeston, but the south side of the district nearest the river Trent suffered last week-end. The February rains caused the river to rise, and last Saturday it overflowed its banks, causing alarm to those who live in the Rylands district. Families had to evacuate to their upstairs rooms, roll up their carpets and lino and remove other belongings. Furniture which was too heavy to be moved was propped up above water level, and boats had to be used to convey many people to their homes.

The river was high on Friday, but it was at noon on Saturday that the real trouble started.

"The water came over here like a tide," Mr. J. D. Russell, the lock-keeper, told our reporter. "The water," he said, "has been higher than I can ever remember it before. It came with such a rush that it could not get away."

Started With A Rush

He went on to say that the river had come up suddenly, more quickly than he had ever seen it, and in his opinion it was considerably worse than the previous flood in May, 1932. "When it started," he said, "it didn't stop to flow in an ordinary manner, it came like the galloping major."

The level of the canal was 13 feet nine inches on Saturday night and Sunday morning, and the greatest depth during the week-end was about 14 feet. On Tuesday morning it had dropped to less than six feet.

Houseboats On Canal Walls

Two barges had been anchored near the lock on Saturday morning, but had had to turn back to Nottingham.

One of the houseboats had needed some attention, as the inrush of water had caused it to collide with the walls and spring a leak, but this was soon repaired. Other houseboats had risen so high that they lodged on the canal walls and had to be pushed off.

But for the houseboat people there had been no great inconvenience apart from that of having to remain in all day, as their homes had risen with the level of the water, although some of their moorings had been pulled out.

The banks of the canal bore testimony to the force of water which had spread over all the surrounding fields, even as far as Clifton woods, for several large concrete slabs about four feet by two feet had been carried several feet.

A huge spare part of the old lock gates, which had been placed across the canal to form a kind of bridge, had been washed completely away from this position, and was lying some eight yards away.

Fortunately the lock house stands fairly high, but even so, Mr. Russell had a depth of ten inches of water in his cellar.

Residents of Prince of Wales-terrace had two feet of water in their gardens and houses.

There is supposed to be a shortage of waders, but nine out of ten people, most of them sightseers, seemed to have them when the floods came.

Mrs. G. H. Mitchell, of "The Boat House," Beeston, had to be evacuated by boat on Saturday night. "I have lived here thirty years," she told our representative, "and this is the second time I have had to turn out." She said the water was an inch less in depth round her bungalow than during the 1932 flood, but believed it had been worse round the lock.

Houseboat on the canal at Beeston Lock. The "Jolly Angler" public house and the Mission Hall are left of centre

"The water ran right through my bungalow," she said, "until there was a foot of water inside."

On Tuesday morning Mrs. Mitchell had nearly finished cleaning her bungalow, which was once more looking spick and span again. As with most people in a similar predicament, her chief difficulty was a shortage of fuel, because she needed large fires to dry out the rooms.

Plight Of 39 Sheep

Staying with Mrs. Mitchell during the winter months are Mr. and Mrs. C. Peaty, and they were evacuated to a friend's houseboat. Mr. Peaty said that on Saturday night it w as discovered that 39 sheep be longing to Mr. P. L. Turner, of Grove Farm, Clifton, were isolated in the meadows on the opposite side of the river.

Three brothers named Blagg, who are boatmen on the river, worked 24 hou rs without ceasing – from Saturday afternoon to Sunday afternoon – to rescue the sheep, and were successful in saving all but three. The sheep were taken in a ferry boat one at a time to the bottom of Clifton Pastures, where they were given attention.

The Rylands district was practically cut off from the rest of Beeston. The water rose as far as the junction of Station-road and Queens-road, and up to the John Clifford Baptist Church on Dovecote-lane. The recreation ground was like a lake.

Day Nursery Evacuated

Water poured into the Day Nursery on the Dovecote-lane Recreation Ground on Saturday morning, and when the flood was at its height there was a depth of nine inches of water throughout the building. Fortunately, the flood had been anticipated and the nurseries evacuated.

Drying-out operations began on Monday, and the place was thoroughly cleaned. As the walls were painted, water marks were easily scrubbed off. The nursery was closed for the week while blankets and beds were put to air, but they are to open as usual next Monday.

Nevertheless, the Rylands were not in such a waterlogged condition as might appear, as the flooding ceased just below the station and there was a large area comparatively dry as far as the Rylands School.

Buses Continue To Run

Mrs. M. J. Maycroft, of 39, Birch-avenue, Beeston, and her neighbours, began to take their lighter furniture upstairs on Saturday, but fortunately the houses kept dry and only the gardens were flooded.

The water was not deep on St ation-road, and t he buses did not stop running to the Cliftonside Estate, but t hey were so packed with sightseers that there was little chance of residents on legitimate business finding a seat.

Several residents of Trent-road near the canal, were marooned from Saturday noon until Monday morning.

Back Home By Boat

Quite a lot of children who had gone to the cinema, and men who were working late or had gone to football matches had to be brought home by boat. The floods did not affect the houses near the canal so much as those further up the road, as the floods came down as far as Mackay's shop on Trent-road.

On South-road and Trent Vale-road the water was as much as four feet deep. One resident of South-road however, said that none of the houses there had been flooded, as they stood fairly high from the road.

Beeston Lock, about 1939

Front steps and yards between Mackay's shop and the Rylands School were covered with a fine silt on Tuesday morning, but housewives were too occupied in cleaning out their houses to bother about outside.

Rushed Under The Door

Mrs. W. Amos, of 107, Trent-road, Beeston, was having a good dry out in her downstairs rooms on Tuesday morning. Having noticed the floods rising on Friday, she had taken up her carpets and lino and propped her larger pieces of furniture above water level.

Like everyone with whom our reporter spoke, she was astounded at the suddenness of the flooding. "On Saturday dinner time," she said, "the water rushed down the entry and spread out all over the garden. It came through the scullery and into the pantry. Despite the fact that there were two deep steps leading up to the front door it then rushed under the door and met in the middle of the house."

Mrs. Amos said that owing to the terrible smell left by the river water she had had to disinfect the rooms.

Cooking In The Bedroom

She and her husband had had to live upstairs and do their cooking there. They had no waders, but had to paddle through the water when they wanted water from the tap.

"When we lay in bed," she said, "we could hear it rushing down the entry and it sounded like the river Trent itself." Marks on the wallpaper above the skirting-board showed that there had been six or eight inches of water in the house. The flood water in the pantry did not go down until Monday.

N.F.S. men were still at work this week pumping water out of Ericsson's field, which was entirely covered.

Extra Food And Fuel

Enquiries at the Food Office revealed that they had been given authority to issue extra rations if need be, but had not been called upon to do so.

The Fuel Office reported that they had authority to issue one cwt. extra coal until the end of February for drying out purposes and had actually issued this ration to four applicants.

Report From The Beeston Gazette & Echo, 16 February 1946

143

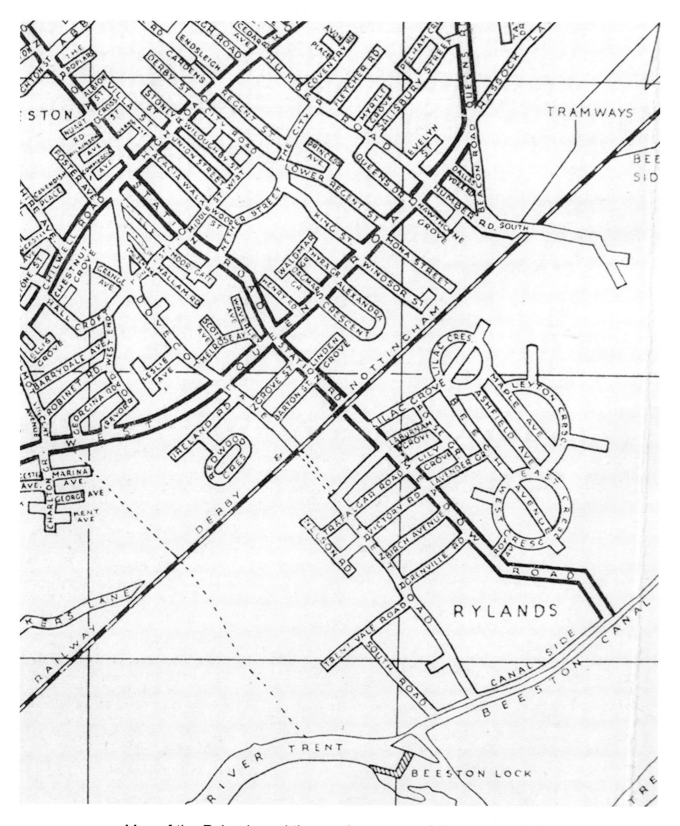

Map of the Rylands and the southern area of Beeston in 1947.
Most of the area below Middle Street was affected by the floods.

Queens Road looking towards the Majestic Cinema, later the Essoldo, at the corner of Station Road

Report from the Beeston Gazette & Echo on Saturday 22 March 1947

BEESTON FLOOD "WORST EVER"

-------0-------

Three Hour Shuttle Service To Clear Factory Workers

BOATS AIDS SHOPPERS

WITH Queens-road completely awash and flood waters surging hundreds of yards up Station-road towards the High-road, the whole of south Beeston was virtually isolated by late afternoon on Wednesday.

Water feet deep drove residents upstairs in the low-lying Rylands district, and around the Beeston Boiler Co's. works the picture was much the same.

Boating To The Shops

In Mona-street the Harrison family came to the rescue of people with empty larders, putting their boat into commission so that housewives could reach the shops.

Rising with a rapidity unprecedented in living memory, the flood quickly engulfed whole areas, filling living rooms, kitchens and cellars.

Looking down Station-road from points near the Ex-Servicemen's Victory Club it was a veritable sea-scape, with white foamed waves lapping the walls of the isolated Majestic cinema. Hundreds stood at the edge of the creeping waters hoping to hitch-hike a lift from lorries which crawled through the flooded streets.

How Workers Got Home

It became apparent on Tuesday night, when the flood began to percolate on to the railway line at Beeston station, that it was merely a matter of time before the factory of Messrs. Ericsson Telephones, Ltd., would become surrounded. While the cinder track between the factory premises and the company's recreation ground was becoming deeper under water. Workmen cut channels through the banks to drain the flood into the recreation ground, but the water continued to rise steadily and the playing pitches soon resembled a lake.

By Wednesday the factory itself was completely surrounded, and lorries working a shuttle service to waiting omnibuses half way up Station-road took three hours to get the workers away to their homes. The company's entire fleet of lorries worked non-stop, reinforced by mechanised contingents from the Beeston and Stapleford Council.

Boots' Works Isolated

Messrs. Boots' factory at Beeston was also isolated, and similar difficulties were experienced in transporting employees to and from work. The position became so serious on Wednesday night that the management decided to bring in only a skeleton staff on Thursday. Employees were unable to reach the canteen, and food was brought by lorry to the drug, soap and "own goods" factories.

The emergency services of the Beeston and Stapleford Council worked to capacity with every available man on the job. All day long lorries were taking families from their homes to the British Restaurants for meals, and military vehicles were called into assist. Food was delivered by lorry to many homes.

Relief services worked all night from a depot at Attenborough, with 40 men and lorries helping families to move furniture to a place of safety.

Late on Wednesday an official stated: "If the position gets any more serious we are in touch with the military authorities, and hope to have amphibious 'ducks' at our disposal."

Aid From N.F.S.

The N.F.S. and the ambulance services carried on admirably, and main-tained an efficient organisation. A detachment of the N.F.S. was called out when the sewerage farm machinery at Dovecote-lane became covered with water. The firemen took pumping apparatus to maintain the service while workmen took out the soaked engines.

The Rylands area was badly affected. Streets inundated included South-road, Trent Vale-road, Trent-road, Grenville-road, Birch-avenue, Meadow-road, Trafalgar-road, Victory-road, and parts of Lavender-grove, Lily-grove and Laburnam-grove.

The floods surged rapidly down the railway line from the Attenborough direction, eventually engulfing Barton-street, Grove-street, Linden-grove, Ireland-road, Redwood-crescent, Leslie-avenue, Melrose-avenue, Waverley-avenue, and a large area of Dovecote-lane.

Police traffic blocks were placed along Queens-road, but a few heavy lorries and omnibuses managed to creep through. Many private cars however, had to be abandoned in deep water.

Sweeping along Queens-road the floods entered Humber-road South, Dallas York-road and Hawthorne-grove, and on Thursday morning had reached Fletcher-road.

Chilwell And Toton

Workers from Chilwell and Toton who had left Beeston factories only after considerable delay and difficulty found further trouble meeting them as they got nearer home.

At Chilwell, Meadow-lane, in the area of its junction with Queens-road West, was under water, and homes were flooded in Trent-crescent, Clifton-avenue, Barker's-lane, and Long-lane, Attenborough.

Attenborough was a badly hit area, many roads, including part of Nottingham-road, being covered, together with Attenborough-lane.

At Toton, parts of the main high-way and other roads were under water.

Queens Road looking west with the Methodist Church in the centre and Beeston Boiler Company's employees' allotments on the right.

ECHO OF FLOOD AT BEESTON

-----0----

Families Evacuated
And Invalids
Taken To Hospital

6,000 MEALS PROVIDED

PRIOR to the normal business of the Beeston and Stapleford Council on Tuesday, Mr. F. W. Litchfield (chairman) referred to the floods which had overtaken Beeston as well as other parts of the country. Locally the Council had formed an Emergency Committee and certain provision made should part of the district be inundated. Their first act was to engage a loudspeaker van, and those who took heed of the warning derived some benefit, but those who took no notice had to put up with the consequences.

The committee made arrangements for the provision of food and fuel in case it was required and the British Restaurant was organised to provide meals in the event of need.

Nearly 6,000 Meals Provided

The need did arise and the British Restaurants played a great part in the distribution of food. To give some idea of the magnitude of the task a total of 5,723 meals were provided and 3,942 hot drinks. There were 3,449 meals and 2,020 hot drinks supplied from the Lads' Club. 1,497 meals and 1,122 hot drinks from Albert-street, Stapleford, and 777 meals and 790 hot drinks from Chilwell.

In addition the Council provided to people who could not leave their homes 2,574 loaves and 838 pints of milk.

Mr. Litchfield paid a tribute to the landlady of the Boat Inn at the Rylands who placed a room at their disposal to provide meals for children and adults. In all 400 meals were taken down to the district. It would be agreed that on this occasion at any rate, smiled Mr Litchfield, that the British Restaurants had proved of great benefit to the community.

*Report from the
Beeston Gazette & Echo
29 March 1947*

Families Evacuated

He would also like to thank the Salvation Army who placed their Citadels at Beeston and Stapleford at their disposal for the use of people who had been evacuated from their homes. In all 29 persons including two expectant mothers and 11 children were safely removed from their homes. They were provided with food and fuel, but brought with them their own bedding.

One public spirited resident rang up the Town Hall and offered to billet a family in distress, and advantage was taken of the offer, an expectant mother and two children being accommodated in the house.

They also rescued from the floods one expectant mother and one chronic invalid who were taken to hospital.

Gallons Of Disinfectant

Other data supplied by the chairman was that 160 gallons of disinfectant had been distributed, and all householders who had had water in their dwellings had received, or would receive, 1cwt. of coal. The Nottingham Corporation were going to deliver 1cwt. of coke to every house in which flood water had penetrated.

He thanked Messrs. Boots for providing 2,500 bottles for filling with disinfectant which they had generously given without charge. The officials of the Council were working day and night and Mr. Litchfield thanked them, and all the staff and workmen and the military for the loan of lorries.

Mr. G. H. Peel moved that an endeavour be made to receive some financial assistance from the Government towards the cost of the damage, contending that the floods were national and should not be borne by individual districts. The resolution was carried unanimously.

The Chairman's Lot

Mr. Jarvis commented that Mr. Litchfield had paid tribute to many people and organisations who had rendered assistance, but he thought that Mr. Litchfield himself should be included in any vote of thanks they intended to pass. He had done a great deal of work and had proved an admirable leader.

The chairman modestly dismissed the matter by saying: It is one of the duties which falls to the lot of the chairman of the Council.

Bottom of Station Road near Queens Road

147

Queens Road, Hassocks Lane centre left

Beeston

Last night flood water was rising in Beeston, and a loud-speaker van toured the area near University - boulevard warning residents to be on the alert.

Water had reached half-way up Humber-road and was waist deep in King-street.

Although Ericsson's telephone works were surrounded by water, the night shift was able to go on duty. and it was expected that work would be able to proceed as usual this morning.

Near Chilwell Ordnance Depot's No. 13 gate on the Nottingham - road. swans were swimming in two feet of water.

Flooding half a mile in extent on Queen's-road and the Chilwell by-pass caused traffic to be diverted through Beeston-square.

Nottingham Journal, 19 March 1947

BEESTON

Flooding in Beeston became rapidly more serious last night. Attenborough village was completely isolated; Ericsson's sports ground went under water in less than half-an-hour; and Chilwell Ordnance Depot was surrounded by water on three sides.

At one time readings taken on the Depot sports ground revealed a rise in water of six inches in 45 minutes.

Lower Trent-road. in the Beeston Rylands district. was flooded to a depth of four feet at 10 p.m

Nottingham Journal, 20 March 1947

A WINTER'S TALE
By Ken Potts

The great freeze of 1947 was to my mind the coldest time I have ever experienced. I was only a nine-year old lad at the time, yet I remember well the long icicles hanging from the gutterings, almost touching the floor. It was only two years after the war and rationing was still tight and getting worse. In winter, fuel rationing was felt most keenly, and anything combustible was saved for the fire - potato peelings, old shoes, orange boxes and rags.

The snow had started to fall sometime in January. Each fall would be followed by a hard frost and so street levels steadily rose. I remember a group of us kids built a snow wall across the mouth of the cul-de-sac where we lived on Trent Road. The Co-op milkman tried, unsuccessfully, to knock the wall down with his float, much to the cheers of the rosy-cheeked children.

The winter dragged on into February and it seemed to get colder. The shortage of fuel was becoming a crisis. Most Sunday mornings we would form a queue at Mellor's Coal Yard on the canal side. If we were lucky,

Snow Clearing

The surveyor reported on the steps taken to clear the main roads of snow and ice. At the beginning of the winter 50 tons of salt were in stock, but as this was used, it was not possible to replace it owing to the salt factory being closed on account of fuel shortage. Twenty additional men had been engaged, and every-thing possible was being done to clear the roads.

Beeston Gazette & Echo, 15 February 1947

we would be able to buy a bag of coke, which was not rationed. Most times the wait was fruitless and I would return home with an empty wheelbarrow. On the way home from school, I would search along the railway line for coal. A resourceful neighbour was employed by the Railway Company and he often worked on the Nottingham/Birmingham line. It was strange how his coal missed the fire grate and fell onto the line whenever his train passed through Beeston!

By late February, the situation was desperate. One Saturday morning, I went with my father to the willow woods, beyond Mitchell's Boat House by the Trent. When we arrived, I am sure the whole of the Beeston Rylands were there, hacking, sawing, chopping and dragging away the trees. That weekend, the whole wood had been reduced to waste. It was a beautiful wood at one time; a favourite playground of my childhood. Many years passed before it recovered. The rest of the family joined us later and on the way home, I slipped on the ice and fell on to my father's bow saw which I was carrying. It cut deep into my left leg. I remember the blood stained the ice where I fell. First Aid was administered and we managed to get home.

Our wooden booty was summarily cut up and piled on the fire, still wet and frozen. After the application of a mug of pork dripping, turpentine-soaked rags and much puffing and blowing, the fire came to life. I remember later that day Mr. Frost, our Insurance Collector (aptly named) complementing our blaze. He said it was the finest sight he had seen on all his calls. He sat down by the roaring fire; the customary cup of tea was placed in his hands. On a cold day, a fireside has no shortage of company eager to relate their news of the day.

February departed and, at long last in March, so did the big freeze. It turned very warm and a rapid thaw set in. All the snow and ice had disappeared within a few days. The River Trent began to rise and was soon a torrent. There was no flood-bank then. The water rose until the cul-de-sac became an island. The problem now was being unable to get to the shops for food. One particular day, a group of the local men decided to row a boat in order to buy provisions. As they were rowing beyond the Prince of Wales Terrace, the fast-flowing current took the boat and smashed it against the metal railings on the side of the road. They were not seriously hurt, only very wet and cold. After a few days, we were relieved of our plight by the Army. Several lorries arrived bringing hot food. Trestles and benches were set up in the pub,

The *Boat Inn* and several local people organized themselves to serve the food. No one had ever been fed so well since before the war. There were daily deliveries until the floods eventually receded. The mud and debris were cleared from the houses, although fortunately at our house at No 110, the flood at its height, had only reached our back door.

Order slowly returned to the area as winter turned to spring and then to summer. It was one of the hottest summers I remember. There were other floods in the following years until the Flood Protection Scheme was completed, but none were as bad as 1947. It was a common talking point for many years after.

Queens Road, Alexandra Crescent centre right

Station Road outside Bostock's, now Foster and Pearson Building Services

THE FLOODS OF '47
By Carole White

We lived on Trafalgar Road in the Rylands and my mother always told me that, during the floods, the day she put her feet in water in the back kitchen was the day things got serious. There was a step down into our back kitchen (or scullery as we used to call it) and the flood water had come over the back door step and seeped under the floor boards of the other downstairs rooms. Mum said you could hear the water slopping about under the house.

The sodden floorboards gave way and the following day dad, who had been a joiner by trade, made a new floor but overnight the trapdoor in the floor had been left open and spores from mould that grew like hanging pieces of fabric, escaped all over the furniture and floor. It looked just as if someone had tipped the contents of a hoover bag all around the room.

For many years after and many changes of floorboards, dad had to shine a torch to check the foundations and use a blowtorch to burn off the mould spores that were still growing. The whole floor had to be replaced many times.

Station Road near the corner of Nether Street

Station Road, Beeston looking towards Queens Road. The Majestic Cinema, later called The Essoldo, can just be seen in the centre

THE 1947 FLOOD
By Dennis Hassell

The winter of 1947 was the most severe in living memory. Snow began to fall early in January, followed by severe frost and was reinforced almost daily by snow falls and more frost, so that ice remained on the roads until April.

When it finally melted it produced the worst flood since 1875 along the whole of the Trent valley. The water in Beeston didn't come straight up from the river but came across the fields from Attenborough. On Station Road it reached as far as Middle Street where lorries picked up Ericsson employees to take them to work. And on Humber Road the water rose as far as Fletcher Road. The whole of south Beeston from the Rylands upwards was flooded and boats were a common sight.

When the water retreated it went fairly quickly, but in the King Street area it remained for several more days.

Flooding near Queens Road

Queens Road, Vincent Avenue on the left

THE FLOODS OF 1947
By AJ Horton

The floods in the winter of 1947 are still strong in my memory. After weeks of snowfalls it suddenly got warmer and all the snow and ice thawed, the River Trent burst its banks and invaded the lower half of Beeston. There was no flood protection scheme in those days and the water ran off the Derbyshire hills and into the rivers and overflowed into Attenborough and along into Beeston. Coal was rationed in 1947 so we couldn't have fires as often as we should and it was a very cold winter.

We lived on Coventry Road then and the floods came up Humber Road as far as Fletcher Road just below us, so luckily we were unscathed. Fleets of lorries and small boats had to take people to work every day. My father worked at Ericsson's and I recall him going off to work every day in a boat from Nether Street.

Cyclists on Humber Road returning home after work at the Beeston Boiler Company

Lower Regent Street

Trent Overflows, Canal Bursts Its Banks, Water Swirls Into 2,000 Homes

LAST YEAR'S PEAK LEVEL PASSED

Hundreds Of Families Marooned : S.O.S. Sent Out For Army Aid

FOOD AND MILK DELIVERED BY BOATS

WATER NOW RECEDING

FOR the second time within 13 months Long Eaton, Sawley, New Sawley. Toton and Attenborough districts have suffered serious and perilous flooding.

On the last occasion, in February, 1946, damage amounting to thousands of pounds was done to property and hundreds of families were marooned in upper rooms of their houses which still bear the effects of the inundation. This time the flood waters have reached a much higher level than ever before. The River Trent has overflowed its banks, the canal bank has burst in five separate places and Sandiacre, which escaped in 1946, has this time also suffered from continuous inundation since Monday, when the Erewash over-spilled so suddenly that residents of houses in many streets were caught quite unawares.

Long Eaton Advertiser, 22 March 1947

Floods at Attenborough in 1947
(Before the Nature Reserve was established)

MEMORIES OF BEESTON FLOODS 1947
By Jean Mellors née Robinson

My widowed mother had not long moved house to King Street when flooding struck there. I was 18 and working in the offices of the Meadow Dairy Company which was where the Beekeeper pub is now, at the corner of Meadow Lane, Chilwell. I was a punch-card operator in the Data Processing Department. Data Processing was new in those days. My future mother-in-law rang me from her house on City Road, Beeston, overlooking King Street, to advise me to come home because she could see the flood water advancing and getting deeper. King Street was deep in flood water when I arrived and I had to leave my bicycle at the City Road house where dinner was ready for me before I made my way home through the water carrying my shoes and stockings. My mother was encamped upstairs at number 22, the water was up two stairs and the whole lower floor looked dreadful. The piano had been hoisted onto bricks by neighbours but the water still reached about a foot up the piano legs. The bedroom had a fireplace and I managed to find some dry firewood and then I paddled to the coal house for coal and we soon had a fire to boil some water in a saucepan for tea. Mum had taken up as much food as she could to keep it out of the water so I scouted round and found bread and cheese and I think we managed OK on that the first day. Mum had taken candles upstairs so we did have some light to help us get to bed. My sister and brother managed to find places to sleep elsewhere; it was pointless for them to come home to such a mess.

The next morning we greeted the folk across the street, also at their bedroom windows. I was alerted to some sort of emergency and on opening the landing window (over the coal house) I discovered a beautiful bedraggled Persian cat cowering terrified on the roof just below me. I gathered towels and cloths for it to cling to and eventually coaxed the cat onto the sill with rewards of milk and food. The poor thing was terrified of me and dashed down the stairs only to be stopped by the flood water. It then dashed back and flew round and round the bedrooms until it was exhausted. I eventually made friends with it and then discovered the cat lived near Nether Street which was just out of the floods. We were getting help by now from a rowing boat with men bringing bread and milk so I asked the boatman if he would take the cat to higher ground as it was still very distressed. We decided to put it into a pillowcase, with its head protruding, to protect us from its claws and after much struggling and very nearly dropping it, we did get this poor moggie into the boat and transported safely to its owners. They rewarded me with a bunch of grapes – quite expensive fruit and a real treat. That teatime the boatman brought us fish and chips from Mrs Downs' fish shop which was next to the Methodist Church on Queens Road, and were they good?! Only the hungry can relish food they have been starved of.

We lived upstairs for three or four nights and the mess when the water receded was quite dreadful. The carpets were covered in inches of black mud and they all had to be dragged into the garden and cleaned and the floorboards scrubbed time and time again. The Council gave us disinfectant to help with the hygiene and no one seemed to suffer any ill effects. Weeks of hard work were needed to rid the house of mud and smells. Of course many items of our property were ruined including furniture, photo albums and personal papers, which could never be replaced.

One good thing came of the experience. We had inherited black beetles when moving to King Street. They were atrocious insects coming out of the skirting boards at night and if we came in late and put the light on there was such a horrible scurry of black creepy-crawlies, my sister and I would scream with terror. The land had been used by the Beeston Boiler Company's foundry as a tip for black sand and clinker that was used at the works before the King Street homes were built, and we thought the insects came from there. After the flood we didn't see any more black beetles. After all the mess and trouble, that was one good outcome of the floods.

I REMEMBER THE FLOODS
By Margaret Hollingsworth née Shipley

When the floods came in 1947 I was a little girl living with my mother and father, sister Edna and brother Tony at 188 Canal Side, Beeston Rylands. Edna and I had gone to stay with grandma in Derby because mum was in hospital. Mum came home from hospital later in the week arriving at 11.30 am. Two hours later my sister and I got off the train at Beeston Station but we only managed to walk up Trent Road to Grenville Road when the flood water met us. There was a rowing boat to take us home and my father was one of the rescuers. The flood waters were rushing through the railings just near to Trent Vale Road and the force of it knocked the oar out of my father's hand and he had to be saved from drowning. What a fright!

The flood water reached almost to the end of the terraced houses but not quite up to the *Boat & Horses* pub. Although the canal overflowed and came half way up our gardens we didn't get any water in the house. The very big army lorries that came to help us were able to get through as far as the *Boat & Horses*. They brought us milk, bread and potatoes. When Saturday evening came a nice army man with a big lorry asked us all if we would like to go to the cinema, and because we hadn't been out we were very pleased. And so we all got in the lorry and were driven up through the floods to the Palladium on Beeston High Road to see Rita Hayworth in *Gilda*. Does anyone remember?

As I recall the floods came again next year. At eight o'clock one morning we could see from our bedroom window that the Weir Field was already flooded and the river came up and soon filled the canal. In about four hours we were cut off once again. What a good job our mums hadn't let us go to school! A year or two later the authorities did a lot of work to prevent flooding. They raised the bank on the other side of the canal and did a lot of work on the river.

Station Road, south of Queens Road

BEESTON FLOODS 1947
By Maisie Waggott ex Newbery née Robinson

When the floods came in 1947 I had just enrolled for extended service in the ATS (Auxiliary Territorial Service) at the Central Ordnance Depot, Chilwell, now Chetwynd Barracks. I was in the Queen Elizabeth Camp high on the hill. The winter of 1946-1947, was very long with extreme cold and will be remembered by many of my generation. Fuel was rationed and there was a shortage of coke and coal. And to add to the misery our water pipes were frozen. When the big thaw came it was a great relief to everyone but being on the top of a hill we escaped the devastation the floods had caused that people in the lower areas experienced.

After the second world war ended we were very busy dealing with stores being returned from war zones around the world as well as organizing the demobilization of many of the ATS girls so when the message spread quickly that parts of the Queens Road area in Beeston were flooded, I knew I must get home to help my family in their home on King Street. There was my mother who was recently widowed, two sisters Jean and Nancy, and my younger brother Cecil, who had just been demobbed from the Royal Air Force. When I arrived Jean and my mother were camped upstairs because the whole of the ground floor was flooded. My other sister and my brother were staying elsewhere. We had to salvage what we could but some things were ruined beyond repair and had to be thrown away.

When we look back and reminisce, we recall the 1947 flood and how hard it was to keep warm and fed and how difficult it was to get everything clean again afterwards and we remember the treasured items we lost forever.

Queen Elizabeth Camp, Central Ordnance Depot, Chilwell,
during World War Two

THE GREAT FLOOD – AND AFTER

Apart from the cleaning and scrubbing, the repairs and re-decoration required to be done, the floods at Beeston are now a thing of the past. It is the fervent hope that such a calamity will never pay a return visit to Beeston, or indeed to the country, especially at a time when we are attempting to re-habilitate ourselves after over six years of a devastating and disastrous war. Many house-holds on the south side of Beeston suffered from the floods, but I have heard nothing but praise for the way the calamity was handled by the Council. They could not stop the flow of water, but they did see to it that no one went without food, and with only limited supplies at their disposal eked out their fuel stock in a praiseworthy way. Where the money to pay for things would come from was of secondary consideration to the succour and relief which was given without hesitation, but it is of interest to record how much was spent. Including wages it is estimated that the total cost of supplying meals will not ex-ceed £320, while the total cost of the services rendered which in-cludes meals, wages, the pro-vision of soap, disinfectant and the hire of vehicles for haulage and other sundry items is esti-mated at £2,140. It is a pity that the district must be saddled with the expense - and, incident-ally, the Council are going to try to get a Government grant – but no one will begrudge the cost, and the Emergency Com-mittee are to be congratulated on their foresight, enterprise and energies. Many letters of appre-ciation of the assistance ren-dered by the councillors and officials have been received. C. A. Wass, of 37, South-road, commenting that "it is this true comradeship that will pull us through these hard times." Mr. J. Hardman, of 90, Trent-road, particularly mentions in his tribute Messrs. F. Stowell, W. and G. Thorley and Biddulph.

Beeston Gazette & Echo, 5 April 1947